One Lord, One Faith, One Baptism

Christians Through the Centuries

Thomas A. Von Hagel

CONCORDIA PUBLISHING HOUSE · SAINT LOUIS

To Eldon Albert and Lois Elaine, my Christian father and mother

Published by Concordia Publishing House
3558 S. Jefferson Avenue, St. Louis, MO 63118-3968
1-800-325-3040 • www.cph.org

Library of Congress Cataloging-in-Publication Data

Von Hagel, Thomas A.

    One Lord, one faith, one baptism : Christians through the centuries / Thomas A. Von Hagel.

      p. cm.

    Includes bibliographical references and index.

    ISBN 0-7586-0760-1

    1. Christian biography. 2. Bible—Biography. I. Title.

BR1700.3.V66 2006

270.092'2—dc22

                                        2006004880

1 2 3 4 5 6 7 8 9 10   15 14 13 12 11 10 09 08 07 06

CONTENTS

One Lord, One Faith, One Baptism

1

Introduction

Since the time of the apostle Paul's preaching in Athens, to Cyril and Methodius's ninth century missionary work among the Slavs, to the apologetic endeavors of C. S. Lewis, the Christian Church has preserved and retold stories of the lives of Christians in numerous and diverse fashions. Christians have been the subjects of autobiographies and passions and sermons. Volumes of church histories, even hymns, chronicle their eventful lives. In these ways and others, the Christian Church has made a concerted effort throughout her entire history to faithfully preserve Christian biographies.

Utilization of these biographies plays a vital role in the Church. Christianity's emphasis upon the lives of Christians has been primarily beneficial, but at times detrimental. The preservation of the biographical data of earlier Christians allows us to look back and reflect upon the lives of our spiritual ancestors. Simultaneously, earlier Christians are given the opportunity to teach their heirs through the documented signs of God's grace in their lives and the manifestation of their faith in cross-bearing words and deeds. Christians today should not ignore the lives of past Christians, but learn from them and recognize the intimate relation between past and present Christians in the one Church. Regrettably, an over-emphasis upon the lives of the saints and the value of their works in medieval Catholicism at times overshadowed the singularly salvific work of Jesus. A balanced and proper emphasis upon Christian lives is a fine line to walk.

Unity

The apostle Paul wrote to the Philippians concerning the proper understanding and correlation of Christian lives: "There is one body and one Spirit—just as you were called to the one hope that belongs to your call—one Lord, one faith, one baptism, one God and Father of all, who is over all and through all and in all" (Ephesians 4:4–6). As is always the case, the starting point is God. God is Father, Son, and Spirit; yet there are not three gods, but one. In the midst of this apparent plurality, there is divine unity. Similarly, though there is a myriad of Christian lives, they are one body that is united in the one true God.

Faith and Baptism

At the heart of this divinely ordered unity, according to Paul, is the Lord Jesus, with faith and Baptism connecting human lives to their Lord. Through the God-given gift of faith, people of all ages and in all locations are united around their dear Lord. According to the Letter to the Hebrews, there existed a great cloud of faithful witnesses, including Abel and Enoch, Sarah and Rahab. These faithful men and women of the Old Testament believed in the promises of God, and though they preceded the fulfillment of these promises in Jesus, through faith they received all that God promised (Hebrews 11:13–16). Similarly, those who lived after the New Testament, though separated from Jesus by time and place, receive, through faith, the same benefits promised by God to all who believe in Him. Not only is Jesus the object of this faith, He is the "founder and perfecter" (Hebrews 12:2) of this faith in all who trust in the promises of the one true God.

Baptism, a much more tangible sign, also unites people around Jesus. Jesus calls Baptism a rebirth. Human beings are born first of a human father and mother, but Christians are born a second time of water and the Holy Spirit (John 3:5). Through this second birth, God becomes the Father of the baptized, and the baptized becomes a child of God and a brother or sister of the Son of God. St. Paul describes Baptism in another fashion: The baptized participates in Jesus' crucifixion and resurrection by being plunged into a watery death and is then raised up out of it (Romans 6:3–5). According to St. Peter, those who are far away from God are brought near to Him in Holy Baptism (Acts 1:39). Scripture repeatedly illustrates how the sacrament of Holy Baptism intimately connects people with the life of Christ.

Faith and Baptism, it must be noted, are not two autonomous components in the Christian life; they work together as one. Jesus promises, "[w]hoever believes and is baptized will be saved" (Mark 16:16). It is not one or the other, but both. Once the Ethiopian eunuch believed in the promises of God, he asked Philip, "What prevents me from being baptized?" (Acts 8:36). Those who believe in the promises of God are baptized because God has promised to give the gifts of His promises through this watery ritual. And the baptized believe these promises.

Lord's Supper and Offices

Christian lives are joined to Jesus in other related fashions. On Maundy Thursday, Jesus "took bread, and after blessing it broke it and gave it to the disciples, and said, 'Take, eat; this is My body.' And He took a cup, and when He had given thanks He gave it to them, saying, 'Drink of it, all of you, for this is My blood of the covenant'" (Matthew 26:26–28). In this sacred meal, baptized Christians eat and drink bread and wine. Most importantly, Jesus' body and blood are present and consumed under these ordinary elements. Cyril of Jerusalem (ca. 315–395) explained that when the Christian eats and drinks the body and blood of Jesus, then Jesus and the Christian are joined together and become one.[1]

Christian lives also parallel the life of Christ and are connected to Him via the myriad of Christian offices: mission work, preaching, martyrdom, prayer, caring for the sick, or a host of other Jesus-like actions in their lives. In these, the Christian "follows after" Jesus and becomes attached to the life of Christ. Four fishermen—Peter and Andrew, James and John—leave their boats and fishing nets, follow Jesus, and at the behest of Jesus become fishers of men (Matthew 4:18–22). The "sheep" who feed the hungry and clothe the naked actually feed and clothe Jesus (Matthew 25:33–40). The Christian Church, then, is made up of Jesus and His people whom He feeds in a sacred meal and leads in their daily lives.

Sum

To protect against abuses, the study of Christian biography must look beyond the life of a particular Christian and even the relation of one Christian life to another. It must focus upon the intimate relation between a Christian life and the life of Christ. For example, it is appropriate to study and be inspired by the lives and works of Cyril and Methodius. Moreover, it is quite valuable to see the correlations between the missionary work of these "Apostles to the Slavs" and the apostle Paul, a mission-minded predecessor in the New Testament. All three traveled extensively and boldly spoke the word of God to foreign people in faraway lands. However, the most important question is: How are their lives joined to the life of Christ? They are most intimately connected to Jesus in Holy Baptism where they are buried and raised with Him. They are also attached to Jesus through their missionary work. Jesus not only heals the servant of a Roman centurion (Matthew 8:5–13) and teaches a Samaritan woman (John 4:1–26) but also commissions His apostles to make disciples of all nations (Matthew 28:19). Mission work begins with Jesus and flows out of Him. The Christian lives and works of Paul, Cyril, and Methodius must be read and understood primarily in their relation to Jesus. This is the principle aim in portraying a Christian life: to show the intimate relation between the Christian life and the life of Christ.

This book will examine Christian lives—in a variety of literary genres from numerous times and places—in relation to the life of Christ. Chapters 2 through 5 will present and evaluate the biographical data of significant Christians in the Bible, the Early Church, and the Eastern and Western Churches. The concluding chapter will provide a final analysis of chapters 2 through 5, while the remainder of chapter 1 will lay the groundwork with an introduction to historical theology, literary genres, and methodology.

Historical Theology

Theology, the study of God, always takes place within the context of history. This is most readily apparent with historical theology, but it is no less true of biblical theology, pastoral theology, and so on. Biblical theology is rooted, grows, and flowers in history—time, place, and people. Christian theology must be studied in light of this historical trinity.

The God who creates time, place, and people reveals Himself in time, place, and people. This is the norm in Christianity. The canonical and historical writings of Christianity overflow with seemingly endless dates, exotic places, and unpronounceable names. Of these, the first two serve the last. Time and place are not insignificant, yet they are not an end to themselves. They are part of God's good creation in that they serve people by providing the surroundings and context for human existence. God primarily reveals Himself and His will through many different people in various times and places, for example, to Moses at Mount Sinai ca. 1446 BC, to James in Jerusalem on the day of Pentecost, and to Christian Beyer at Augsburg in AD 1530, to name a few.[2] This is God's modus operandi. The God of creation works exclusively through His creation.

The incarnation is the supreme example of this. Athanasius, the eminent fourth-century Alexandrian bishop, taught that the principle act of God's salvation for humanity takes place in history. As humanity wishes to worship creation rather than the Creator, the Creator becomes part of the creation so that humanity can worship the Creator in a created form. With the nativity of our Lord, the Son of God becomes the Son of Man, and the Father's gracious will for all of creation is fulfilled through the salvific work of Jesus in first century Israel.[3] So the study of God first and foremost takes place within the study of history.

In Christianity, one must study history—time, place, and people—to study God. Apart from the created order, Christianity knows nothing of God. God's revelation of Himself and His will is seen and heard and must be interpreted according to the historical context of time and place. Initially, theology focuses upon the historical event of the incarnation and proceeds from there with the examination of other historical figures in the Church. Though they are secondary to the life of Christ and His work, they are intimately related to Him in that their lives and works point to and flow out of His. Just as God worked in and most fully revealed Himself through the life of Christ (Colossians 1:19), the same is true, to a lesser degree, in all Christian lives. Theology is historical or, more precisely, God is studied in the examination of His words and actions in Christian lives, within the context of their corresponding times and places.

Literary Genres

The biographical data of a number of Christians—apostle and bishop, martyr and ascetic, emperor and soldier, hymnographer and confessor, teacher and servant, spouse and child—has been preserved in a variety of literary genres. In many instances, a single literary form can properly depict the varied lives of numerous Christians. At other times, a different literary form better illustrates God's unusual graces in the diverse lives of His people. For example, a historian and a poet may describe the same event or person, but in quite contrasting fashions. Thus, it is necessary for the reader to discern one literary genre from another—genealogy and martyrology, life of a saint and church history, to name a few—for the sake of reading and analysis.

Holy Bible

Scripture portrays many lives with a variety of literary forms. The main categories of the Old Testament include the Pentateuch, Historical Books, Writings, and the Prophets.

The Pentateuch contains quite a few prominent figures: Adam and Eve are the first. Their firstborn son, Cain, kills his brother, Abel (Genesis 4:8). In the eighth generation, Methuselah lives 969 years (Genesis 5:27), the longest life recorded in the Bible (Genesis 9:22). In the tenth generation, Noah and his wife become the new progenitors of the human race similar to Adam and Eve (Genesis 1:28). The twentieth generation begins with Abraham (Genesis 11:27) and is followed by his son Isaac and his grandson Jacob. While much biographical data is provided for Jacob's son, Joseph, Jacob's heir was Judah. The remainder of the Pentateuch—Exodus, Leviticus, Numbers, and Deuteronomy—includes an abundance of biographical data, the great majority focusing upon Moses and his siblings. The quantity of Moses' biographical data is second only to the amount written about Jesus.

The Historical Books and the Writings of the Old Testament provide a large supply of biographical data. The life of Job falls under the category of Wisdom Literature, a sub-category of the Writings. The lion's share of biographical data for Joshua is considered a Historical Book, whereas David's biographical data is spread out over the Historical Books of 1 and 2 Samuel, and 1 Kings. Biographical information is utilized extensively to show that God continues to act in and through a variety of people in various times and places.

A sapiential biography[4] is a hybrid of a Historical Book and Wisdom Literature (Writings). Ruth and Esther fit this category, though they are more commonly and improperly referred to as moral biographies. Some number them among the Historical Books because they provide biographical data. Because of their ethical lessons they are often classified as Wisdom Literature that reveals divine wisdom versus human foolishness (Proverbs 1:7). These sapiential biographies, however, demonstrate the aforementioned wisdom and foolishness in a historical setting. In the Book of Esther, for example, Esther and Haman are historical characters, but they are much more than that. In the gracious preservation of Esther's life and the violent death of Haman, they serve as a historical illustration of the divine wisdom as revealed through Solomon: "The fear of the LORD prolongs life, but the years of the wicked will be short" (Proverbs 10:27).

Genealogy is another sub-category that is utilized throughout the Old Testament. It provides raw biographical data: lists of fathers and sons, with the occasional female component. Of greatest importance, it chronicles God's promise in the garden that "[the woman's seed] shall bruise [the serpent's seed]" (Genesis 3:15) through successive generations. Genealogies are primarily included in the Pentateuch and the Historical Books, like 1 Chronicles and Ezra.

The Prophets also contain biographical data. The Historical Books, 1 and 2 Samuel, and 1 and 2 Kings provided sundry biographical facts for a number of prominent prophets, for example, Samuel and Nathan, Elijah and Elisha. The writing prophets, like Isaiah and Hosea, include a miscellany of biographical details for themselves. In the initial verses, they generally provide a bit of genealogical data—one or more generations of ancestors—and the historical context of their prophetic work, such as contemporary kings, is often named. In addition, various facets of their lives are occasionally sprinkled throughout their writings.

The New Testament carries over the genealogies from the Old Testament and adds a few other genres. The authors of the Epistles slipped a few bits of biographical data into their writings, be it Paul's thorn in the flesh (2 Corinthians 12:7) or Peter's presence in Rome (1 Peter 5:13). In addition, Luke's Acts of the Apostles depict the lives and works of the apostles, primarily Peter and Paul.

The Gospels are a biography-like literary genre that report the life of Christ. Far beyond any other biblical characters, an abundance of biographical data details the life of Christ in the Gospels according to Matthew, Mark, Luke, and John. A few biographical components are common in this literary form: Jesus' family members, forerunner, baptism, teachings, miracles, crucifixion, and resurrection. Each Gospel, though, is more selective concerning His nativity, childhood, temptation, transfiguration, and ascension. Yet all of these are utilized in the larger corpus. The large amount of data provided in the Gospels, the emphasis of four different perspectives, their subject matter (Jesus), and their canonical placement at the beginning of the New Testament elevate them to be the pinnacle of literary genres in the New Testament and all of Holy Scripture.

The variety of literary forms in the Bible revolves around the Gospels. The biographical data in the Old Testament points ahead to that of Jesus in the Gospels. For example, Esther was a type of Christ: her willingness to sacrifice her life for her people foreshadows Jesus offering Himself as a sacrifice on behalf of all people. The biographical data in the rest of the New Testament flows out of the life of Christ. The preaching of Peter on the day of Pentecost is clearly a continuation of the missionary work of Jesus and obedience to Jesus' apostolic commission. Consequently, the Gospels are the biographical basis for the rest of the Bible.

Passion, Martyrology, and Synaxarion

A passion is an early and significant literary genre in the Christian Church that describes the suffering and death of a Christian. Luke not only includes a passion of Jesus in his Gospel but also portrays the passion of Stephen, a deacon at Jerusalem, in his Acts of the Apostles (Acts 6–7). Using this literary form, second and third century Christians preserve the sufferings and deaths of those who continue to be persecuted for the sake of Jesus and the Gospel. Numerous passions describe the suffering and death of martyrs from the entire Mediterranean world, for example, Polycarp in Asia Minor, Perpetua in Africa, and Lawrence in Italy.

Individual passions are subsequently collated into larger collections called martyrologies. While a passion was often read at the liturgical celebration of a local martyr's earthly death and simultaneous heavenly birth, a martyrology chronologically ordered the passions to be read throughout the church year. Wherever and whenever the Church has been persecuted, martyrologies have been produced. The Martyrs of Palestine composed by Eusebius of Caesarea (ca. 260–ca. 340) portray the passions of those Christians persecuted in Palestine under the Roman Empire. The Acts and Monuments of Matters Happening in the Church by John Foxe (1516–87) chronicles the history of Christian martyrs beginning in the first century and culminating in the sixteenth century, with particular emphasis upon those in England during the reign of Queen Mary (1516–58). A. A. Valentinov's Black Book (1924) records the persecutions of Orthodox Christians under early Soviet Communism. These and other martyrologies faithfully remind Christians today that many have suffered and died for the sake of their dear Lord who first suffered and died for the sake of all creation.

Martyrology has another definition that is related to the term Synaxarion. Later martyrologies by Bede (ca. 673–735), Usuard (d. ca. 875), and ultimately an official Roman martyrology in 1584 include the names of bishops and other notable Christians. A few brief comments concerning their lives along with their geographical location are read on the day of their simultaneous earthly death and heavenly birth. It is traditionally read at Prime in the Roman Catholic Church. In the Eastern Orthodox Church, the Synaxarion is read at Orthos, where more biographical data is often included. Both churches, on a daily basis, include brief narratives of the lives of martyrs, bishops, and other Christians worthy of remembrance in the Church.

Both the Roman Catholic martyrology and Eastern Orthodox Synaxarion incorporate biographical data into their respective liturgical families. The Roman martyrology primarily cites Christians from the west, while the Synaxarion from the east, though the renowned are included in both. Nonetheless, both clearly recognize God at work in His people throughout the history of the Church and the value of assimilating these past Christians into the (liturgical) life of contemporary Christians.

Life of a Saint

In the study of Christian biography, the classic literary genre is a life of a particular saint. More often than not, it describes not the average Christian, but one who abounded with interesting and pious stories. The cup of Patristic, Medieval, and Byzantine Christianity overflows with lives: Athanasius's Life of St. Antony, a fourth-century ascetic; Leonitius's Life of

John the Almsgiver, a seventh-century patriarch of Constantinople; Reginald of Durham's Life of St. Goderic, a twelfth-century merchant. On and on goes the list of lives, some of which are well known, while others remain obscure.

More than a few characteristics are common to this literary form.

- The first three are genealogical background, an interesting birth, and a significant childhood. The Life of St. Declan, a fifth-century Irish bishop from noble ancestry, includes all three. On the night of his birth a blazing ladder stretched up from his house to the heavens and was surrounded by an angelic host. Even in his childhood, people clearly noticed his grace and charity and goodness.

- Another characteristic is that a life-changing event often takes place. Following this event, the saint's life changes dramatically—spiritually, morally, and even physically—as happened after Jesus spoke to Martin of Tours (d. 397) in a dream. Immediately, Martin forsook his military life, was baptized, and took up the ascetic life.

- Demonic temptation of the saint is another characteristic. Upset with the ascetic life of Irene, an abbess of Chrysobalanton (d. ca. 940), Satan appeared to her in the form of a repulsive man and unsuccessfully threatened her and accused her of witchery.

- Two other features include visions and notable services rendered. After miraculously multiplying a store of wine, St. Dominic (1170–1221) was raised up to heaven and saw the Virgin Mary clothed in blue and seated to the right of our Lord who informed him that Mary would care for his order.

- An eighth characteristic describes notable events surrounding the end of a saint's life. At the death of Gildas (ca. 500–ca. 570), angels attended his fragrant body, radiating with angelic brightness.

- Finally, divine guidance and protection often overshadow the life of the saint. While this may be more evident with some than with others, it is a common theme. While each of these characteristics is not necessarily utilized in the life of every saint, all are commonly incorporated in the larger corpus.

The life of a saint shows two very different, but related, components of the Christian life. On one hand, the saint is quite human: the names of family, places, and earthly surroundings are clearly delineated. On the other hand, there is a supernatural aspect to the saint's life that is evident, such as visions and miracles. Both of these components make the saint. The saint is not an angel, but a fleshly being through whom God actively and tangibly works.

Church History

The copious writings of church historians exhibit the appreciation of Christianity for her historical character. While there are numerous contemporary church histories, those composed in earlier times and in different places are of great interest for this study as they provide insight into the then-contemporary views and interpretations of past Christians and their historical context.

In the ten books of his Ecclesiastical History, Eusebius of Caesarea (ca. 260–ca. 340), an eminent fourth-century church historian, chronicled the first three centuries (and then some) of the Christian Church from Jesus and the apostles to Constantine. He included both orthodox Christians, such as Origen (ca. 185–ca. 254), and the lives of heretics, like Menander and Cerinthus.[5] Most importantly, Eusebius had access to and utilized an abundance of early fourth-century sources, both written and oral. He was the curator of Origen's literary works at the library in Caesarea, so Origen was a favored subject.

In the early Middle Ages, Bede composed the Ecclesiastical History of the English Nation (731). He begins with Gaius Julius Caesar's visit to this isle in 60 BC and concludes with the death of Archbishop Bertwald and the consecration of Tatwin as the archbishop of Canterbury in AD 731. Pope Gregory I is credited with initiating the missiological work in England. Bede does not shy away from the miraculous. Not only does Cuthbert, bishop of Lindisfarne perform miracles in his life, but miracles are associated with his tomb and relics. It must be noted that historical accuracy is a vital concern for Bede. Consequently, he utilizes the best contemporary sources to which he had access, which were learned scholars of his day and the archives at Rome.[6]

The Russian Primary Chronicle (1116) recounts the history of Christianity among the Slavs and Russians. Though it begins with Bible times, it focuses upon the Christianization of Russia under Prince Vladimir of Kiev (965–1015). It concludes in the early twelfth century.

In conclusion, church histories have proven to be a valuable literary genre for Christian biography. They are, at times, subjective in their collection and analysis of data, yet their principle value lies in their broad scope. That is, they do not portray one Christian life, but a collection and chronological series of Christian lives, providing a historical context for the larger Christian community. By beginning with the life of Christ, church histories also show the Christological basis of later Christian lives.

Hymn, Prayer, and Sermon

The Christian Church Year unswervingly revolves around the life of Christ. The most noticeable events in the life of Christ include His Nativity, Epiphany, Triumphant Entry, Passion, Resurrection, Ascension, sending of the Holy Spirit on the Day of Pentecost, and Final Advent. At the same time, a number of days commemorate Christian lives. While this practice first begins with the martyrs in the second century, bishops and other notable Christians are introduced into the Christian Church Year within a few centuries. The value of this practice has been the incorporation of biographical data into the liturgical life of the Church. This has already been noted in regard to the passion, martyrology, and Synaxarion. It is manifest also in hymn, prayer, and sermon.

The saints' days are considered minor festivals—second to the major festivals, the life of Christ—in the Church Year. Both biblical and extra-biblical characters are commemorated. Hymns and prayers used on a saint's day are often replete with biographical data for that particular saint. In his Book of the Martyr's Crowns, Prudentius (348–ca. 410) compiles fourteen hymns that narrate and interpret the passions of early Christian martyrs, such as Peter, Paul, Lawrence, and Cyprian. Horatio Bolton Nelson (1823–1913) composed the hymn, "From All Thy Saints in Warfare, For All Thy Saints at Rest" (1864). Verse one is introductory and verse three concluding. Dependent upon the saint's day being commemorated, one of more than twenty verses portraying New Testament saints is inserted as verse two. Prayers often provide a bit of biographical data as does the collect at Lauds for the commemoration of the martyr Lawrence (August 10) in the Roman Catholic Church: "Give us grace, Lord, to extinguish the fires of our evil passions, as You gave St. Lawrence the strength to triumph over the flames of his cruel torture."[7]

Biographical data also works its way into sermons. Funeral orations proclaim Jesus crucified and risen, but also depict, in part, the life of the deceased as it was connected to the life of Christ. The same is true for sermons preached on saints' days. Even with the objection in the sixteenth century by the Protestants to the overabundance of saints' days and the undue emphasis upon them, the House Sermons of Martin Luther (1483–1546) include homilies for the days of biblical saints as well as those from the Early Church, like Martin and Lawrence.[8]

In sum, the saints' days serve as an excellent example of the fine line that the study of Christian biography must walk. Undue emphasis upon the lives of the saints in worship can eclipse the honor due the Savior but this need not be the case. Instead, the lives of the saints can serve as appropriate examples and illustrations of God working mercifully and powerfully in and through His people.

Authorship

The authorship of Sacred Scripture is in one sense humanly manifold and in another divinely singular. While Moses penned the Pentateuch and Luke penned the Acts of the Apostles, the apostles Paul and Peter suggested a divine author: the Holy Spirit (2 Timothy 3:16; 2 Peter 1:21). For this reason Sacred Scripture serves as an unquestionable source for biographical data in the Christian Church. Even when the name of a human writer is in question, divine authorship trumps this concern. This is not to say that there are no difficulties with this position. For example, one question arises with the narrative of the rich man and Lazarus (Luke 16). Is the author telling a parable or depicting real people in an actual historical event? Nonetheless, the divinely inspired Bible holds center stage for credible and accurate biographical data in the Church.

Tradition also creates an umbrella of authorship. The history of Christianity has been generously sprinkled with biography-filled literature. Many of these have come to be incorporated into the liturgical life of the Church—martyrologies and Synaxarion, prayers and hymns. Their human writers are a diverse group: some are known, others are only cryptically known through pseudonyms, while many remain anonymous. Through their incorporation into the life and tradition of the Church, the human writers are not as significant as is the principal actor in the Church: the Holy Spirit. It was not that the Spirit of God had inspired these writers in a fashion identical to that in the Bible, but the Spirit who descends upon the Church on the day of Pentecost remains with the Church, preserving and directing her ways and works and words. This is not to say that these writings of tradition must not be critically examined; questionable writings have, from time to time, erringly rested under the umbrella of tradition. Even so, the numerous writings of tradition have great spiritual value in the Church.

Other authors must be more critically assessed; many questions must be asked. Who was the author? What access did the author have to appropriate data? How was the author qualified? What was the intent of the author? These are great concerns when looking at ancient documents, but are no less important with those that are more contemporary.

Clearly, there is a hierarchy of authority with authorship: divine authorship is the most authoritative, while human the least. However, this does not imply that all biographical data in the Bible is of equal importance. For example, the genealogies of Ham or Japheth are not without importance, but that of Shem bears the messianic line (Genesis 10–11). The value of the biographical data of Jehoram (2 Chronicles 21) cannot rival that of Jesus in the Gospels. Moreover, the importance of biographical data for significant historical figures such as Augustine and Martin Luther certainly rival that of a variety of minor biblical figures. At the same time, they remain secondary to and flow from the life of Christ. While authorship is significant and must be carefully analyzed, it does not provide all the answers in determining the values and corresponding relations of biographical data in the Church.

Sum

This brief survey of literary genres is not exhaustive, but imparts a modicum of background to a few of the many literary forms that have been utilized in the history of the Christian Church in preserving biographical data. Moreover, these and others—biography and autobiography, dictionary and encyclopedia—will be referred to in the following chapters. Furthermore, it illustrates the Christian Church's diverse employment of biographical data in her life: Holy Gospels are read aloud in the Divine Service and passions at the Prayer Offices; lives of the saints are studied for personal inspiration and church histories in academia.

Methodology

The study of Christian biography can take one of two routes. One option is to use the volumes of contemporary literature that portray and analyze the lives of Christians throughout the history of the Christian Church. Instead, this study will examine several Christian lives according to the literature of their respective times and traditions. The documents employed here are most commonly from earlier eras and from a great variety of authors and geographical locales. Please note that, with a few exceptions, each Christian life depicted in this volume is based upon one historical document.

A threefold methodology will be employed in the choice of biographical documents. The first choice of a document will be one that has been composed by the subject himself or a contemporary author. For example, the Confessions of Augustine (354–430) is an autobiography, while the Life and Acts of Martin Luther is penned by Philip Melanchthon (1497–1560), a younger contemporary of the great reformer. The second option will employ authors who have written within a few generations of the subject, for example, Bede (ca. 673–735) is born approximately 69 years after the death of Pope Gregory I (ca. 540–604) and includes biographical data for Gregory in his Ecclesiastical History of the English Nation. On occasion, later authors from the same tradition will be used as when the Synaxarion of the Orthodox Church depicts her saints, such as Gregory Palamas (ca. 1296–1359) and others. Third, a modern dictionary or church history may contain biographical data for those of earlier periods, but will be used here only for contemporary Christians.

This study of Christian biography cannot examine Christian lives with perfect objectivity apart from a contemporary perspective. Nonetheless, its intent is to make a historical argument. To make this argument, not only is the specific biographical data historical in nature, each chapter will include an analysis of Christian biography from that period and/or tradition. The purpose of this historical analysis is to show that a common theme pervades Christian biography throughout the history of the Church: Christian lives point to and flow out of the life of Christ.

Summary

The sources and literary genres and uses of biographical data in the Christian Church are quite diverse and complex in their relations of one to another. However, one cannot ignore such data. The theology of the Church is historical, which requires that she cannot ignore the created order through which her God works and, thus, reveals Himself and His will. Instead, the Church must continue to analyze (critically) the great multitude of literary genres of Christian biography for use in pedagogy and study, praying and hymning, and in countless other fashions. The following chapters will survey an assortment of literary genres and their Christian subjects from many different times and places and authors in order to view these Christian lives in relation to the life of Christ.

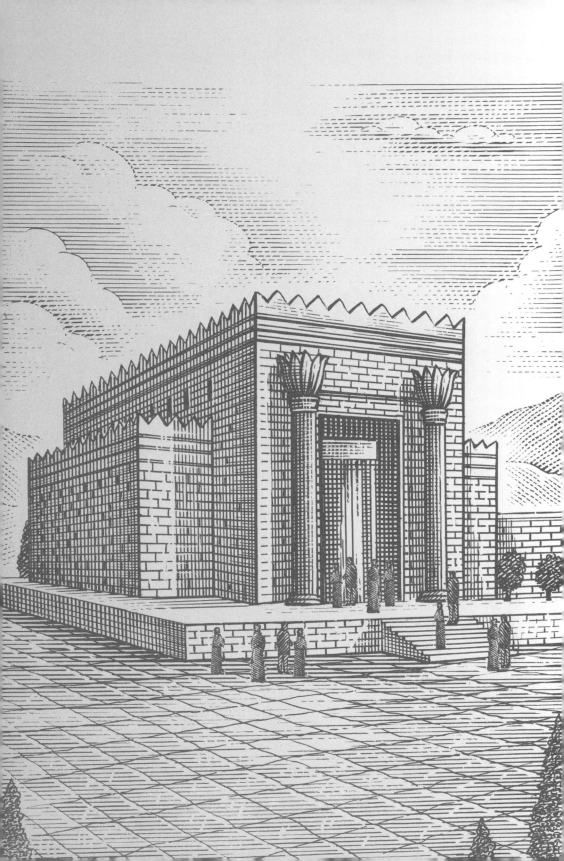

2

BIBLE TIMES

Creation to AD 100

The Bible is awash in biographical data. It cites births and deaths, friends and foes, offices and travels, times and places, and many other components common to human life. The reason for this is quite simple: God works through and reveals Himself in people. Scripture therefore chronicles the lives of these people and those around them. The Bible documents the lives of a select few—Isaac, Jacob, Joseph, Moses, Samson, Samuel, Solomon, Jeremiah, John the Baptist, and Jesus—from birth to death.[1] The provision of biographical data for other biblical figures ranges from quite extensive, for example, Abraham and Paul, to the most minimal, like Shamgar (Judges 3:31) and Aeneas (Acts 9:32–35).

The immense amount of biographical data in the Bible can be organized in a number of ways, but the data may be collated most simply under three categories, each with three subcategories. The initial category is birth with the subcategories of pre-birth, birth, and post-birth events.

An important person often has a more than interesting birth and, on occasion, astounding incidents occur both before and after this birth to draw attention to it and emphasize its significance. The next category is life and includes the subcategories of childhood, life-changing events, and specific events. Again, significant people often have interesting childhoods that seem to foreshadow their greatness and one or more events specifically associated with their lives. In addition and usually most interesting, there is often a single incident upon which one's life pivots: The old life is left behind and the new life is begun. The last category is death with the subcategories of pre-death, death, and post-death events.

Much of the collections of biographical data are preserved and analyzed chronologically: parents bear children, a high priest or judge or king is succeeded by another. This is quite pronounced in many genealogies, particularly in the oft-mentioned succession of patriarchs Abraham, Isaac, and Jacob. Also, a hero and a villain are often paired up against the other. Adam and the serpent in the Garden of Eden establish this paradigm and are followed by their respective ancestors, Isaac and Ishmael, Moses and Pharaoh, John the Baptist and Herod, to name a few.

At the peak of this biographical mountain of data is Jesus. The intent of this book is to illustrate that all Christian lives are directly related to the life of Christ, through faith and Baptism, the Lord's Supper and various offices, like mother, martyr, reformer. (While Baptism and the Lord's Supper are New Testament sacraments, there are similar rites—circumcision and the Passover—in the Old Testament that serve analogously.) This chapter will demonstrate that the principle relation between biblical Christian lives and life of Christ is familial. Once it is recognized that all of these have the same heavenly Father, then numerous family traits become evident. Consequently, this chapter serves as a sort of family portrait for the Old Testament people of God and New Testament Christians with Jesus at the very center.

The Two Adams

The assertion that Jesus is at the very center of the biographical data in the Bible is true, yet somewhat misleading. Technically, there are two centers, two Adams: 1) Adam and 2) Jesus, the Second Adam. Nonetheless, the latter fully eclipses the former. Consequently, these two must be carefully compared. Adam's life serves as the initial basis for the lives of all people, but Christ, following after Adam and replacing him, serves as the new basis and is the true center from which all Christian lives emanate.

Adam Time: Creation
Place: Garden of Eden
Office: First Adam
Biography: Genesis
Biographer: Moses

Adam, the First Adam, is the archetype for all biographical data in the Bible. He is the first human created, and he is created in the image of God. All of the creation makes known to some degree the nature of its creator, with its orderliness, beauty, goodness. Adam, along with Eve, reveal God and His will in a special way: God speaks animals into existence, and in kind Adam speaks their names into existence (Genesis 2:19); God creates all of creation for Adam and Eve, and Adam and Eve become caretakers of all creation (Genesis 1:26); God creates, and humanity procreates (Genesis 1:28). Adam is the archetype of human life in that he reflects the divine image. As such, his descendants are intended also to reflect the divine image.

The biographical data of Adam is brief, but meaningful. While he is not born of a father and a mother, he is conceived of the earth and the breath of God (Genesis 2:7) on the sixth day of creation (Genesis 1:27, 31) and placed in the Garden of Eden (Genesis 2:8). The determinative component in Adam's life is a single, life-changing event: He succumbs to the serpent's temptation (Genesis 3:1–6). Rather than obeying and seeking God, he disobeys and hides (Genesis 3:8). Rather than living in and tending to the garden, he is cast out of Eden (Genesis 3:24) and toils in the newly cursed land (Genesis 3:17). Rather than living, he dies when he is 930 years old (Genesis 5:5). With Adam succumbing to the serpent's temptation, Adam loses the divine image. Devoid of the breath of God, Adam is but earth or soil. Adam no longer reflects the divine image, but rather, is only a muddy human image. The descendents of Adam inherit this muddy human image: brotherly love is replaced with anger and murder (Genesis 3:6–8), fertile women with barren (Genesis 11:30, 29:31;

Judges 13:2; 1 Samuel 1:6; Luke 1:7), health with disease, a home with nomadism, food with hunger, life with death. According to the apostle Paul, Adam remains the archetype of humanity, not in reflecting the divine image as initially intended, but a muddy human image that sins and dies.

Therefore, Adam is the first archetype of humanity. With creation, his life initially reflects the image of God with his descendants set to follow in his footsteps. Because Adam fell into sin and death, so do his descendants. With the fall, there is need for a Second Adam: one who can replace the first—one who can serve as the divinely intended archetype for all human biography—and one who can overshadow the consequences of the first. The life of the Second Adam must reflect the image of God so that the image of God may be reflected in the lives of His heirs and, thus, restore the original intent of God's creation of humanity.

Jesus	Time: ca. 5 BC–ca. AD 30
	Place: Promised Land
	Office: Second Adam
	Biographies: Gospels according to Matthew, Mark, Luke, and John
	Biographers: Matthew, Mark, Luke, John

Jesus, the Second Adam, takes center stage in the Bible. Quantitatively, the biographical data of Jesus in the four Gospels—Matthew, Mark, Luke, and John—is extensive, if not exhaustive (John 21:25). Textually, the life of Christ in the four Gospels introduces the New Testament as the life of Adam introduces Old Testament. Genealogically, God first promises to Eve that her seed shall crush the seed of the serpent (Genesis 3:15), and the Gospel according to St. Luke shows that Jesus is this culminating descendant (Luke 3:23–38). Theologically, the apostle Paul claims that the two are inextricably connected. Adam brought into the world sin and death, whereas Jesus brought righteousness and life. Jesus is the Second Adam: God fully reveals His divine image in the life of Christ. As such, the life of Christ replaces the life of Adam as the archetype for all human biography.

- The first category of biographical data concerning the life of Christ consists of His birth and the many astonishing events surrounding it.

Prior to Jesus' conception, the archangel Gabriel foretells His birth to Mary, Joseph's fiancée (Luke 1:30–35). After His conception, an angel of the Lord announces to Joseph that this child has been miraculously conceived by the Holy Spirit, and that he would be called "Jesus" and is "Immanuel" (Matthew 1:18–25). Moreover, Mary's Magnificat (Luke 1:46–56) and Zechariah's Benedictus (Luke 1:67–79) prophesy of Jesus. Furthermore, the census of Caesar Augustus (27 BC–AD 14) causes the Holy Family to travel from Nazareth to Bethlehem for His birth (Luke 2:1–4). Jesus' birth itself is rather common and unadorned, yet it sets Jesus in time (ca. 5 BC), at a place (Bethlehem), and among people (Caesar, Joseph, and Mary). Following the birth of Jesus, there are heavenly and angelic signs (Matthew 2:2, Luke 2:8–12), foreign and local visitors (Matthew 2:1–11, Luke 2:15–16), and amazed hearers and the praise of God (Matthew 2:11, Luke 2:13–14, 18).

Jesus' birth not only parallels, but greatly surpasses the creation of Adam, His fleshly ancestor. Jesus' birth shows Him to be the Second Adam and serves as the rebirth of humanity. In both, God initiates and is intimately involved. More specifically, just as God breathes His divine breath—Spirit—into the soil-turned-flesh of Adam, so God speaks His Holy Spirit—divine breath—into the virgin Mary to conceive Jesus. Jesus is the new and greater Adam in that He has a human mother and is the Son of God.

Jesus' birth becomes the new archetype of birth! Through human procreation, the descendants of Adam reflect not the image of God, but Adam's muddy human image: They sin and die. Through the second birth of the Sacrament of Holy Baptism, the descendants of Adam are born again like Jesus' birth—God's Spirit is breathed into their human flesh and blood, and they become sons and daughters of God, heirs of Jesus (John 3:3–8, Titus 3:5–7).[2] Consequently, all who are reborn in Baptism reflect, at least partially, the image of God (Romans 6:3–5, Galatians 3:27). Jesus' birth eclipses the creation of Adam and becomes the archetype for the new birth of Baptism in Christian lives. The Gospels' inclusion of numerous extraordinary events surrounding the birth of Jesus underscores its significance.

- The second category of biographical data is comprised of Jesus' childhood, Baptism, and ministry.

Shortly following Jesus' birth, King Herod learns from the Magi about whom they claim is born King of the Jews. Fearful of losing his throne, Herod puts to death all boys two years and younger in and around Bethlehem. Jesus is spared as the Holy Family flees to Egypt (Matthew 2:13–18). While still a young boy, Jesus is filled with wisdom and divine grace (Luke 2:40). At age 12, he exhibits advanced maturity and intellect in conversing with the teachers in the temple at Jerusalem (Luke 2:46). And most uncommon to young boys, he obeys his parents and "increased in wisdom and in stature and in favor with God and man" (Luke 2:51–52).

An extremely bright facet in the life of Christ is His Baptism. It is a life-changing event, not that Jesus changes, but others do. From the time this 12-year-old boy sits in the temple to the time this same man at approximately 30 years of age stands in the Jordan River, Jesus lives a quiet life according to the silence of the four Gospels. This changes dramatically when Jesus is unequivocally revealed as the Son of God in His Baptism. After He is baptized by John the Baptist, the Son of God rises from the water, the heavens open so that the Holy Spirit may descend upon Him, and the Father says, "This is my beloved Son, with whom I am well pleased" (Matthew 3:16–17). Immediately following, sides are chosen: Jesus is spirited off to the wilderness where Satan unsuccessfully tempts Him (Matthew 4:1–11). The apostles and sundry disciples follow after Jesus. On Satan's side gather many of the Jews and their leaders, numerous Roman soldiers and the Roman Governor Pontius Pilate. With His baptism, Jesus' life shifts from being relatively calm to being quite contentious.

The ministry of Jesus begins immediately following his Baptism and temptation, and continues for approximately three years as he travels through Judea, Samaria, and Galilee.

With his teaching, Jesus reminds the people of God's creation how they are to reflect the image of God in their lives. While the Ten Commandments earlier attempted to redefine the divine image in humanity, Jesus clarifies: "You have heard that it was said to those of old, 'You shall not murder', . . . But I say to you that everyone who is angry with his brother will be liable to judgment" (Matthew 5:21–22), and then, "Love your enemies and pray for those who persecute you" (Matthew 5:44). God did not murder and was not angry without reason, but loved even His enemies (Romans 5:6–8). This is how humans are to reflect the image of God in their lives. One other example—Jesus' teaching on marriage—must suffice: "Because of your hardness of heart Moses allowed you to divorce your wives, but from the beginning it was not so" (Matthew 19:8). The marriage of Adam and Eve reflects the image of God: just as the Father, Son, and Spirit are one God, so Adam and Eve become one flesh. In sharp contrast, divorce distorts the image of God in humanity: an emphasis upon plurality rather than singularity, division rather than unity. Jesus' teachings are neither arbitrary nor legalistic, but point to the way God intended human life to be in the beginning.

With the fall, the image of God has been lost in Adam and his descendants; rather than health there is illness, rather than life, death. With His miracles, Jesus shows God's initial intent of human life and the manifestation of the divine image in people. With His miracles, Jesus begins to recraft the image of God in humanity. To the Baptist's disciples, Jesus recited the litany of His miracles: "the blind receive their sight and the lame walk, lepers are cleansed and the deaf hear, and the dead are raised up, and the poor have good news preached to them" (Matthew 11:5). The divine image of health and life in Adam that was lost through the fall is replaced in Jesus' miracles. As it had been in the beginning, so it becomes again with Jesus' miracles.

Jesus' giving sight to the blind, other similar actions, or even His birth to the virgin Mary are commonly but somewhat inappropriately termed miracles. Miracles transgress the laws of nature. And while Jesus' miracles appear to transgress the laws of nature after the Fall, they actually restore life as life had been prior to the Fall. They restore humanity to the way it was first created: reflecting the image of God in every aspect of life. In addition, Jesus reflects the image of God in his miracles in that just as God first created Adam with the divine image, Jesus replaces the dirty image of the descendants of Adam with the divine image in his heirs.

In all three components, the life of Christ clearly reflects the image of God. In Jesus' infancy and youth, he shows divine wisdom. In his Baptism, Jesus most clearly and fully reveals the image of the Triune God: Father, Son, and Holy Spirit. In Jesus' teachings and miracles, he imprints the image of God upon others, as first, if only briefly, reflected in the first Adam. In all three components, the life of Christ becomes the archetype of life for all Christian lives both following and preceding.

• The third category of biographical data depicts Jesus' death.

While there are many allusions in the life of Christ to His death, both cryptic (Matthew 2:11, Luke 2:34–35, John 12:24) and obvious (Matthew 16:21), the events surrounding Jesus' death shine as precious gems in His kingly crown. The death of Jesus is painstakingly portrayed, not in morbid interest, but because it is the ironic pinnacle of the life of Christ.

Jesus' death takes place on Friday upon a cross. He is mocked as the King of the Jews (Matthew 27:37), speaks seven words (phrases),[3] and between two criminals (Luke 23:33) dies. The simplicity of this event betrays its cosmological depth. In His death, Jesus redeems humanity. God first looks at or judges all of humanity through Adam. Adam sinned and was punished with death, which was to be the fate of his descendants. God once again looks at or judges all of humanity, but this time, through Jesus. Jesus is without sin, but receives the punishment that the descendants of Adam deserve. Consequently, the heirs of Jesus are declared innocent and live (Romans 5:6–11; Hebrews 10:11–18).

In the week prior to His death, Jesus rides into Jerusalem upon a donkey (Matthew 21:1–11), cleanses the temple (Matthew 31:12–17), is anointed (Matthew 26:6–13), and institutes the Lord's Supper (Matthew 26:26–30). In His last hours, Jesus is betrayed by Judas (Matthew 26:14–16), arrested (Matthew 26:47–56), condemned by the Sanhedrin (Matthew 26:57–66), denied three times by Peter (Matthew 26:69–74), judged by Pilate (Matthew 27:26), and mocked by the Roman soldiers (Matthew 27:27–31). At the very least, these many details accentuate the significance of Jesus' death.

Immediately after Jesus' death, a centurion exclaims, "Certainly this man was innocent!" (Luke 23:47); the temple curtain tears in two (Mark 16:38); the earth quakes (Matthew 27:51); the sun darkens (Luke 23:45). In addition, Jesus descends to hell (1 Peter 3:19), rises from the dead, and ascends to the right hand of the Father (Luke 24:51). With these actions, Jesus demonstrates that humanity is not meant to live in a prison, but paradise; humanity is not meant to die, but live; humanity is not meant to be apart from God, but with God. With these events, Jesus provides humanity with the hope of freedom, eternal life, and communion with God.

Jesus' death locates Him in time (ca. AD 30), at a place (Golgotha), and among people (soldiers and two criminals). It also shows how the death of Christ fully supercedes that of Adam. While initially having judged all of humanity through the fallen Adam, God judges humanity anew through the crucified Jesus. The crucified Jesus perfectly reveals the divine image: "God shows His love for us in that while we were still sinners, Christ died for us" (Romans 5:8). Any questions about who God is and what He is like are answered there. In His death and the surrounding events, Jesus is the archetype of death for humanity: it reveals God's love and serves others and leads to life with God!

Sum

The contrast of the biographical data between these "distant cousins", Adam and Jesus, is quite stark quantitatively and qualitatively, yet the two are really "close relatives". God creates Adam as the archetype of humanity. The divine intent is this: The image of God is reflected in Adam, and Adam's descendants are to reflect the image of God, His righteousness and life. With the fall, the image of God in Adam is lost, however, Adam remains the archetype of humanity. Adam's descendants do not reflect the image of God, but rather, Adam's dirty image: sin and death. Consequently, God sends the Second Adam to replace the first. Jesus soundly defeats Adam's antagonist in the wilderness, through His miracles and teachings, upon the cross at Golgotha, and in His resurrection from the tomb. Where Adam fails through the fall, Jesus perfectly reflects the image of God in His birth, life, and death. While Adam brings sin and death to all humanity, Jesus brings righteousness and life. The life of the Second Adam fully eclipses the first and becomes the new archetype for all of humanity.

The lives of Adam and Christ, then, are the dual starting points for analyzing the lives of all people in the Old and New Testaments. All are the descendants of Adam and, thus, bear the family traits of a muddy human image: sin and death. In contrast, the heirs of Jesus inherit the image of God, so numerous familial resemblances to Jesus are manifest in various components of their lives. Throughout the biographical data in the Old Testament, these divine images and christological resemblances are signs that point forward to Jesus, while those in the New Testament point back to the same. Christian biography in the Old and New Testaments, then, include sins and signs that physically and spiritually link them respectively to their two archetypes: Adam and Jesus.

Old Testament

The great multitude of biographical data in the Old Testament creates a labyrinth of biographies: the data of one connects to, intersects with, overlaps, and/or parallels others. Analysis and comprehension, though, are not impossible. The great assortment of raw data must be categorized concerning birth, life, death, and their corresponding components, as well as evaluated in light of its chronological and theological placement between Adam and Jesus. Everyone in the Old Testament is a descendent of Adam and, thus, exhibits the appropriate family trait: a muddy human image. At the same time, many of the descendants of Adam are also the heirs of Jesus. These heirs are often biologically related to Jesus, but always according to faith. For example, Abraham is an ancestor of Jesus because he is in the genealogical line from Adam to Jesus, but he is also an heir of Jesus through faith. Abraham believes the promises of God that will culminate in Jesus (Genesis 15:6; John 8:56).

These heirs of Jesus manifest the divine image, but as they are also the descendants of Adam, they do so only partially and in varying fashions. This section will analyze the biographical data in the Old Testament according to the sins of the soiled images that point back to Adam and the signs of the divine image that point forward to Jesus. Analysis of these lives is also dependent upon their many different offices.

Patriarch. A patriarch is the leader of an extended family or tribe. This term is utilized for the male leaders in the early history of the Old Testament. For the people over whom they watch, they bear both physical and spiritual responsibilities. In the absence of a priest, they stand between God and His people. The three most august patriarchs are Abraham (ca. 2166–ca. 1991 BC), Isaac (ca. 2066–ca. 1886 BC), and Jacob (ca. 2066–ca. 1859 BC). The twelve sons of Jacob constitute the twelve tribes of Israel, and so, each becomes the patriarch of his respective tribe. Rueben is the firstborn, Joseph (1915–1805 BC) gets the most ink in Genesis, but the genealogical line from Adam to Jesus passes through Judah (Genesis 49:8–12).

Priest. A priest stands between God and His people, be it for prayer or sacrifice or a host of other rituals. Melchizedek, an early and rather obscure priest, blesses Abraham (Genesis 14). With the covenant at Mount Sinai, God institutes a more ordered, two-tiered priesthood among the Israelites. Aaron is the first high priest, with his sons constituting the

Aaronic Priesthood. All of the males of the tribe of the Levi form the Levitic Priesthood and assist the high priest.

Judge. A series of judges lead the Israelites following the leadership of Joshua (d. ca. 1375 BC) and preceding the first king of Israel, Saul (ca. 1050–10 BC). During this time, the Israelites are a loose confederation of tribes. Whenever a considerable uprising of the indigenous peoples in the Promised Land occurs, God raises up a judge to lead the Israelites to victory. There are a number of judges ranging from the obscure, like Othniel (Judges 3:7–11) and Shamgar (Judges 3:31), to the well-known, like Gideon (Judges 6–8) and Samson (Judges 13–16), and even a woman, Deborah (Judges 4–5).

King. Unhappy with God's use of judges and desirous to be like other nations of their day, the Israelites demand of God a king (1 Samuel 8). The king is anointed with oil to signify that he has received the Spirit of God, and speaks and acts on behalf of God for the people. The prophet Samuel anoints first Saul and then David as his successor. Solomon, the son of David, succeeds his father. Following the death of Solomon, the Israelites experience civil war and two parallel series of kings rule the Northern and Southern Kingdoms.

Nazarite. A Nazarite's life is not his own: He takes a vow and sets apart a portion or all of his life for a consecrated purpose. The regulations for a Nazarite are quite specific. He can neither drink alcohol nor cut his hair, and he may not go near a dead body. On the day that his vow is fulfilled, he shaves his head, burns the hair, and offers a sacrifice (Numbers 6:1–21). Only Samson is specifically called a Nazarite, though it is sometimes suggested of Joseph (Genesis 49:26) and Samuel (1 Samuel 1:11), and general references are made to others (Amos 2:11; Acts 21:23).

Prophet. A prophet unequivocally proclaims the word of God. The principle qualification of a prophet is that God's words are placed in his mouth, and he speaks God's words to the people (Deuteronomy 18:18). In various prophets and their prophesies, God consistently works in time, place, and among people to reveal Himself and His will. In so doing, these prophets consistently point to Jesus[4] or at least His near vicinity.[5] And as with the other Old Testament characters who are heirs of Jesus, the prophets clearly reveal the image of God in their lives and foreshadow the life of Christ. The many prophets are quite diverse geographically; Jonah was a prophet to Nineveh in Assyria, Elijah was a prophet to the Northern

Kingdom, Isaiah to the Southern Kingdom, and Haggai to postexilic Judea.

Wife and Mother. The numerous father-son-styled genealogies in the Old Testament intimate a corresponding quantity of wives and mothers. Eve is the wife of Adam and bears Cain and Abel, and later Seth. Sarah, the wife of Abraham, gives birth to Isaac. Rebecca, the wife of Isaac, gives birth to Esau and Jacob. Leah and Rachel, the wives of Jacob, give birth to numerous sons and daughters between them. Ruth is the wife of Boaz and bears Obed. While the lineage from Adam to Jesus is generally chronicled according to the respective fathers and sons, Eve, Sarah, Rebecca, Rachel, Ruth, and ultimately Mary in the New Testament are integral components, to say the least.

Eve	Time: Creation
	Place: Garden of Eden
	Offices: Wife, Mother
	Biography: Genesis
	Biographer: Moses

On the sixth day of creation, God created Eve, the second human and the first woman. She, in her intimate relation to Adam, reflects the image of God in her marriage, procreation, and stewardship of Eden. So closely connected to Adam, she cannot but fall with him and participate in losing the divine image in humanity. Simultaneously, she is both an ancestor and heir of Jesus.

Eve has neither father nor mother, but is formed from Adam's rib. Here the relation between man and woman is established and revealed: She is bone of his bones and flesh of his flesh (Genesis 2:23). Not only their lives, but their very beings are inextricably intertwined. One becomes two in creation and then the two become one in marriage, and as such, they reflect the image of the Triune God—plural yet singular.

The life of Eve begins in the Garden of Eden. There, she lives under three divine commands: be fruitful, subdue the creation (Genesis 1:28), and "You may surely eat of every tree of the garden, but of the tree of the knowledge of good and evil you shall not eat, for in the day that you eat of it you shall surely die" (Genesis 2:16–17). The determinative event in Eve's life is her ill-fated encounter in Eden. The serpent hisses to her, "Did God actually say, 'You shall not eat of any tree in the garden' "? To which Eve mistakenly remarked, "We may eat of the fruit of the trees in the garden, but God said, 'You shall not eat of the fruit of the tree that is in the midst of the garden, neither shall you touch it, lest you die." The serpent then lies, "You will not surely die" (Genesis 3:1–4). The serpent began with a false question to which Eve followed with a wrong answer. The serpent deceives Eve and she succumbs to this temptation. She actively participates in the fall.

The life of Eve is tragic, but given a gracious promise: the seed of the serpent will strike the heel of Eve's seed, but the latter will crush the head of the former (Genesis 3:15). It is not fulfilled in her firstborn son, Cain, who would kill his brother, Abel (Genesis 4:8). Instead, there will be a long line of descendants who will partially fulfill this promise. This promise will finally culminate in the birth of the Second Adam. He will defeat the serpent and restore fallen creation to its original state.

Eve is created to help Adam. Rather than helping him reflect the image of God, she assists in his fall, and so, she shares in his fall and all of its ramifications, sin and death. At the same time, she is the biological root from which the Savior of creation will ultimately sprout. She is the fore-mother of the Second Adam.

Isaac	Time: ca. 2066–ca. 1886 BC
	Place: Promised Land
	Office: Patriarch
	Biography: Genesis
	Biographer: Moses

Isaac is often overlooked in light of such luminaries as Abraham, the father of faith, and Jacob, the father of the twelve tribes of Israel. Between these two significant fathers is an amazing son. He is the first person for whom the Bible portrays all three categories: birth, life, and death. In addition, the many recorded components of his life show not only sins that pointed back to Adam's life but also many signs of the divine image that point forward to the life of Christ.

The first category of biographical data includes Isaac's birth and corresponding components. Prior to Isaac's birth, God establishes His covenant with Abraham promising him a son (Genesis 15:4). After Abraham errantly sires a son, Ishmael, with Hagar, the maid of his wife, God again and more specifically promises Abraham a son with his wife, Sarah, and God provides the name. Later in the form of three men, God visits Abraham and in no uncertain terms reiterates to him that he will have a son by Sarah who is too old to bear a child (Genesis 18:1–15). The conception of Isaac is divinely worked (Genesis 21:1). Following his birth, Isaac is circumcised on the eighth day according to the divine command (Genesis 21:4). While the actual birth of Isaac is rather uneventful (Genesis 21:2), the actions surrounding the birth of Isaac are nothing short of amazing.

In the events leading up to Isaac's birth, God is beginning to re-craft the divine image in humanity. God promises Abraham that he will have a son. This is how, in part, humanity originally reflected the image of God: God creates, and humanity procreates. Prior to the fall, God tells Adam and Eve to be fruitful, multiply, and fill the earth (Genesis 1:28), and so, reflect the image of God. Infertility, then, is a result of the fall. Abraham and Sarah, too old to have children, are the descendants of Adam. God restores His image in Abraham and Sarah with the promise of a son. This divine foretelling, providing a name, and Isaac's miraculous conception are signs that point to Jesus' annunciation, divinely provided name, and miraculous conception. God acts in both, restoring His divine image in humanity.

The youth of Isaac is not without incident. Early on, an antagonistic relationship develops between he and his half-brother, Ishmael, and between their mothers, Sarah and Hagar (Genesis 21:8–21). According to Paul in the New Testament, Hagar represents Mount Sinai and Ishmael bondage, while Sarah signifies the promise and Isaac freedom (Galatians 4:25–26, 28–29). Symbolically, Ishmael is a descendant of Adam while Isaac is an heir of Jesus. Ishmael's birth takes place according to human will as did the fall. In contrast, Isaac's birth is the result of the divine will as is the creation of the First Adam and the conception of the Second. Ishmael's birth is a result of the fall, while Isaac is the son of the promise first made to Eve and finally fulfilled in Jesus.

While still a youth, God instructs Abraham to take his son of the promise to Mount Moriah. Isaac travels with a donkey, carries the wood for the offering, ascends the mount, lays bound upon the altar, and is offered as a sacrifice, only to be replaced at the last minute by a ram caught in a thicket (Genesis 22:1–19). This near-sacrifice of Isaac not only tests the faith of Abraham (Genesis 22:1–12) but also foreshadows Jesus' passion. Just as Isaac travels with a donkey, so will Jesus ride a donkey on Palm Sunday. Just as Isaac carries wood for the sacrifice upon his back to Mount Moriah, so will Jesus bear His cross to Golgotha. Just as Isaac is bound upon the altar, so will Jesus be nailed to the cross. And just as a ram replaces Isaac as the sacrifice, so Jesus will replace the entire sacrificial system of the Old Testament. In addition, the divine image is revealed twice in the relation between Abraham and Isaac: Abraham offers his son as a sacrifice as the divine Father will do with His only begotten Son, and Isaac obeys the will of His father even to the point of death as Jesus obeys His Father (Matthew 26:39, 42, 44).

In his life, Isaac's wife, Rebecca, comes from Nahor, Mesopotamia, the land of Abraham's family. The miraculous conception in the womb of Rebecca follows after Sarah and also points to Mary, the mother of Jesus. In all three, God is responsible, and with Rebecca, she has not just one son, but twins. The antagonism between Isaac and his half-brother continues with Isaac's sons, Jacob and Esau. The parallel lines run as follows: Adam, Isaac, Jacob, and Jesus versus the serpent, Ishmael, Esau, and Satan. Esau is the elder twin and his genealogy is extensive (Genesis 36), but Jacob becomes Isaac's heir and stands in the line from Adam to Jesus. He lives 180 years, and his two sons bury him (Genesis 35:27–29), just as Jesus will be buried by two men (John 19:38–39).

Clearly, Isaac is both a descendant of Adam and an heir of Jesus. The procreative problems with his mother and wife depict him a descendent of Adam. On the other hand, he is an heir of Jesus in that he is born into the lineage from Adam to Jesus. He also bears many of the traits of Jesus' family: an annunciation of his birth, a heavenly provided name, an antagonistic relation, obedience to his father, near-sacrifice, and burial by two. This son, and later patriarch, is a member of the family of God.

Aaron	Time: sixteenth century BC
	Place: Egypt, Wilderness
	Office: High Priest
	Biographies: Exodus, Leviticus, Numbers, Deuteronomy
	Biographer: Moses

Aaron is the brother of two famous siblings, Moses and Miriam. The former is the leader of the Israelites who speaks on behalf of God and performs many wonders. The latter is a prophetess. In contrast, Aaron becomes the high priest for the Israelites. The biographical data provided for him far surpasses that of his sister, but is much less than that of his brother.

The biographical data for Aaron begins just prior to the Exodus. Upon hearing the cries of His people, God determines to deliver the Israelites from slavery in Egypt. God appears to Moses and sends him to deliver the Israelites. Aaron both speaks on behalf of Moses and performs signs (Exodus 4:14–17).

Aaron's assisting relation to Moses is again portrayed at Rephidim where the Israelites fight against the Amalekites. Joshua leads the Jewish warriors into battle. As long as Moses keeps his arms raised up the Israelites prevail, but if they fall, the Israelites begin to lose the battle. Aaron, along with Hur, hold up Moses' arms and the Israelites finally defeat the Amalekites (Exodus 17).

The principle biographical data for Aaron begins at Mount Sinai where God reveals Himself and His will through the Law. With Moses upon Mount Sinai receiving the Law from God, the people grow restless and demand that Aaron make them an image of their god. Succumbing to their wishes, he collects their gold jewelry and fashions a calf and declares it their god. God tells Moses to descend and take care of this problem. Moses burns the golden calf, grinds it into powder, mixes it with water, and makes the Israelites consume their "god." When questioned by Moses, Aaron decries any responsibility, putting the blame wholly upon the people. He simply did as they commanded him.

At Mount Sinai, God establishes the formal priesthood for the Israelites. Aaron becomes the high priest and his sons are to follow after him in this office. The Aaronic Priesthood becomes responsible for overseeing the newly instituted and rather complex worship life of the Israelites. One of the more important aspects in this worship is sacrifice. When an Israelite disobeys the divine law and breaks the covenant, a sacrifice must be offered to appease God's anger and divert His punishment. These sacrifices are many and varied. When Nadab and Abihu, two of Aaron's sons, come into God's presence and offer improper sacrifices to God, they are consumed in fire. Attempting to right the previous wrong, God institutes the Day of Atonement (Leviticus 16) and the high priest is to come before God in the Holy Place only once a year for this ritual. Two goats are chosen. One is slaughtered for the sins of the Israelites that have been committed during the entire year, while the other is sent into the desert bearing the guilt of the Israelites for the entire year. This office and its duties are so important that the priests must wear special clothing to illustrate this. Aaron dies and is buried at Mount Hor. His son, Eleazar, succeeds him as high priest and the Israelites mourn his death for 30 days (Deuteronomy 20).

Aaron is a man and, as such, is a descendent of Adam. This is portrayed in his succumbing to temptation as did Adam and his grievously sinful sons. In contrast, his work as a priest and the sacrifices themselves point ahead to the life of Christ, or rather, His death. A hierarchy of sacrifices develops. First, a particular sacrifice was offered for a particular sin of an individual. Later, the Day of Atonement took care of the sins and guilt that had accumulated among the Jews throughout the year. Finally, the crucifixion of Jesus is a sacrifice that appeases God's anger and diverts His punishment for all of the sins of all people in all times and places.

Samson	Time: d. ca. 1055 BC
	Place: Promised Land
	Offices: Judge, Nazarite
	Biography: Judges

Samson's biography occupies only four chapters (13–16) in the Book of Judges, yet cannot be brushed aside. Samson is a heroic character and appears to be larger than life with his superhuman strength, however, his life is also quite tragic. The weaving together of these contrasting aspects in Samson's life produces a compelling biography.

The actual birth of Samson does not appear to be too significant, but the events surrounding it suggest otherwise. The angel of the Lord appears to Samson's barren mother and promises her that she will give birth to a son. He will be no ordinary man, but a Nazarite who will deliver the Israelites from the oppression of the Philistines (Judges 13:3–5). After the angel of the Lord appears later to Samson's father, Zorah, his father offers a sacrifice, and the angel of the Lord ascends to heaven in its smoke (Judges 13:20). Following Samson's birth, "the young man grew, and the LORD blessed him" (Judges 13:24).

The life of Samson revolves around two groups of people: Philistines and Philistine women. As a young man, he marries a young Philistine woman of Timnah. At his marriage festival, he poses a difficult riddle to the Philistine men present and makes a sizeable wager. These countrymen of Samson's wife seduce her into obtaining the answer from Samson. He reprimands his wife and reproaches her countrymen. Samson then lashes out in anger killing thirty other Philistines in Ashkelon and taking from them the wager he lost to the others.

Samson is an extremely powerful man. One day, he kills a lion that attacked him (Judges 14:5–6). His primary demonstrations of physical prowess, though, are executed against the Philistines. He set fire to their fields and groves and killed many Philistines because he was not allowed to visit his Philistine wife (Judges 15:4–8). When the Philistines threaten to attack the Israelites unless they turn over Samson, an Israelite army seizes Samson, binds him, and turns him over to the Philistines. As soon as he has been handed over to the Philistines, the Spirit of the Lord comes upon Samson, the ropes fall apart, and Samson kills a thousand Philistines with a donkey's jawbone (Judges 15:9–15).

Samson later falls in love with Delilah, another Philistine woman. The Philistines promise Delilah that if she finds out the secret of Samson's strength and tells them, they will pay her richly for they wish to subdue him. After Samson falsely confesses to Delilah that seven fresh bowstrings leave him powerless, she ties him up while he sleeps. When the Philistines attack, Samson easily breaks the strings and is not harmed. This happens a second time with new ropes and a third time with seven woven locks of hair. Finally, Samson truthfully confides to Delilah his secret: no razor has touched his head as he is a Nazarite. After Delilah shaves his head, the Lord leaves him and he loses his strength. The Philistines capture and blind him. They take him to Gaza where he is imprisoned and forced to grind meal (Judges 16).

The death of Samson is quite astonishing. The Philistines, gathered at their temple to worship Dagon, their god, summon Samson to dance for them. As Samson stands between the pillars that supported the temple, he prays for God's help: "O Lord GOD, please remember me and please strengthen me only this once, O God, that I may be avenged on the Philistines for my two eyes!" (Judges 16:28). Receiving strength from God, Samson knocks over the pillars, the temple falls in, and he along with three thousand Philistines die.

Samson judges Israel forty years (Judges 16:31). Like Adam, he has trouble with women: taking their advice lead both to forsake their God. Like Jesus, an angel announces his birth. Like Jesus, God is with him as he heroically fights against his enemies. Like Jesus, his death is not an ignoble defeat, but a great victory! Thus, Samson clearly bears the family traits of the people of God and is an heir of Jesus.

Ruth	**Time: ca. 1375–1050 BC**
	Place: Moab and Bethlehem, Judea
	Offices: Daughter-in-Law, Wife, Mother
	Biography: Ruth

The book of Ruth portrays a short segment in the life of a non-Jew during the time of the Judges. While it does not describe her birth or death, it depicts a few remarkable components of her life.

Ruth is a Moabite who marries into a family of Jewish immigrants. Immediately preceding this, her future father-in-law dies. Ten years into her marriage, her husband and brother-in-law die (Ruth 1:3–5). When her widowed mother-in-law, Naomi, decides to return to her homeland, Ruth returns with her to Bethlehem in Judea, rather than stay in Moab with her sister-in-law, Orpah. There, Ruth gleans fields to provide for the two of them, and makes known to Boaz her marital eligibility (Ruth 2:1–2). Immediately following, Boaz redeems Naomi, marries Ruth, and the two have a son, Obed.

The book of Ruth tells a delightful story, but to what purpose? The most obvious is its concluding, albeit brief, genealogy. This oft-used literary genre in the Old Testament is not insignificant. Genealogies chronicle God's promise first made in the Garden of Eden—the seed of Eve will crush the seed of the serpent—and finally fulfilled in the life of Christ. Between the two lay a string of names, one after another, that connect Adam and Jesus. Boaz and Obed are traced back as far as Perez, who was the son of Judah, the great-grandson of Isaac, and ahead to David, a royal ancestor of Jesus. And so, Boaz and Obed become an integral part of that promise, and Ruth, though she was a Moabite, is brought into this family through marriage. At the very least, the life of Ruth serves as a human-interest story attached to an otherwise less-than-exciting series of names.

Another purpose for the life of Ruth consists of moral modeling. Ruth exhibits high ethical standards: she is faithful to and remains with her mother-in-law; she gleans, providing for Naomi and herself; she acts chastely toward Boaz, a sought-after suitor. Consequently, this piece of literature is often termed a moral biography.

While both of these purposes are not without merit, by themselves, they are incomplete. The former aligns itself with Ruth's placement in the Christian canon, situated between Judges and 1 Samuel, numbered among the Historical Books. The latter fits more closely with the Jewish canon, where it sits between Proverbs and Song of Solomon, counted among the Writings and more specifically Wisdom Literature. Ruth is a sapiential biography.[6] The historical data in the life of Ruth is so organized as to reveal divine wisdom, the divine wisdom as drawn out and developed in the Song of Solomon (and Proverbs).[7]

The Song of Solomon draws heavily upon Ruth. The unnamed bride in the former has dark skin because she works in a vineyard (Song of Solomon 1:6), not unlike Ruth who gleans in the fields (Ruth 2:7). The unnamed bride loves, seeks, and desires her lover, as Ruth for Boaz. The unnamed bride has companions, while Ruth was both the companion of Naomi and, because Naomi is too old, Ruth becomes the bride. The unnamed bride passes through a pasture (Song of Solomon 1:7–8), a garden (Song of Solomon 5:1), and vineyards (Song of Solomon 7:12) in seeking her lover, while Ruth works in the field (Ruth 2:1–2) and then rests upon the threshing floor (Ruth 3:3–14) in her quest for Boaz. While the actions of these two are not identical, clearly, Ruth and Boaz serve as models for the marital portrait of the bride and groom in the Song of Solomon. This shows that the purpose of Ruth's life is more than a historical interlude or moral signpost, but rather, a revelation of divine wisdom. The lives of Ruth and Boaz lay in the past and those of Jesus (groom) and the Church (bride) lay to the future. Between these pairs, the Song of Solomon acts as a lens through which the lives of the former were brought into focus so as to point toward and more clearly reveal the lives of the latter.[8]

In sum, the biographical data gleaned from the Historical Books and the Writings is not only copious, but must be analyzed sympathetically in relation to Jesus if the book of Ruth serves as a proper indication. This biographical narrative of Ruth is not simply raw data. Instead, it serves specific purposes: it exhibits God's actions in time, place, and among people; it reveals God and His will; it always points to Jesus!

David	Time: 1010–970 BC
	Place: Bethlehem and Jerusalem
	Office: King
	Biographies: 1 and 2 Samuel, 1 Kings

David reigns as king during the golden age of Israel. Following after Saul, Israel enjoys political and economic prestige in the Middle East. In addition to being king, David is a shepherd and psalmist, yet he is of special interest for this study in that he is very much both saint and sinner. He takes both to their extreme, and his excesses are well documented, sometimes painfully.

Though the lineage of David is noted in the genealogy that concludes the book of Ruth, the actual biographical narrative begins with his youth. When King Saul falls from divine favor, God sends the prophet Samuel to the House of Jesse in Bethlehem where he is to anoint Saul's successor. The proud father parades his sons before the prophet. Samuel first sees Abinadab, Jesse's oldest son, but declares that he is not the one. The same happens for the second through the seventh sons. Samuel then asks Jesse if he has more sons, to which Jesse responds that he has one younger son who is shepherding. Upon his arrival, Samuel anoints David and David receives the Spirit of God. David will become the actual king of Israel following the death of Saul (1 Samuel 16).

Two events from the life of David will suffice to illustrate his familial ties. While still quite young, David becomes a hero. David is taken into the court of Saul to play his harp and soothe Saul's soul. At this time, the Israelites were battling against the Philistines. For forty days, Goliath, a giant and the greatest warrior from among the Philistines, had insulted the Israelites and challenged them to send out their champion against him, winner take all. All of the Israelite warriors were frightened, except the youthful David. Setting aside Saul's armor, he entered the contest with a sling and five stones. Goliath took the name of God in vain, insulting David. As Goliath finally approached him, David struck him in the head with a stone thrown from his sling, killing him. David took the giant's sword and cut off his head. The Philistines fled, and the Israelites chased and killed them. The people sang: "Saul has struck down his thousands, and David his ten thousands" (1 Samuel 18:7).

The reign of David is quite impressive: he conquers the Jebusites and the Philistines and the Moabites, to name a few. At the same time, his reign is marred with grievous sin. Though David is married, his eye wanders and desires Bathsheba, the wife of Uriah. David consummates his love for Bathsheba, and she is with his child. To cover his sin, David sends Uriah into battle and orders his fellow warriors to retreat and let him be killed. Consequently, the great King David broke the tenth commandment by coveting his neighbor's wife, and then the sixth and fifth commandments by committing adultery with Bathsheba and having Uriah put to death. The punishment for this is that their son, conceived in adultery, dies.

David is both a descendant of Adam and an heir of Jesus. He succumbs to sinful temptations, and at the same time, is chosen by God and becomes an agent of the divine will. Before David dies, he proclaims his son, Solomon, to succeed him. After ruling Israel for forty years, David dies and is buried in Jerusalem.

Elijah	Time: d. ca. 848 BC
	Place: Northern Kingdom
	Office: Prophet
	Biography: 1 and 2 Kings

Elijah was one of the foremost prophets in the Old Testament. His birth and any surrounding events are not mentioned other than that he was a Tishbite of Gilead (1 Kings 17:1). He prophesies in the spiritually corrupt Northern Kingdom from the reigns of King Ahab to King Jehoram, the former being his chief antagonist (1 Kings 18:17).

The life of Elijah exhibits exceptional prophesies and miracles. Elijah begins his career during the reign of wicked King Ahab who worships false gods, Baal and Asherah (1 Kings 16:31–33). During his reign, Jericho is built literally upon the sacrificial deaths of children (1 Kings 16:34). In response, Elijah prophesies to Ahab a drought over the land (1 Kings 17:1). To safeguard him, God sends Elijah into hiding at the Brook Cerith where he is divinely provided with bread and meat sent by ravens (1 Kings 17:5–6). When the water dries up at this brook, God sends Elijah to Zarephath, Sidon. There, he meets a widow and her son who are impoverished and at the brink of death. After Elijah moves in with them, their bin of flour and jar of oil never empties (1 Kings 17:14). And when her son dies, Elijah raises the dead boy to life (1 Kings 17:22).

God then sends Elijah to King Ahab. Elijah challenges the prophets of Baal to a contest: each would offer a sacrifice to their respective God and call upon their God to consume it in fire. Having sacrificed their bull, the prophets of Baal cry out and lacerate themselves all morning and into the evening, but to no avail. After this, the people help Elijah repair the altar of the Lord with twelve stones representing the twelve tribes of Israel. Elijah lays the sacrificial bull on wood upon the altar and drenches it all with water, not two times, but three. After Elijah prays to God, fire falls from the heavens and consumes the burnt offering. Immediately following, the prophets of Baal are put to death and Elijah prophesies that the drought is over (1 Kings 18:1–41).

Interestingly, Elijah's death is not portrayed, not because it is unimportant or passed over, but rather, because he does not die. Instead, Elijah ascends to heaven: "And as they still went on and talked, behold, chariots of fire and horses of fire separated the two of them. And Elijah went up by a whirlwind into heaven" (2 Kings 2:11).[9]

The life of Elijah clearly shows the Creator at work in His creation. God reveals His will, providing nourishment for Elijah, the widow, and her son, not unlike His actions toward Adam and Eve in the Garden of Eden. Moreover, the life of this Tishbite reveals the image of God: God creates life and Elijah gives life to a boy who lost his life. This miracle points ahead to Jesus who will raise the dead to life and ultimately die and rise from the dead Himself. Furthermore, Elijah stands in a long line of Christian heroes who victoriously fight against their antagonists, i.e., King Ahab and Baal. And finally, Elijah's ascension not only serves an exclamation point to the end of a distinguished career, but clearly resembles and foreshadows Jesus' Ascension.

Nehemiah	**Time: ca. fifth century BC**
	Place: Susa, Elam and Jerusalem, Judea
	Offices: Scribe, Reformer
	Biography: Nehemiah

Nehemiah is a scribe among the Judean exiles in Babylonia. Following the defeat of the Babylonian Empire, the Persians allow the Israelites to return to the Promised Land. Nehemiah leads a Jewish contingent back and is instrumental in re-organizing the spiritual life of the Israelites in and around Jerusalem.

While serving in Susa in Elam, Nehemiah hears that the walls of Jerusalem remain in ruin and this causes great concern for his fellow Jews in Jerusalem for they cannot protect themselves against attack. In response, he fasts and prays to God: he confesses the sin of his people and asks God to send him to Jerusalem. Speaking of this to Artaxerxes, the king of Persia, Nehemiah is granted safe passage to Jerusalem and royal permission to harvest timbers from the King's forest to rebuild Jerusalem's walls.

Nehemiah's work in Jerusalem involves considerable changes. First, the walls are restored, the many names of those involved in the building project being cited (Nehemiah 3). Second, Nehemiah restores many of the ancient commands of God that had been forgotten by the Israelites. He reiterates the prohibitions against usury (Nehemiah 5:10), intermarriage with non-Jews (Nehemiah 13:23–27), and working on the Sabbath (Nehemiah 13:15–22). Under the direction of Nehemiah, the word of the Lord is read to the people (Nehemiah 8:1–8) and they confess their sins to God (Nehemiah 9:1–37). Finally, Nehemiah, the governor of the people (Nehemiah 5:14), sees to the cleansing of temple after the mismanagement of priest Elisashib (Nehemiah 13:4–14).

Nehemiah prefigures Jesus. Just as Artaxerxes sends Nehemiah to the place of his fathers' tombs, Jerusalem, so the heavenly Father will send His divine Son to the place of his ancestors' tombs, this world. And just as

Nehemiah cleanses the temple and restores the lives of the people, so Jesus would do in His life.

Sum

The biographical data in the Old Testament is quite extensive, yet not without order and purpose: There are two families. These people are shown to be the descendants of Adam; they bear the family traits of sin and death. (Elijah is an exception, as he did not die.) In various ways, many of these are also shown to be the heirs of Jesus, and so, they bear, not fully but partially, the family traits of the divine image as revealed in Jesus: a remarkable birth or near sacrifice, a marriage or inclusion in a genealogy, a prophesy or a miracle, an antagonist or ascension. Thus, the Old Testament is not filled with arbitrary biographical data, but rather, it shows brief glimpses of the future fulfillment of the promise concerning the seed of Eve. Its biographical data includes sins that point back to the First Adam, but primarily signs that point forward to the Second Adam! These signs clearly illustrate that many in the Old Testament were joined to Jesus through birth and faith, and so, were brought into the family of God.

Excursus: Old Testament Apocrypha

The Old Testament Apocrypha[10] contains biographical data. Of its value and purpose, there are varying analyses. On the one hand, the Roman Catholic and Eastern Orthodox churches recognize their canonicity and, thus, hold them in high regard. On the other hand, many Protestants do not, and so, immediately dismiss them. Lutherans and Anglicans, though, have historically recognized their devotional and historical nature. Be the perspective Catholic or Orthodox, Lutheran or Anglican, the biographical data of the Apocrypha is not without import.

Biographical data is included in many different literary genres throughout the Apocrypha: Tobit and Judith may be termed Sapiential Biographies; 1 Maccabees chronicles the early history of the Hasmonean Dynasty; 4 Maccabees depicts Jewish martyrs; and Psalm 151 briefly describes the life of King David. While the historical accuracy of many of these writings is sometimes questioned and their canonicity is rejected by most Protestants, they are often not inconsistent with the Old Testament in their presentation of biographical data. In regard to time, the writings of the Old Testament and Apocrypha overlap from the United Kingdom (ca. 1050–930 BC) to the postexilic period (ca. 537+ BC). In terms of place, both describe people and events in the Promised Land, Egypt, Assyria, and Babylon. A few characters, e.g., David and Daniel, are common to both and figures in the Apocrypha are often identified according to their Old Testament tribe. Throughout both, the same God is portrayed as working in His created order.

A high point of biographical data in the Apocrypha is the "Hymn in Honor of Our Ancestors" in Ecclesiasticus (Wisdom of Jesus, Son of Sirach) 44:1–50:24. It must be noted, however, that it principally does not portray Apocryphal characters. Instead, it names not less than 28 noteworthy Old Testament figures, beginning with Enoch (Sirach 44:16) and concluding with Nehemiah (Sirach 49:13); and it provides varying amounts of biographical data for each character. The lone character not from the Old Testament is a late third, early second century BC priest named Simon, son of Onias,[11] clearly mentioned after the canonical figures and their brief summary (Sirach 49:14–16). While most are described rather briefly, his priestly duties are extensively detailed (Sirach 50:1–21).

According to this hymn, the biographical data of the Old Testament is not a disjointed list of individuals, but rather, continuous and ordered. All are famous and remembered (Sirach 44:1, 8). Of much greater import, all have been blessed by God (Sirach 44:2); play important roles in Israel (Sirach 44:3–6); perform righteous deeds (Sirach 44:10); and stand in the covenant (Sirach 44:12). They are related according to varying levels: Moses, Aaron, and Phineas rank as the three highest in glory; Enoch, Joseph, Shem, Seth, and Enosh are honored above others (Sirach 49:14–16); and Simon is portrayed as a priest above all priests. At the same time, none of these, according to this hymn, has approached the stature of Adam. Adam is the first man and created in the image of God. No one throughout the Old Testament can compare.

The biographical data of the Apocrypha very much continues after the pattern of the Old Testament. It shows Adam as the archetype of humanity and humanity as the descendants of a fallen Adam. At the same time, it emphasizes heroes of the faith, showing that God continues to work in time, place, and among people. The "Hymn in Honor of Our Ancestors" leaves the door wide open for a Second Adam: one who is greater than those memorialized, one who will finally and fully replace the First Adam.

New Testament

Biographical data permeates the New Testament. In addition to the life of Christ, other figures include the immediate family of Jesus and His relatives, friends, and followers, ecclesial and governmental leaders, and miscellaneous others. These figures are portrayed in the Gospels, Acts of the Apostles, the Epistles, and Revelation. Their lives occur at a pivotal time in the Bible: chronological proximity to Jesus. A few barely precede the life of Christ, one clearly overlaps, while most follow. All are shown to be the descendants of Adam: bearing a muddy human image, and so, they sin and die. Many are portrayed as heirs of Jesus: the image of God is partially and in various fashions revealed in their lives. This section will analyze the biographical data of the New Testament according to sins that point back to Adam and signs of the divine image that point to Jesus. This is done through various offices.

Forerunner. The forerunner of Jesus was John, and his life stood in close proximity to Jesus. All of the signs and the prophesies of the Old Testament funneled through him to Jesus. Even the Old Testament prophesied of him (Isaiah 40:3–5). John was a cousin of Jesus and baptized Him in the Jordan River. In addition, his is the only life in the New Testament (other than the life of Christ) that included birth, life, and death narratives. What did Jesus say of his life? "Truly, I say to you, among those born of women there has arisen no one greater than John the Baptist. Yet the one who is least in the kingdom of heaven is greater than he" (Matthew 11:11). John's life was quite unique and, at the same time, not at all. Like many, many others, he was both a descendent of Adam and an heir of Jesus.

Apostles. The twelve apostles are those who had followed Jesus during His ministry through His Ascension (Acts 1:21–22) and those Jesus specifically called and sent (Matthew 10:1–5). Most of their biographical data is contained in the Gospels, though the Acts of the Apostles and various Epistles add additional information.[12] They leave families and jobs to follow Jesus (Matthew 4:18–22). Peter, James, and John witness His transfiguration (Mark 9:2). Peter, the leader, first confesses Jesus (Matthew 16:16) and later denies Him three times (Matthew 26:69–75). Thomas first doubts Jesus' resurrection and later confesses it (John 20:24–29). Judas betrays Jesus (Matthew 26:14–16), and consequently neither receives the Apostolic Commission nor views the Ascension (Mark 16:14–20), and is replaced by Matthias (Acts 1:26). The apostles continue the work of Jesus. Paul is not one of the twelve, but becomes, nonetheless, an apostle.

Deacon. A deacon serves. In the New Testament, it becomes a technical term for one who serves according to a specified role in the Christian Church. Paul enumerates the qualifications: reverent and holding the mystery of faith, not given to wine or greed, the husband of one wife and ruling well his family (1 Timothy 3:8–12). They serve the people of God under the direction of the bishop. With the explosion of converts in Jerusalem following the day of Pentecost, seven are appointed to assist the apostles in caring for the widows. While these assistants are not called deacons, their service to the apostles parallels that of a deacon to a bishop. Only two of the seven, Stephen and Philip, are mentioned again in the Acts of the Apostles.

Missionary. The Christian faith is mission-minded. There are glimpses of this in the Old Testament, but this comes to full fruition in the New Testament. Jesus first interacts with Samaritans and Gentiles. Just prior to His Ascension, He speaks His apostolic commission: the apostles are to preach the Gospel to every creature (Matthew 28:16–20; Mark 16:15–18). And on the day of Pentecost, the twelve apostles speak the message of Jesus in foreign languages (Acts 2:4). The implication of the last is that the message of Jesus is to be spoken to all peoples of all languages. Immediately following, the missionary work of Philip, Peter, and Paul are portrayed in the Acts of the Apostles. The travels of each spiral outward from Jerusalem and Judaism: Philip converts an Ethiopian as he travels from Jerusalem to Gaza (Acts 8:28–40). Beginning in Joppa and traveling to Caesarea, Peter converts Cornelius and his Gentile family. Paul begins at Antioch and travels throughout the northern portion of the Mediterranean world converting Jews and Gentiles alike to the Christian Faith.

There are connections between the offices of the Old and New Testaments. The patriarchs of the twelve tribes of Israel are replaced with the twelve apostles. All of the prophets in the Old Testament culminate in John the Baptist. Deacons worked under their bishop, just as the Levites served under the Aaronic Priesthood. Eve was the precursor of Mary. The many offices of the New Testament differ from those in the Old Testament, yet they all fit together around Jesus.

John	Time: ca. 5 BC–AD ca. 28
	Place: Promised Land
	Office: Forerunner, Baptist
	Biographies: Gospels according to Matthew,
	Mark, Luke, John
	Biographers: Matthew, Mark, Luke, John

John's life, at times, is almost indistinguishable from the life of Christ. God sends John to witness of Jesus. The people, however, have difficultly telling one from the other. On one occasion, John explains that he "was not the light, but came to bear witness about the light" (John 1:7–8). At another time, "[John] confessed, and did not deny, but confessed, 'I am not the Christ.' . . . He who comes after me, the strap of whose sandal I am not worthy to untie" (John 1:20, 27). Some thought that John was the Christ, but rather, he points to the Christ.

The birth of John and the events surrounding it are more than worthy of note. John's parents are both righteous (Luke 1:6) and too old to have children. One day when Zacharias, his father, is burning incense in the temple, an angel of the Lord appears to him and promises him that he and his wife, Elizabeth, will have a son, and will call him John. Their son, according to the angel, will not be ordinary, but rather, be filled with the Holy Spirit and be like unto Elijah, turning the hearts of the people back toward God. When Zacharias questions the plausibility of this promise, he becomes mute.

Between his conception and birth, a rather startling event occurs. Mary, pregnant with Jesus, visits Elizabeth. When Mary speaks to Elizabeth, John leaps in his mother's womb, and Elizabeth is filled with the Holy Spirit upon hearing the voice of Mary (Luke 1:41). Following the birth of John, his father receives his lost voice after John is named at his circumcision (Luke 1:64) and sings the Benedictus (Luke 1:67–79); people rejoice (Luke 1:58) and talk about these things (Luke 1:65–66). These events are not common to the descendants of Adam.

The life and death of John are quite abrasive and abrupt. In his youth, he grows and becomes strong in spirit (Luke 1:80). During the reigns of the Roman Emperor Tiberius Caesar, Pontius Pilate the Tetrarch of Judea, Herod the Tetrarch of Galilee (Luke 3:1), and the high priesthoods of Annas and Caiaphas (Luke 3:2), and after living in the desert, he preaches a baptism of repentance in the area of the Jordan River (Luke 3:3). John baptizes Jesus (Luke 3:21–22). He then points to Him and says, "Behold, the Lamb of God, who takes away the sin of the world!" (John 1:29). Later John sends two disciples to question Jesus (Matthew 11:1–6). Finally, Herod imprisons John and beheads him.

The comparisons to the life of Christ are quite obvious. In both pre-birth narratives, an angel announces a miraculous conception and provides the name of the child; the times are clearly delineated; the parents are righteous; a parent sings a canticle. Both births are miraculous. In both post-birth narratives, there are signs people are amazed. In both lives, they preach, are associated with baptism, and persecuted by Herod. Both suffer violent deaths.

The lives of John and Jesus are intimately related, so much so that John has to deny that he is the Christ. Their parallel birth narratives at the beginning of the Gospel according to Luke closely connect them, yet John is not Jesus. He is born six months prior to Jesus and precedes him like many other Old Testament figures. John is a descendent of Adam in that his parents' inability to have a child reveals the muddy image of Adam. John is also an heir of Jesus; the image of God is clearly revealed in his birth and baptizing, and his life and death are fraught with Christological resemblances.

Mary	Time: b. ca. 20 BC
	Place: Promised Land
	Office: Wife, Mother
	Biographies: Gospels according to Matthew, Mark, Luke, John
	Biographers: Matthew, Mark, Luke, John

The four evangelists provide seemingly little biblical data for Mary, considering her unique and vital role as the mother of Jesus, the biographical focal point of the entire Bible. While neither her birth nor her death are included in the New Testament, more than a few other components of her life are strategically placed in relation to the life of Christ.

The biblical portrayal of Mary's life commences with the Annunciation. The archangel Gabriel visits Mary in Galilee. Gabriel addresses Mary as the "favored one" and "blessed among women" (Luke 1:28), while Mary dubs herself the "servant of the Lord" (Luke 1:38). Gabriel informs Mary that she will conceive by the Holy Spirit and bear the Son of God (Luke 1:35). Mary then gives birth to Jesus in Bethlehem of Judea (Luke 2:6). After the shepherds arrive and visit the baby Jesus, they tell others of this happening. Many marvel. Mary does not forget, but holds these events close to her heart. Immediately following she is purified according to the law of Moses and witnesses her son's presentation to God in Jerusalem (Luke 2:22) and the words and actions of two of the faithful. Simeon, a righteous man and filled with the Holy Spirit, takes Jesus in his arms and sings the Nunc dimittis (Luke 2:29–32) while Anna, a prophetess, gives thanks to God that He has sent the Savior.

Mary is very much involved in her son's childhood. After the magi visit the Holy Family, the latter flee to Egypt for safety from King Herod. Upon returning, they regularly visit Jerusalem. On one occasion, Mary and her husband have departed the city without Jesus. Upon returning and searching for him, they find him in the temple. When Mary questions his actions, he responds, "Did you not know that I must be in my Father's house?" (Luke 2:49). Under her guidance, Jesus is obedient to his parents and matures before all (Luke 2:51–52).

Mary continues to play an active role in the life of Jesus during His brief ministry. She seems to push Jesus toward performing a miracle at a wedding in Cana of Galilee (John 2:1–12). She infamously appears while her son was teaching thinking that she deserves special treatment (Matthew 12:46–49). She is present at Jesus' death (John 20:6) when Jesus consigns her to the care of John, the apostle. Mary is in Jerusalem on the day of Pentecost (Acts 1:14).

The life of Mary has a single purpose: Jesus. For this reason, Mary conceives and gives birth to the Son of God. Moreover, she encourages a miracle from her Son and serves as an object lesson. Furthermore, this mother's soul is pierced (Luke 2:34) as her son suffers and dies upon the cross. The life of Mary encompasses the life of Christ like no other, first in her womb and then throughout her life. The Baptist dies prior to Jesus and presumably so does Joseph, the Baptist's parents, Simeon and Anna. The twelve apostles, Paul, and others miss His birth, but continue their lives after Jesus' death. As such Mary's life is significant, and yet, Jesus' comments about His mother parallel those He spoke concerning John, "[More than the womb that bore Jesus] Blessed rather are those who hear the word of God and keep it!" (Luke 11:28). Mary is a descendent of Adam. She is also the mother of Jesus. Though she does not always understand the circumstances surrounding Jesus, she conceives Jesus by the Spirit of God and gives birth to the perfect image of God in human flesh and blood.

Stephen	Time: d. ca. AD 30
	Place: Jerusalem, Judea
	Offices: Deacon, Martyr
	Biography: Acts of the Apostles
	Biographer: Luke

Stephen is a deacon in Jerusalem. As a second-generation leader in the church, he clearly demonstrates that the New Testament Church does not stray from Jesus after His Ascension, but rather, stays the course, preaching the Gospel and exhibiting traits of the divine image as the heir of Jesus. On the day of Pentecost, the Holy Spirit converts 3,000 to the Christian faith. As the Christian Church continues to grow numerically, the twelve apostles cannot fulfill all their duties, so assistants are needed. Stephen, along with six others, are chosen by the people and appointed by the Apostles to care for the various needs of the people.

Stephen stands out among the six. Performing miracles and speaking of God (Acts 6:8), he draws the ire of the Jews who bring him before the Sanhedrin on the false accusation of blaspheming Moses and God (Acts 6:9–15). He does not fear these charges, but glories in them. In fact, his face shines like that of an angel (Acts 6:15). Before the council, Stephen reiterates the history of God and His people, particularly their Adamic descent. He reminds the Jews that the sons of Jacob sell their brother, Joseph, into slavery, and the Israelites rebel against Moses. Similarly, but much worse, the present Jews have rejected Jesus and put to death the

"Righteous One" (Acts 7:52). Accused of resisting the Holy Spirit, the Jews stone Stephen. Just prior to the stoning, he looks into heaven and sees Jesus at the right hand of the Father, and just before he dies, he prays, "Lord, do not hold this sin against them" (Acts 7:60).

Stephen is intimately connected to Jesus: The apostles who were appointed by Jesus appointed him to his office. Moreover, he understands his family history: He sees Jesus as the culmination of those through whom God worked and were persecuted. Furthermore, Stephen exhibits the family traits: He is put to death and prays like Jesus (Luke 23:34).

Paul	Time: d. ca. AD 68
	Place: Mediterranean World
	Offices: Apostle, Missionary
	Biography: Acts of the Apostles
	Biographer: Luke

Saul turned Paul is the arch-persecutor of Christianity turned arch-missionary of Christianity. Trained as a Pharisee (Acts 25:6), he vigorously persecutes Christianity (Acts 8:1–3). His antagonistic actions toward Christianity paint him worse than a descendent of Adam: his ancestry is of the serpent.

Saul's life is turned upside down on the road to Damascus. In the midst of his persecution of Christianity, the ascended Jesus speaks to him out of a blinding light: "Saul, Saul, why are you persecuting me? . . . rise and enter the city" (Acts 9:4, 6). Blinded and terrified, Saul obeys Jesus and travels to Damascus where Ananias lays hands on Saul. Immediately, Saul receives his sight and is baptized (Acts 9:17–18). A persecutor who put to death many Christians becomes a Christian through his Baptismal death (and resurrection).

Following his conversion, Paul's life is a flurry of activity. Heeding Jesus' Apostolic Commission (Matthew 28:19–20), Paul makes disciples throughout the Mediterranean world, e.g., Galatia and Ephesus, Corinth and Thessalonica. In every town, he visits first the Jews and then the Gentiles. Like Jesus, Paul is poorly received by the Jewish ecclesial leaders (Acts 9:23–25, 23:1–22) and persecuted by civil rulers (Acts 14:19–20). Like Jesus, Paul questions the rituals of Judaism (Acts 15). Like Jesus, Paul preaches and performs miracles. At the Areopagus in Athens, Paul informs his hearers that the "unknown God" they worship has become incarnate in Jesus of Nazareth, that He has been crucified upon the cross and raised from the dead (Acts 17:22–31). In Asia Minor, the diseased are healed by merely touching a cloth that had been in contact with Paul (Acts 19:12).

Paul is an antagonist turned hero: Ishmael turned Isaac; Herod turned John the Baptist. In addition, Paul is one of the first chronological steps of Christian biography after Jesus. He teaches the Christian faith and establishes churches and writes letters to congregations and pastors. His life flows from the life of Christ and will be paralleled by the lives of many later Christians.

Summary

The biographical data in the New Testament is quite varied in the figures portrayed, yet they are intimately related to one another. They are all shown to be the descendants of Adam, inheriting his muddy human image, sinning and dying. Many, though, are portrayed also as heirs of Jesus, inheriting and reflecting his divine image. Because the latter are both descendants of Adam and heirs of Jesus, they receive both inheritances and inconsistently, at times, bear both images. The former happens according to the will of man, while the latter the will of God (John 1:12–13). The will of God is this: God perfectly reveals His divine image in the Second Adam so that His heirs inherit the divine image originally intended for the descendants of the First Adam. This divine image is shown in births and baptisms, teachings and miracles, persecutions and deaths. Thus, the New Testament is not filled with arbitrary biographical data, but rather, it demonstrates numerous sins that point to Adam and many more signs that point to Jesus. With the promise concerning the seed of Eve being fulfilled in Jesus, Jesus is not the end of the genealogical line, but rather, the beginning. Out of the life of Christ flows Christian lives. Through Holy Baptism, they become part of the family of God and reveal, in part and in many different fashions, the image of God.

Biblical Analysis

The Bible's preservation of biographical data is extensive and, more importantly, ordered. Although the times, places, peoples, and literary genres differ, the God who works in and through these remains constant.

As such, these many biblical characters are closely related, physically and spiritually. And they are all related intimately to Jesus the Son and fullest revelation of God.

The divinely inspired authors of Holy Scripture go out of their way to demonstrate and analyze the intimate relations between the people of God in the Old Testament, Jesus, and the Christians in the New Testament. Time and again, they portray the people and events in the Old Testament being fulfilled by Jesus. In his polemic to the Sanhedrin, Stephen argues that just as the Israelites rebel against Moses in the wilderness, so also the Israelites reject Jesus at Golgotha (Acts 7). They also show that the people of God in the Old Testament and Christians in the New Testament are not two disconnected communities, but one. Though they are separated by time and sometimes place, they participate in the same events: both are baptized, the Israelites in the mist of the Red Sea and the Christians in Holy Baptism; and both are nourished by God, Christians in the Lord's Supper and the Israelites in the wilderness eating manna and drinking water from the rock which was Jesus (1 Corinthians 10:1–4). Consequently, the people of God in the Old Testament and the Christians in the New Testament are one people in Jesus.

The relation of Jesus with those around Him is familial. On one occasion, Jesus is teaching a large crowd of people. When His mother and brothers arrive, they cannot get to Jesus and request to speak to Him. When Jesus has been informed, He responds, "For whoever does the will of my Father in heaven is my brother and sister and mother" (Matthew 12:50). Jesus does not denigrate the biological family, but rather, emphasizes the spiritual family: the circumcised and baptized. Through circumcision in the Old Testament and Baptism in the New, the descendants of Adam are brought in, adopted as it were, to the family of God. This family exhibits family traits: Christians imitate Jesus and other Christians imitate Christians who imitate Jesus (1 Thessalonians 1:6–7).

The Bible paints a family portrait: the Old Testament people of God and New Testament Christians are lovingly positioned around Jesus. Mary and John the Baptist are part of Jesus' immediate family; while Eve, Isaac, and Paul are much more distant relatives. Ruth is an in-law and proselytes are adopted through circumcision and Baptism. There is one Lord, one faith, one family portrait.

Summary

The Bible's biographical clutter—immense quantity, intersecting lives, pecking orders, and sprawling genealogies—is set in order around Adam and Jesus, the archetypes of humanity. The first Adam loses the divine image, so his descendants bear Adam's muddy human image. The Second Adam perfectly reflects the divine image, so His heirs reflect the divine image, but imperfectly because they remain at the same time descendants of Adam. Jesus supercedes Adam as the divinely intended archetype of humanity, so all Christian biographical data in the Bible revolves around Jesus primarily and secondarily Adam. This, then, is the hermeneutic for interpreting Christian biography.

This paradigm is multi-faceted. First, an antagonist is often pitted against a hero. Just as Satan first attacks Adam, so Satan similarly attacks Jesus, and the satanic ancestry attacks over and again the heirs of Jesus. Second, genealogies chronicle generation-after-generation the promise first made of Eve's seed and finally fulfilled in Jesus. Third, the categorization and evaluation of the biographical data demonstrate that the God who creates Adam on the sixth day and places him in the Garden of Eden continues to act in time, place, and people as He first restores His divine image in Jesus and subsequently in His heirs. Fourth, common "family" traits illustrate Jesus' relation with His heirs, and also the relations between heirs. For example, just as Jesus' conception is foretold so were those of Isaac and Samson and John the Baptist. Elijah and Paul perform miracles not unlike Jesus. Samson and Stephen both die in fashions like Jesus. Isaac and Aaron are involved with sacrifices that point ahead to that of Jesus upon the cross.

This multi-faceted paradigm is best illustrated by family. Just as Adam and Eve are joined together so that two became one, so also are all the heirs of Jesus joined together and become one in their relation to Jesus. They all have the same heavenly Father through a common birth. They all share familial traits that are exhibited in any number of fashions.

This biblical paradigm serves as the initial and necessary step for examining Christian lives in relation to the life of Christ. These biblical figures are closest to Jesus chronologically. They not only immediately follow after Jesus, but even precede Him. Chronologically, the next step in this examination is the categorization and evaluation of the biographical data of Christians in the Early Church.

3

EARLY CHURCH

AD 100–500

This examination of Christian lives proceeds from the time of the New Testament to the Early Church. In this short stride, a twofold succession of Christian lives occurred. One was quite natural. The apostle Paul reminded Timothy that his faith was received from his mother, Eunice, who received her faith from her mother, Lois (2 Timothy 1:5). This faith was handed down from one generation to another, from the New Testament period to the Early Church. The other succession was missiological. Where no Christian parents were present to hand down their faith to their children, Paul and other early Christian missionaries broke the chain of unbelief and converted many to the Christian faith. In so doing, they provided an alternate route for the succession of Christian lives. In both manners, New Testament Christian lives were succeeded by Early Church Christian lives. The relatively intimate family of God during biblical times expanded to include many more Christians from the furthest corners of the Mediterranean world.

The period of the Early Church was quite pivotal. On the one hand, these first Christians were closely related to Jesus and His apostles. It has been suggested that Ignatius of Antioch (d. ca. 107), as a child, was held in the arms of Jesus.[1] Polycarp (d. ca. 155) was a student of the apostle John at Ephesus. Clement of Rome (ca. 97) followed Peter as the fourth bishop of Rome. On the other hand, the Christian Church was growing geographically, and by the end of this period two distinct traditions were beginning to develop within the Christian family: one in the west (Northwest Africa and Europe) and the other in the east (Egypt, Palestine, Syria, Asia Minor, and Greece). The fifth century Christians, Augustine and Patrick, very much influenced later western Christianity, while the same was true in the east for Mary of Egypt and Daniel the Stylite.

The biographical literature written during the Early Church period was plentiful and varied, including passions, lives, church histories, homilies, and poems. This chapter will illustrate how the biographical literature of the Early Church utilized the sacraments and other pious components of the Christian life to portray the familial relations between Early Church Christians and Christians in the biblical period and, of course, Jesus.

Ante-Nicenes

The first portion of the Early Church is commonly called the Ante-Nicene Period (100–325) as it preceded the first Ecumenical Council at Nicaea (325). The most notable features of this period includes chronological proximity to the New Testament, persecution by the Roman Empire, and early formation of the teachings and practices of Christianity. In light of the last two, the most significant Christian offices during this time included bishop, martyr, apologist, and catechist. It must be noted that often one office overlapped another in a single Christian life. For example, while Ignatius was a bishop and Justin an apologist, both were martyrs. Early Christian biography employed these and other offices to illustrate the intimate relation between Ante-Nicene Christian lives and the life of Christ.

Martyr. Prior to the Edict of Milan (313), martyrs held the most prestigious position among Ante-Nicene Christians. They confessed the Christian faith to a hostile audience and subsequently lost their lives for this confession. Ignatius of Antioch, during his journey from Syria to martyrdom in Italy, wrote seven letters that were generously seasoned with his praise of martyrdom: The chains of persecution are spiritual pearls. In addition, he pleaded to the Christians in Rome that they not attempt to secure his release, but allow him to receive divine grace and achieve this worthy goal. In death, the martyr is united with Jesus.[2] Consequently, martyrdom was not to be feared, but recognized as a glorious event in the Christian life. The names of the martyrs were copious and their stories abundant, if not inspiring. For example, in Prudentius' portrayal of Eulalia's passion, a snow-white dove wings from her mouth and into heaven.

Apologist. An apology is a defense. Christian apologists authored written defenses of the Christian faith in the face of the many early critics of Christianity: Jews, pagans, and heterodox Christian sects. Justin (ca. 100–ca. 165) was a traveling Greek apologist who ended up in Rome. Two of his Apologies were addressed to the Roman emperor and Roman citizens. He argued that Christians should not be persecuted because of their apparently obscure beliefs. Instead, they made exemplary citizens because their God demanded a strict morality and, at the same time, they believed that their God watched them unceasingly.[3] While not all apologists forfeited their lives for the Christian faith, as did Justin, all of these literary warriors fought on the front lines for the sake of Jesus and the Gospel.

Catechist. Pedagogy was a vital component in the Early Church. Even in the face of persecution and martyrdom, many were curious of the teachings and practices of this "new" religion and flocked to catechists for instruction in the Christian faith. Alexandria was a key center for Christian catechesis. After being a student of Pantaenus (d. ca. 190) at the catechetical school in Alexandria, Clement (ca. 150–215) became the teacher. Origen (ca. 185–ca. 254) succeeded Clement at Alexandria and later moved to Caesarea in Palestine. In the classroom and out, these catechists were influential: Clement penned Protrepticus, Paedagogus, and Stromateis; while Origen's corpus included biblical commentaries, homilies, and theological treatises. These and other catechists laid much of the theological groundwork in the Early Church.

Bishop. First appointed by the apostles (Acts 14:23), the bishops followed as their successors. Their role as leaders was immediately addressed in the Ante-Nicene Period. Two early bishops, Clement of Rome (d. ca. 97) and Ignatius of Antioch, broached this topic in their letters to the Christian communities in Corinth and Magnesia, respectively. Each community had a single bishop who was responsible for the souls of the people and oversaw the work of the priests and deacons. Early key bishops included Melito of Sardis and Irenaeus of Lyons in the second century, and in the third century Serapion of Antioch and Peter of Alexandria. Slowly a hierarchy developed that was based upon geography. Rome, Italy; Alexandria, Egypt; and Antioch, Syria were early key bishoprics.

The Ante-Nicene Period was an exciting time in the Christian Church. Bishops and catechists attempted to direct a fledging church. Martyrs and apologists fought the good fight. Through all of this, many were brought into the family of God through Holy Baptism, and a myriad of Christians fearlessly stepped forward to model their Savior's life and death.

Polycarp	Time: d. ca. 155
	Place: Smyrna, West Asia Minor
	Offices: Bishop, Martyr
	Biography: Passion of Polycarp[4]
	Biographer: Church of Smyrna

The Passion of Polycarp vividly portrayed an Early Church hero who answered Jesus' call: "If anyone would come after Me, let him deny himself and take up his cross and follow Me" (Mark 8:34). The biography provided no data from the birth or life of this bishop, focusing exclusively upon Polycarp's death and the events surrounding it.

This passion narrative begins with a series of events setting the stage for Polycarp's death. Labeled an atheist by the people,[5] the local authorities began their search for him. While this faithful bishop wished to remain in Smyrna to care for his flock, others persuaded him to flee. His brief exile was devoted to prayer. He envisioned a burning pillow, which foretold his manner of death. A young servant of his was captured, tortured, and betrayed Polycarp. With his arrest imminent, he refused to flee and responded, "The will of God be done."[6] Showing no fear of torture and death, he waited, ate a meal, and prayed for two hours. Following his arrest, Polycarp rode into town upon a donkey. Before Herod and Nicetes, he refused to acknowledge Caesar as Lord or offer incense to him.

The proceedings intensified as Polycarp was brought to the stadium. A heavenly voice cried out, "Be strong Polycarp, and be a man."[7] When he was commanded to revile the Christians condemning them as atheists, he instead turned to heaven and said the same concerning his Roman persecutors. When asked to reject Christ, he responded, "Eighty-six years I have served him and He has done to me no wrong. How can I blaspheme my King who has saved me?"[8] First threatened with wild beasts, he was partially stripped of his clothing and tied to a post to be burned alive. Polycarp prayed to God: "Lord God Almighty, Father of your beloved and blessed Son, Jesus Christ, . . . I bless you because you have considered me worthy of this day and hour, that I should be numbered among your martyrs in the cup of Christ to the resurrection of eternal life, both of soul and body, through the incorruptibility of the Holy Spirit. . . . Amen."[9] Immediately following, the fire was lit. It surrounded Polycarp, but he remained unsinged. There was no smell of burning flesh, but the sweet smell of baking bread. Desirous of blood, his persecutors ordered him to be stabbed with a knife. From his wound came a dove and much blood that extinguished the fire.

Immediately following his death, both Nicetes, at the behest of the evil one, and the Jews from their remembrance of the Christ, requested that Polycarp's body not be released to the Christians. A Centurion, however, burned his body, and the Christians collected his bones. These "precious treasures" were preserved for the annual celebration of Polycarp's "birthday," the single day of his earthly death and heavenly birth.[10]

The numerous correlations between Polycarp's martyrdom and the passion of Jesus are unmistakably obvious. For example, Polycarp's equine mount was reminiscent of Jesus' ride on Palm Sunday (Matthew 21:7), and his words, "The will of God be done" echoed those of the Savior in the Garden of Gethsemane (Matthew 26:39, 42). Moreover, the young servant turned traitor mirrored Judas, while the infamous name of Herod surfaced in both. Furthermore in his prayer at the stadium, Polycarp connected his death with the death of the other martyrs, and through his martyrdom hoped to participate in the resurrection of the arch-martyr, Jesus. The Passion of Polycarp clearly and repeatedly connected his life with the life of Christ via their respective passions.

Perpetua	Time: d. ca. 203
	Place: Carthage, North Africa
	Office: Martyr
	Biography: *Passion of Perpetua and Felicitas*[11]
	Biographers: Perpetua, Tertullian
	(ca. 160–ca. 225)

The Passion of Perpetua and Felicitas told the tender story of a martyr who was also a daughter and young mother. This willing victim heeded Jesus' pronouncement that "Whoever loves father or mother more than Me is not worthy of Me, and whoever loves son or daughter more than Me is not worthy of Me" (Matthew 10:37). This martyr, Perpetua, kept a journal during her passion that preserved the most personal details of her passion.

Prior to Perpetua's twenty-second year, all was well in her life according to the standards of this world. She came from a good family, was educated, was married, and had an infant son. As soon as she became a catechumen in the Christian Church her idyllic life was shattered. Roman soldiers arrested her, along with her fellow catechumens—Revocatus, Felicitas, Saturninus, and Secundulus. Imprisoned, she awaited her death.

Perpetua suffered severe temptations. Three times her father visited her in the dungeon of her imprisonment and pleaded that she renounce the Christian faith and live for his sake. At a public interrogation, her father entreated her to renounce the Christian faith and live for the sake of her little boy. There, her father was severely beaten. When Perpetua was ordered back to the dungeon, she lost custody of her nursing boy. Despite all of this, Perpetua's faith did not waver.

Perpetua enjoyed great delight during her captivity. Following the first departure of her father, she was baptized and received the gift of the Holy Spirit after which she laid aside all earthly cares. Moreover, she was comforted by a series of visions. In one, she stepped upon the dragon's head as she ascended to her heavenly home. There, she glimpsed her dear Lord who was clothed as a shepherd and fed her. In another, rather than being thrown to the wild beasts, she fought an Egyptian gladiator, and won. Upon awaking from the latter vision, she realized that her battle was not with man or beast, but the devil, and her victory was at hand. In yet another vision, she surveyed the heavenly realm and saw her dear Lord surrounded by four angels, the twenty-four elders, and a multitude clad in white robes hymning "Holy! Holy! Holy!" Consequently, Perpetua did not mourn in her present suffering, but rejoiced in her future victory.

At the amphitheater, Perpetua sang psalms while her companion, Felicitas, rejoiced that she had given birth and so was allowed this death, this "Second Baptism"—the first being washed in water, the second in blood. When the people called for her male companions to be scourged, they exulted in the opportunity to bear the same suffering of Jesus. When it was her turn, Perpetua was thrown to the ground. Picking herself up, she showed no fear of torment, but rather, covered herself with her torn garment out of modesty, and she straightened her hair lest it appear that she was lamenting her passion rather than reveling in the glory. Finally, Perpetua assisted a gladiator in her own death.

The martyrdom of Perpetua illustrated that she was a precious child of God twice. Through Baptism, she was born again of the Spirit into the family of God upon earth. She no longer looked to her earthly father to protect her, and she deserted the fruit of her womb. She filled the void with a sure and certain hope; she trusted in the care of her heavenly Father. Upon her arrest and imprisonment, she forsook her earthly family. Through martyrdom, she was born again in this "Second Baptism". In this second birth, she was born again into the family of God in heaven.

Origen	Date: ca. 185–ca. 254
	Places: Alexandria and Caesarea
	Offices: Catechist, Confessor
	Biography: *Ecclesiastical History*[12]
	Biographer: Eusebius of Caesarea
	(ca. 260–ca. 340)

In his Ecclesiastical History, Eusebius recorded numerous events from Origen's rather amazing childhood and life. While Origen was known primarily as a catechist, he was a prolific author—Hexapla, homilies, biblical commentaries, apologies, and theological treatises—and an extremely influential theologian in Ante-Nicene Christianity.

Origen's childhood was anything but ordinary. His father, Leonides, often uncovered his son's breast and kissed it as though it were the shrine of the Holy Spirit. During the persecution of the Roman Emperor Severus, his father was arrested and Origen wished to be martyred with him. His mother unsuccessfully pleaded with him and finally hid his clothes to keep him home and safe. With his father awaiting a martyr's death, Origen wrote to him: "Hold fast, do not change your mind because of us."[13] With the death of his father and his family destitute, Origen began to work at the age of seventeen. In his work, though he had to associate with a known heretic, Origen clearly confessed the Christian faith and never prayed with him.

The life of Origen was multi-faceted. At the age of 18, he became head of the catechetical school in Alexandria. He visited those in prison awaiting martyrdom, and this infuriated the pagans. Consequently, they sought to take his life, but he miraculously escaped harm by the protective hand of God as he found sanctuary in a series of Christian homes. Origen's courage in the face of persecution drew ever more students who sought his tutelage and a goodly number—Plutarch, Serenus, Heraclides, Hero—became martyrs. He dedicated his treatise, On Martyrdom, to two who suffered under the reign of Emperor Maximus. Origen devoted his life to the study of Holy Scripture. He frequently fasted. He slept little, and when he did it was upon the ground. He lived a life of poverty, charging his students only a minimal amount. For many years he abstained from shoes and wine.

Rather infamously, Origen castrated himself. For Eusebius, who greatly revered Origen, this event was more than a bit troubling, yet he neither ignored it nor interpreted it metaphorically. Instead, he recorded it to illustrate Origen's Adamic ancestry; he took the words of Jesus—there are eunuchs who have made themselves eunuchs for the kingdom of God (Matthew 19:12)—too literally and too far. Origen was also concerned with how the public viewed himself and Christianity. As a catechist, he often instructed women, and by castrating himself he attempted to allay any suspicions of improper behavior on his part. Eusebius credited this action to a rash and fanatic act of his youth. At the same time, he claimed that Origen's motives were pure, for he fulfilled a divine command and showed significant "faith and self-control." In fact, it added to his already growing reputation and was even overlooked when he was ordained a priest in Caesarea.

During the reign of Emperor Decius, Origen was captured and severely tortured. He was placed in stocks, stretched, and threatened with fire. Yet he did not suffer at the hands of men, but recognized that all of this was demonic in nature and the devil could not destroy him. Therefore, Origen was a confessor, not a martyr. Not long after these tortures, Origen died at the age of 69.

Origen lived an extremely pious Christian life. More specifically, Origen's life was connected to Adam secondarily, but primarily to the life of Christ. Even when Origen acted like Adam in castrating himself, he obeyed the words of Jesus. Finally, Origen understood the value of martyrdom in the life of Christ and in Christian lives. While he may not have been martyred, he greatly honored it and taught its excellence to his students.

Gregory Thaumaturgus

Date: ca. 213–ca. 270
Place: Neocaesarea, Pontus
Offices: Bishop, Miracle Worker
Biography: *The Life of Gregory the Wonderworker*[14]
Biographer: Gregory of Nyssa (ca. 330–ca. 395)

The life of Gregory Thaumaturgus is honored by Gregory of Nyssa with this panegyric. Thaumaturgus means wonderworker. Hence, the latter Gregory chronicles the many miracles attributed to the former Gregory, along with numerous other aspects of his life.

Gregory was not raised in a Christian family, yet his youth was not without virtue. He was sent to Alexandria to study where he became knowledgeable of Greek wisdom as had Moses of Egyptian wisdom. Because he was such an excellent student, envious fellow students hired a prostitute to falsely charge Gregory for services rendered. Gregory, though, remained calm by neither denying the claim nor seeking witnesses. Instead, he forgave his perpetrators. Immediately the prostitute was overtaken by a demon that finally suffocated her. While yet a young man, Gregory chose virtue over vice.

After Gregory studied under the great teacher, Origen, in Caesarea of Palestine, he returned to his homeland. There, Gregory was ordained into the Holy Ministry. His bishop wished him to assume the appropriate duties, while Gregory sought to suppress them and live a more contemplative life. Finally, God revealed Himself to Gregory in a vision and he realized he must begin his priestly duties.

Gregory entered a town to establish a Christian Church in a place that was filled with heathen altars and dominated by satanic demons. On the first day there, a storm forced Gregory into a heathen temple that was inhabited by demons. Gregory did not flinch, but cleansed the temple with the sign of the cross, and stayed up the entire night praying and hymning, and then continued in the morning. When the pagan priest arrived the following day to offer sacrifices, he could neither enter because of Gregory's presence nor invoke the demonic forces. The pagan priest hurled insults and threats at Gregory, but Gregory remained calm. The pagan priest began to admire Gregory for his great power over the demons, and when Gregory miraculously moved an unmovable stone, the pagan priest forsook all and was instructed in the Christian faith. Many in the town forsook their pagan ways as well and became Christians.

Gregory preached and taught. He consoled the ill and corrected the young. He instructed all to fulfill their god-given vocations. Children are to be obedient to their parents and parents are to care properly for their children. He reminded the poor that their treasure is virtue and the wealthy that they are to share their abundance with the impoverished.

Reminiscent of the wisdom of Solomon, Gregory judged the case of two brothers and their inheritance. Upon their father's death, they quibbled over a lake, each wanted sole possession of it. Gregory instructed them to put aside their greed and share their father's gift to them. The brothers could not do so, so each hired an army: winner take all. Just prior to the battle, Gregory miraculously dried up the lake in order to pre-empt the battle. The strife between the brothers was resolved, and they returned to their past and pleasant relations. Where there had been a lake, there was now a beautiful meadow.

On another occasion, Gregory was teaching the people when a young man accused Gregory of being demon possessed. The young man was brought to Gregory and Gregory immediately saw that the young man was demon possessed. Gregory breathed upon him and laid his hand upon him. The young man fell down and writhed about on the ground. He arose healthy and free of demons.

The accomplishments of Gregory spread about the land and enraged the Roman emperor. All Christian services and practices were prohibited and Christians were threatened with severe forms of torture, like fire, beasts, and the rack. Even youth, women, and the elderly were shown no mercy. Children betrayed their Christian parents, and parents their Christian children. Christians were fearful and in disarray and many fled. Gregory, though, remained calm. Surrounded by the enemy that was about to attack, Gregory raised his arms in prayer and they could not find him. Gregory continued to intercede on behalf of the Church, and finally, God answered his petitions and peace returned for the Christian Church. A feast was declared and the martyrs were honored.

The life of Gregory was quite amazing, yet not out of the ordinary for the Christian family. He was educated like Moses, had wisdom comparable to Solomon, and had the missionary zeal of Paul.

Lawrence	Date: d. ca. 258
	Place: Rome
	Offices: Deacon, Martyr
	Biography: *Hymn in Honor of the Passion of Blessed Martyr Lawrence*[15]
	Biographer: Prudentius Aurelius Clemens (348–ca. 410)

Prudentius's verse portrays Lawrence as a Christian champion who fought against pagan Rome. He was fearless before the power of the Roman Empire. In his death and apparent defeat, this humble Roman deacon was a martyr and actually victorious.

Two events precipitated Lawrence's martyrdom. The first was a prophecy. The persecution of Christianity was in full swing with the crucifixion of Pope Sixtus. With Lawrence, the archdeacon at Rome, lamenting at the foot of his cross, Sixtus prophesied that Lawrence would follow him into martyrdom in three days.

The second event occurred on the same day as the first. The Roman prefect, desirous of money, summoned Lawrence who was responsible for the Church of Rome's treasury. The prefect complained that Christians condemned the Roman gods and noted greedily that the Christian Church was extremely wealthy: silver chalices and golden candlesticks and great deposits of coins. For the welfare of the empire, he demanded that Lawrence hand over the treasures of the church. To encourage Lawrence, the prefect cited Jesus: The image on a coin is not God, but Caesar (Matthew 22:19–21), and poverty is a virtue (Luke 6:20). In the following three days, Lawrence gathered the impoverished and crippled and diseased for whom the church cared, also virgins and widows, presented them to the prefect, and declared that these are the treasures of the Church. Chosen by God and hated by man, Lawrence trod the path of martyrdom.

The prefect, expecting riches and receiving the impoverished, was so infuriated with Lawrence that he promised him a long and painful death by fire. Led to the pyre, his face glowed as had those of Moses in the Old Testament and Stephen in the New Testament. As the flames scorched his flesh, Lawrence made a mockery of this torment. Rather than crying out in pain, he calmly noted to the prefect that he was well done on one side and needed to be turned to the other. With his final breath, he prayed to God on behalf of pagan Rome and prophesied of a future Christian emperor.

The martyrdom of Lawrence turned the spiritual tide of the day. Many Romans—senators and pagan priests and others—were converted to the Christian faith. While the pagan temples emptied, multitudes flocked to Christian altars. Satan was defeated in this battle.

In his martyrdom, the countenance of Lawrence shone like those who before him who had been in the presence of God. Lawrence was a Christian warrior like Jesus. Neither used a sword nor led an army. Both suffered and died. Both wrestled not "against flesh and blood, but against the rulers, against the authorities, against the cosmic powers over this present darkness, against the spiritual forces of evil in the heavenly places" (Ephesians 6:12). Both were victorious in death.

Cyprian	Date: d. 258
	Place: Carthage, North Africa
	Offices: Bishop, Martyr
	Biography: *Life and Passion of Cyprian*[16]
	Biographer: Pontius the Deacon (d. ca. 260)

Pontius, a deacon under Cyprian, portrayed an extremely humble and devout Christian leader in the Life and Passion of Cyprian. The life of this bishop began with his Baptism and concluded with his passion as two jewel-encrusted bookends support a greatly treasured book.

With Cyprian's Baptism, everything changed in his life. He began to question the darkness of his earlier secular learning and look only to the divine light of spiritual wisdom. Moreover, he rid himself of earthly possessions, dispersing his wealth among the needy. Furthermore, his good works were myriad. In fact, his countenance glowed with holiness. Soon after his Baptism, he was raised to the bishopric in Carthage. He remained in Carthage to care for the sick during a plague, but voluntarily withdrew to the countryside during a persecution.

With Cyprian's martyrdom, he was enrolled among those who had shed their blood for the sake of Jesus. The light of the sun revealed the glory of this event. He was an enemy of the pagan gods; the sentence was read; he succumbed to the sword. This priest was offered as a sacrifice and received the crown of glory.

Second and possibly the principle reason for his biography, Pontius defended Cyprian's bishopric. Cyprian left himself wide open for criticism when he was made bishop within two years of his conversion. This clearly conflicted with an apostolic prohibition (1 Timothy 3:6). Consequently, Pontius argued that in the life of Cyprian, faith was much more important than time. In addition, he illustrated the events surrounding Cyprian's appointment: the people demanded that Cyprian become their bishop; Cyprian's humility proved his worthiness to be bishop; after becoming bishop, even his enemies were befriended. A second problem for Cyprian was his voluntary exile to the countryside during persecution rather than reception of martyrdom. Pontius claimed that Cyprian's action stemmed not from "faint-heartedness," but "Divine Providence." Later, God visited Cyprian and showed him that he would soon be martyred.

Third and quite interesting, Pontius closely connected a variety of biblical characters with Cyprian's life. Like the eunuch in the Acts of the Apostles, Cyprian was a quick study. Just as the former was baptized immediately, Cyprian was quickly ordained a bishop. Similar to Job, Cyprian was not concerned with loss of property, but rather, freely gave to all in need. As with Elijah and Daniel, Cyprian was exiled from the pleasures of society to inhospitable surroundings. Following after Zacharias, God's messenger to Cyprian made signs instead of speaking. Like Zacchaeus, many Christians climbed trees so that they could view the martyrdom of Cyprian. With these examples, Pontius placed Cyprian within the sacred throng of biblical saints.

Pontius did not at all attempt to be exhaustive in nature, but carefully selected his biographical data. It logically began with Cyprian's Baptism and ended with his martyrdom. The heart of this life showed Cyprian as the bishop that he was: virtuous and guided by God, closely related to Jesus and many others who had preceded him in the Christian faith.

Eulalia	Date: d. 304
	Place: Merida, Spain
	Office: Martyr
	Biography: *The Passion of Agnes*[17]
	Biographer: Prudentius Aurelius Clemens
	(348–ca. 410)

Prudentius writes of Eulalia: "noble by birth, and far nobler in death."[18] Eulalia was the daughter of wealthy Spanish parents during the reign of Diocletian and Maximian who ruled the western half of the empire. She, though, would far surpass this honor as a child of God. Even as a young child, she was a mature Christian. Eulalia was both the child of noble parents and a martyr in the Christian Church.

At the tender of age of 12, Eulalia was not like other children. She was not interested in childish games and toys. Scented oils and precious stones held no place in her life. Instead, her life was filled with her love and devotion to God. She had no desire for an earthly husband, but only the one in heaven.

When persecution broke out against Christians, Eulalia relished the thought of combating these pagan enemies, so her mother took her to the countryside, not only to protect her from persecution, but to prevent her from joining the fray. Unhappy, Eulalia snuck away through barred doors and traveled miles through rugged countryside. She was escorted by heavenly messengers and a heavenly beacon shone on her path like the pillar of light that led the Israelites!

Finally arriving in Merida, she presented herself before the pagan persecutors of Christianity and questioned their actions. How could they worship false gods and persecute the one true God? Then she ridiculed their pagan rituals and threatened to dispose personally of their so-called gods. Finally, she insulted the western ruler, Maximian, calling him a puppet of false gods and his gruesome acts of torture against the Christians heinous.

The officials then chastised Eulalia and attempted to put her in her place in relation to their gods and government and her parents. No doubt, her parents were looking for her and were concerned for her well-being and were crying over her. Moreover, death now means no future betrothal for Eulalia. Then they impotently attempted to scare her with death by sword and beasts and fire. Simply recant, they said, and offer incense to the gods, and you will live. When she spat in their faces, her flesh was torn from the bone. For Eulalia though, the cuts were but inscriptions of Christ upon her, and blood that flowed from her wounds proclaimed the name of Christ. They did not withhold their malice from this young girl. They ripped her flesh apart and blood flowed everywhere and they finally set her on fire. As her hair became ablaze, the fire surrounded her face like a veil! A white dove flew from her mouth. When the prefect saw the dove, he fled from scene of this crime. Immediately snow covered her like a pall.

According to Prudentius, Eulalia's bones remain in Merida. Those who gather in around the remains of this youthful saint are not to mourn, but to honor the work that God worked through her. In addition, some bring garlands and sing hymns. Even the land is favored that bears her remains. It is like a beautiful meadow.

Eulalia bears resemblances to her Christian relatives: the pillar of light before the Israelites in the wilderness and all those who have lost their life for the sake of Jesus and the Gospel. Eulalia is not unlike Jesus in His youth. When both were young, both knew their destiny and did not shirk from it. Most notably, just as the Spirit of Jesus departs from Him upon the cross, so also the spirit of Eulalia departs from her upon the martyr's pyre.

Summary

The Ante-Nicene period included a goodly number of influential figures. These biographies demonstrated a sharp interest in differing portrayal of Christian lives with a variety of literary genres. Polycarp was the subject of a passion, Origen was depicted in a history book, and Gregory was portrayed in a life. The common thread running through all of these was the intimate relation that each Christian had with the life of Christ. Perpetua and Cyprian were baptized into Jesus. As bishops, Gregory and Cyprian followed after Jesus, the head of the Church. Perpetua, Origen, and Cyprian heard the Word of God and obeyed it. The Holy Spirit, sent from Jesus, resided in the breasts of Polycarp and Origen. Divine realities were revealed to Perpetua and Cyprian. Most strongly emphasized, martyrdom was the principle office; just as Jesus suffered and died, many of His early followers followed in His train. If it were not possible to hold this office, it was greatly desired and its importance impressed upon others. Although the Ante-Nicene Christians lived one to two centuries after Jesus, they were portrayed as closely related to Him.

Post-Nicenes

The Post-Nicene Period of the Early Church followed the first Ecumenical Council at Nicaea (325). Included in this period are Nicene Christians, those who whose lives overlapped this preeminent council, like Antony, Constantine, and Eusebius of Caesarea, and Post-Nicene Christians, those clearly after this council, like Augustine and Patrick. With the Edict of Milan (313) enacting toleration of Christianity, the reverence for martyrs did not diminish, though the number in their ranks did. Hence, this period emphasized the importance of pure doctrine, Christian piety, and missionary endeavors. These are manifested in the Christian offices of emperor, ascetic, bishop, miracle worker, and missionary. Post-Nicene Christian biography employed these offices to illustrate the intimate relation between Post-Nicene Christian lives and the life of Christ.

Emperor. The role of the Roman emperor changed drastically in the Early Church. Throughout most of the Anti-Nicene Period, the Roman government and its leaders severely persecuted the Christian Church. This had begun in the New Testament with Pontius Pilate, a Roman Governor, sentencing Jesus to death by crucifixion. This was followed by a series of Roman emperors who persecuted Christianity, the most brutal being Decius (250–51) and Diocletian (303–11). The tide began to turn with Galerius (d. 311). Though an adamant opponent of the Church, he issued the Edict of Toleration (311) that first legalized Christianity. The first and great Christian emperor was Constantine (d. 337). As a friend of the Church, he issued the Edict of Milan (313) that gave Christianity freedom in the Roman Empire. Following this, he greatly supported the Church in numerous fashions. Post-Nicene Christianity variously addressed the Roman emperors: Julian the Apostate (332–63) was assailed in a series of hymns by Ephraim the Syrian (ca. 306–73), while Pacatus's panegyric (389) to Emperor Theodosius I (d. 395) praised him.

Helena (d. ca. 330), the mother of Constantine, lived a virtuous life and was responsible for the construction of Christian churches throughout the Roman Empire, particularly in Rome and Palestine. So influential was she that Eusebius, the great patristic historian, preserved much of her biographical data.

Ascetic. The ascetic rigorously exercised his Christian faith through acts of prayer, fasting, alms, celibacy, and caring for the sick. These were components of the Christian life that Jesus performed in His own life and commanded of His followers. Consequently, the ascetic held a prominent position in the Early Church. Christians lived ascetic lives in the Ante-Nicene Period, like Origen and Cyprian. At the same time, they generally did not seclude themselves from the local Christian community. Following the Edict of Milan, numeric growth in the Church spawned hypocrites, and those living extremely rigorous lives began to leave the Christian communities in towns for a more devout and pious life in the desert. Hermits lived in relative solitude, while coenobitics lived with other like-minded ascetics. Stylites lived atop pillars for extended periods of their lives. At the close of the fourth century, Palladius (ca. 365–425) visited Egypt to learn about asceticism from Evagrius (346–99), a prominent ascetic and author. Early in the fifth century, he returned to Asia Minor and penned Lausiac History, an account of no less than seventy fourth-century desert ascetics. The preeminent position of martyr among the Ante-Nicene Christians was quickly supplanted by the ascetic among the Post-Nicenes.

Asceticism was not restricted to men. Macrina and Mary of Egypt were notable ascetics, the former a coenobitic and abbess, the latter a hermit. The lives of numerous Christian women were considered important enough to preserve in writing. Palladius included female desert ascetics in his Lausiac History.

Miracle Worker. The successors of Jesus—apostles, bishops, martyrs, and others—carried on the work of their Lord. They not only preached and baptized, but many performed miracles. The Acts of the Apostles recorded many of the apostles' miracles. Later and similarly, Gregory Thaumaturgus (ca. 213–ca. 270), bishop of Neocaesarea in Pontus, and Hilarion (ca. 291–371), a Palestinian ascetic, were noted miracle workers: the former an Ante-Nicene, the latter a Post-Nicene. In regard to their miracles, the question among the Early Church Christians was not "are these miracles possible?", but rather, "Is God revealed in a fashion that is faithful to His revelation in Jesus and the rest of the Bible?" These miracles did not glorify the saint. Instead, they showed the intimate relation between the Christian's life and the life of Christ in that the miracles of the former flowed out of the latter.

Missionary. The missionary, early on, was quite important in light of Jesus' apostolic commission at the conclusion of the Gospels according to Matthew and Mark. The Acts of the Apostles described the mission work of Philip and Peter, Paul and Barnabas. The apocryphal Acts of Thomas had this apostle traveling to India, while Eusebius' Ecclesiastical History placed the evangelist Mark in Alexandria. Such work carried over into the Early Church. The Didache mentioned traveling prophets. The mission of the Church was also extended through the martyrs' public confessions of faith and by the writings of the Apologists. Other early missionaries included Pantaenus to India, Gregory the Illuminator to Armenia, and Frumentius to Abyssinia.

With the Edict of Milan and the subsequent support of Christianity by a number of Roman emperors, the Church grew in number and influence. Both the role and amount of biographical data increased in direct proportion to the multiplication of significant Christian lives and literary genres utilized. Significant collections of Christian lives serve as an apt example. Two such collections were the Lives of Illustrious Men by Jerome (ca. 342–420), and its continuation by Gennadius (d. 471). They provided biographical data for well over two hundred Christians, beginning with the apostles and extending into the Post-Nicene Period. Other literary genres employed by the Post-Nicenes with biographical data included: life, panegyric, funeral oration, autobiography, and hymn.

Constantine	Date: d. 337
	Place: Constantinople
	Office: Emperor
	Biography: *Life of the Blessed Emperor Constantine*[19]
	Biographer: Eusebius of Caesarea (ca. 260–ca. 340)

Eusebius of Caesarea was thoroughly enamored with Constantine and praised him effusively in the panegyric, Life of the Blessed Emperor Constantine. As the first Christian emperor of the Roman Empire, Constantine integrated the church into the empire.

Constantine had a noble pedigree. His father, Constantius, was courageous and victorious in battle, and, at the same time, a benevolent ruler who was said to be loved by all. He rejected polytheism, and did not persecute Christianity. God rewarded him with supreme authority over the Roman Empire, a large family, a worthy heir (Constantine), and eternal life.

The youth of Constantine was compared to that of various biblical figures. Just as Moses was raised in the Pharaoh's court and later had to flee, so Constantine was raised among the Roman nobility prior to his flight. While Constantine was in Palestine, his troops honored and revered him like God's ancient prophet. He had "natural intelligence and divinely imparted wisdom", not unlike the child Jesus (see Luke 2:52).

A momentous event occurred in Constantine's life. After succeeding his father to the throne and achieving numerous military victories, he began to ponder spiritual matters and he looked for a worthy god. He noted that his polytheistic predecessors had met with ignoble ends. In contrast, the God of his father had provided well for him and his empire. One day at noon, a cross with the inscription, "conquer by this", came into sight above the sun. This was seen by Constantine and his army. Later in a dream, Christ appeared to Constantine, confirmed him, and promised that this sign would protect him. From this time on, Constantine utilized a superimposed chi-rho (χ-ρ), the first two Greek letters of Christ ($\chi\rho\iota\sigma\tau\acute{o}\varsigma$), upon his helmet and standard. This proved beneficial in Constantine's future military campaigns.

Constantine's life was thoroughly Christian. He was catechized, and Christian priests became his counselors. He honored the Christian clergy, financially supported the building of churches, provided for the poor, and frequented the bishop's gatherings. Constantine's Christian life quickly accelerated.

Constantine's antagonist was Licinius, ruler of the eastern portion of the Roman Empire. Licinius severely persecuted Christianity: Synods of clergy were prohibited; Christian property was confiscated; men and women were forbidden to assemble together in church; Christians were removed from the military. Moreover, churches were destroyed, and clergy killed. By far the worst, Licinius called upon the magical arts, and had his heart hardened by God as did the Egyptian Pharaoh (Exodus 7:13). In contrast, Constantine prepared for battle with Licinius through prayer, proudly bore his new standard, and finally was victorious. Constantine's battle against Licinius followed in the train of previous heroes and antagonists: Jesus and Satan, Isaac and Ishmael, Moses and the Pharaoh of Egypt.

Constantine's life reached its pinnacle as a Christian emperor when he called a church council. While he forced Christianity upon no one, he was deeply concerned with the theological troubles brewing in Alexandria between Bishop Alexander and Presbyter Arius. Desiring peace and unity in the Christian Church, he summoned the bishops of the church to Nicaea.

The perspective of Eusebius was clear: God worked through Constantine. Constantine summoned church leaders from throughout the Mediterranean world. A new Pentecost occurred: Christian leaders were present from Syria and Sicily, Phoenicia and Arabia, Palestine and Egypt, Libya and Persia. At the assembling of this august body, a church building was miraculously enlarged to contain those present. The emperor addressed the council, patiently listened to both sides, and in the end, persuaded all to true Christian unity. Constantine restored peace to the Christian Church through the Council of Nicaea I and then upheld its decisions among the bishops and throughout Christianity.

The death of Constantine was preceded by prayer and baptism in a church dedicated to the martyrs. The irony was obvious: This emperor received a water Baptism in a church that commemorated Christians baptized in blood at the hands of previous emperors. Following his Baptism, Constantine vested himself no longer in purple, but only the purest of white. Constantine died on the day of Pentecost, the feast of feasts. The death of Constantine was followed with mourning and honors, worship and prayer, and a coin depicting his entrance into heaven.

Eusebius' biographical data for Constantine was quite extensive. Constantine was portrayed as extremely spiritual: He had a pious father (and mother); he exhibited a biblically-styled youth; he received visions from God; he called the Council of Nicaea I to establish peace in the church. Of no less value, Baptism was a significant, albeit late, event in Constantine's life. In all of this, Constantine was the proto-typical Christian emperor. Through Baptism, his life was associated with the life of Christ, and as an emperor, he was a divine agent.

Athanasius	Date: ca. 296–373
	Place: Alexandria
	Office: Bishop
	Biography: *Oration*[21]
	Biographer: Gregory of Nazianzus
	(329–89)

In this panegyric, Gregory lauded Athanasius, who lived an exemplary Christian life. Athanasisus, Gregory argues, heaped virtue upon virtue in his life, and the least virtues in his life would be considered the greatest in the lives of most Christians. Greater yet, Athanasius was a theologian of the incarnation. This was true of all of the faithful in the Old Testament. Priest and prophet and apostle, Isaac and David and John, to name a few, had faith in the divine promise of a Savior. They prophesied and foreshadowed in many fashions the nativity of Jesus. Like them and perhaps to a greater degree, Athanasius looked to Jesus alone.

Athanasius' youth is mentioned rather briefly, but not without importance. He was born into a Christian family where he learned both love and respect for the Christian faith. A life-changing event occurred in his academic studies. Athanasius studied philosophy, but Holy Scripture captured his mind and heart. He studied and contemplated upon both testaments until he learned that he had no reason to fear God. Rather than being a slave, he became a friend and, better yet, a beloved son of God.

Athanasius was well-suited for ecclesial life. After holding a series of offices, the people chose him to become bishop of Alexandria. In so doing, he occupied the same office of the evangelist Mark who was the first bishop of Alexandria. Athanasius was a splendid bishop. He had no interest in earthly power and did not lord his authority over the people. Instead, he was a faithful shepherd. His qualities as overseer had already been delineated in Paul's first letter to Timothy (1 Timothy 3:1–7). Athanasius was concerned with the true teachings of the Christian Church. He sought to drive out heterodoxy and unite the orthodox.

Arius was the chief antagonist of Athanasius. He denied that the Son and the Holy Spirit were true God, the Father only being fully God. Arius taught this and it infected others, so much so that 318 Church fathers were united by the Holy Spirit at the Council of Nicaea (325) to address this issue. Though Athanasius was not yet the bishop of Alexandria, he was greatly respected by all present. The battle was fierce, but Arius was deemed a heretic and the doctrine of the Holy Trinity: one God and three persons—Father, Son, and Holy Spirit—won the day. Arius was a Judas in that he betrayed his Savior and died when his bowels burst apart.

Gregory, a native of Cappadocia, was a second antagonist of Athanasius. Though Athanasius won the day at Nicaea and would later become the bishop of Alexandria, a new emperor, Constantius, who was Arian, meant an Arian bishop in Alexandria. Gregory was an Arian, and Athanasius went into exile, living among the desert ascetics for a brief time. He was terribly persecuted, falsely accused of murder, tormented, and hunted as though he were an animal. However, Athanasius found comfort in the Holy Scripture, both imitating the life of Job and taking counsel from the wisdom of Solomon: "For everything there is a season, and a time for every matter under heaven" (Ecclesiastes 3:1).

Gregory caused great havoc. He taught the heresy of Arius, embezzled, and lived an immoral life. So sinful, it was as if he was the forerunner of the Antichrist. With the death of the Emperor Constantius, Gregory lost his position and Athanasius returned triumphantly to Alexandria on a colt, welcomed with branches and clothing, with cheers and joyfulness. Once again the bishop of Alexandria, Athanasius purged the temple of false doctrine and taught the doctrine of the Holy Trinity for the salvation of all who believe.

With his death, Athanasius transcended this temporal life. He left behind the sinful flesh that tied him to Adam and all of his descendants. In death, Athanasius is united with all the faithful who preceded him: patriarchs in the Old Testament, apostles in the New Testament, and martyrs in the Ante-Nicene Period. Greater still, Athanasius has come into the pure light and even now is one with the Holy Trinity.

Antony	Date: ca. 251–356
	Place: Egypt
	Office: Ascetic
	Biography: *Life of Antony*
	Biographer: Athanasius (ca. 296–373)

Antony was not the first ascetic in the Egyptian desert, however, he was one of the more interesting. The Life of Antony was penned by Athanasius (ca. 296–373), a notable, fourth century theologian and Bishop of Alexandria. The mixture of its exciting narratives and authoritative author granted it an immediate and widespread influence in portraying early Egyptian asceticism.

The birth of Antony and the events surrounding it were minimal. He was born of wealthy Egyptian parents. As a child, Antony was not like others his age. He did not play with his peers. In contrast, he showed great interest in matters spiritual; he gladly attended church, listened carefully to the readings, and contemplated them. Also, he did not complain, content with the care provided by his parents.

At the age of 18, his parents died and he became responsible for his younger sister. Soon after, a life-changing event occurred. As he approached church one day, the actions of the apostles came to mind— they left everything and followed Jesus. Upon entering church, he heard the Gospel reading: "If you would be perfect, go, sell what you possess and give to the poor, and you will have treasure in heaven; and come, follow me" (Matthew 19:21). And so he did. He sold his earthly inheritance and gave the proceeds to the poor. He placed his sister with a community of virgins and began his ascetic life.

The ascetic life of Antony began quite simply. He traveled about, seeking advice from other, more experienced ascetics. He worked and gave surplus income to the poor. He prayed constantly and read the Bible. He was admired by many and called "God's friend". His ascetic life then quickly accelerated. Intolerant of such a devout life, the devil tempted him with earthly concerns: possessions, family, food, fame, and the like. Unsuccessful, he appeared to Antony in the form of a woman to seduce him, but to no avail. In the face of these temptations and deceits, this ascetic was victorious. Seeking to further exercise his Christian faith, Antony took up residence in the tombs. There he prayed to God and announced his presence to the demons. Many monstrous demons attacked and beat and almost killed Antony. The assault was so fierce, that riotous sounds shook the tombs. Specters of leopards and scorpions and snakes surrounded Antony, but were unable to vanquish him. Jesus came to his side when the fighting was most fierce. Antony's attackers disappeared, and Jesus delivered him.

The majority of Antony's life was spent in solitude, where he was a martyr not of the body, but of the spirit. On occasion, he directed other ascetics, and many Christians often sought spiritual guidance and direction from one as holy as Antony. At other times, he performed miracles like healing various physical maladies and casting out demons as Jesus had done.

During the Arian controversy, the Arians claimed that Antony supported their position. This promoted Antony to enter Alexandria and denounce the impious and demonic teachings of Arius. There, he confessed the Christian faith that Jesus was the "Eternal Word" and that the Son of God was equally God with the Father. He supported the teaching of Athanasius.

Prior to his death, Antony received a premonition and looked forward to his death with fondness. The ascetics with him at the time embraced him briefly. He then instructed them in living virtuous lives and rejecting heresy. At 105 years old, he died—his health unimpaired, his eyes strong, his teeth intact though worn, and his demeanor cheerful. Following his death, he was buried and at place unknown except to the two who buried him.

Antony's life was shown to be related to the faithful who preceded him. He followed the example of the apostles who left all behind and followed Jesus. Like Moses, Antony's long and productive life concluded with a secret burial. In addition, Antony's life flowed directly from the life of Christ. Antony obeyed the words of Jesus to begin his ascetic life. Early in their careers, both Jesus and Antony were unsuccessfully tempted by Satan. Antony's miracles paralleled those of Jesus. Most significantly, while Jesus died upon a cross, Antony died daily in his ascetic life. The preeminent role of martyr was being replaced by the ascetic in Antony's life.

Hilarion	Date: ca. 291–371
	Place: Palestine
	Offices: Ascetic, Miracle Worker
	Biography: *Life of Hilarion*
	Biographer: Jerome (ca. 342–420)

Jerome vividly portrayed the well-traveled life of Hilarion. He was a notable ascetic and celebrated miracle worker. In the introduction to this life, Jerome lamented that many would be overly critical of this ascetic because he was out and about. Jerome argued that these same people complained that Paulus, of whom Jerome also wrote a life, was too much of a recluse. Jerome, then, compared these complainants to the Pharisees in the New Testament who had similarly criticized John the Baptist and Jesus (Matthew 11:16–19).

Hilarion was born in Thabatha, a small village in southwest Palestine. His pagan parents sent their young son to Alexandria to receive an education. He was an exceptional student, but soon converted to Christianity. He rejected societal pleasures and delighted in the church alone. While still at the tender age of 15, he visited Antony in the Egyptian desert. This encounter changed his life: He was so impressed with the asceticism of Antony, he returned to his homeland to thoroughly exercise his Christian faith in the same way.

The ascetic life of Hilarion was quite rigorous. He forfeited his inheritance, part to his brothers and part to the needy. Remembering the calamity that fell upon Ananias and Sapphira, he kept nothing (Acts 5:1–11). Unburdened with earthly possessions and unafraid of local criminals, he set out into the desert, east of Gaza in Palestine. He had little clothing and only one rough blanket. He never washed his clothing, though he cut his hair once each year on the day of the Lord's Resurrection. His first years were lived in a small, crude shelter. His nourishment was minimal. During one three year period, he consumed nothing but lentils and water. Following the example of the Egyptian ascetics, he wove baskets to support himself. He prayed and sang; he memorized the entire Bible.

On one occasion, thieves approached him and asked if he was afraid of robbery. Hilarion responded, "He who has nothing does not fear thieves." They then asked him, what if they take your life? Hilarion countered, "I do not fear thieves because I am prepared to die." These thieves then confessed their past transgressions to Hilarion and vowed to renew their lives.[20]

The devil was always about and after the soul of Hilarion. The evil one attacked with the cries of babes, the bewailing of women, the snarls of wild animals, and the din of military. Hilarion was tempted in his celibacy with apparitions of unclothed women and lavish meals as he fasted. Hilarion endured mightily under the manifold temptations of the devil.

Hilarion did not perform his first miracle until he was 38 years old, but after that these wondrous signs multiplied greatly in his life. A blind woman from Egypt approached Hilarion. She complained that she had spent all of her money on physicians, but remained without sight. Rather than comforting her, Hilarion spoke harshly, "If you had given to the poor rather then spent your money on doctors that perish, then Jesus, the true Physician, would have cured you."[21] Unwilling to leave, the woman kept petitioning Hilarion until he spit in her eyes and she could see again. He healed three sickly children. He exorcised countless demons from both man and beast. He countered the demonic actions of magicians. His miracles were heralded far and wide in his day!

In his later years, Hilarion became the abbot of a great monastery. He also traveled about the Mediterranean world as a servant of God. In the deserts of Egypt, he blessed some oil so that it cured all who had been bitten by asps. On his voyage to Sicily, he cast out a demon from the son of the captain. In Epidaurus of Dalmatia, he prayed to his dear Lord and then summoned a beast- and man-eating serpent upon a pyre where it was consumed in fire. At the age of 80 and in Cyprus, he died, repeating the phrase, "Proceed, what do you fear? Proceed, my soul, why do you wait?"[22]

Hilarion's life appeared spectacular, but simply flowed from the spectacular life of Christ. They were born in the same land, lived without luxuries, had followers, performed analogous miracles, and similarly desired their heavenly home. Hilarion, like Jesus, was ever the faithful servant of God.

Macrina	Date: ca. 327–79
	Place: Pontus
	Office: Ascetic
	Biography: *Life of Macrina*
	Biographer: Gregory of Nyssa (ca. 330–ca. 395)

Macrina (ca. 327–79) was a Christian woman in the Early Church. She faithfully served two families, one in the home and the other in the church. The overlap between these two is quite evident in the Life of Macrina that was authored shortly after her death by Gregory of Nyssa, her brother and one of the Cappadocian Fathers.

Macrina's parentage was exemplary. Her father's parents lost their possessions because of their confession of Jesus, and before that, her mother's grandfather was martyred. In addition, her mother was quite virtuous. With this, Gregory showed that while Macrina was a Post-Nicene Christian, her spiritual heritage was rooted in the martyrdom of the Ante-Nicenes and ultimately Jesus.

As Macrina was raised in a Christian family, she was taught the Sacred Scriptures from her youth. She learned particularly well the Psalter. By the age of 12, her extraordinary beauty began to flower. Surrounded by many suitors, her father promised her to one. Although he died before the marriage, Macrina declared that she would wed no other as her fiancé was not dead, but alive in heaven because of the resurrection of Jesus Christ. She remained faithful to him, her husband. This event was pivotal for Macrina in that it showed her early spiritual resolve and set the stage for her devout Christian life.

In the absence of her "husband", Macrina remained close to and very much influenced her family. She converted her brother, Basil (the Great and future bishop of Caesarea), from oratory to philosophy, poverty, and virtue. Macrina never left her mother so that she could physically and spiritually support her. Macrina directed her mother, after the death of her husband and the raising of her children, away from the world and into a community of virgins and widows.

Macrina lived an ascetic life and became the superior of a religious community. Three miracles were associated with her life. One certainly called to mind the work of Jesus. Macrina healed the eye of a young daughter of a military leader named Sebastopolis. Another miracle was a bit more elaborate. Afflicted with a life-threatening abscess below her neck, Macrina refused a doctor's care because of modesty. In fervent prayer, she shed tears. With these tears and the ground upon which they fell, she produced a poultice and placed it upon the sore. Later, when her mother made the sign of the cross upon the abscess, it was healed, yet a small mark remained as a sign of the miracle. Christological echoes abounded: Jesus shed tears prior to rising Lazarus from the dead (John 11:35); Jesus anointed the eyes of a blind man with a mixture of spit and dirt (John 9:6); and Jesus retained the marks of His crucifixion after His resurrection (John 20:27).

The death of Macrina was quiet, yet significant events preceded and followed. Seriously ill, she lay not upon a couch, but upon a board on the ground, not unlike Job. As the end of her life drew near, she reflected upon the beauty of the Bridegroom and trusted in the hope of the resurrection of the dead. Macrina no longer desired to remain in this world, but rather, to travel to the heavenly realm where she could be present with and gaze upon the Holy One. She prayed audibly of the work of Jesus and forgiveness and the resurrection. After the fever dried up her tongue, her lips and hands moved as she continued in evening prayer. She made the sign of the cross immediately prior to her death. Following Macrina's death, the women in her religious community mourned and held a vigil like those for the martyrs. Finally, the procession of her body to be buried alongside her parents included the bishop and priests and deacons, monks and nuns, and a great multitude of people. The procession took most of the day, with choirs singing.

Macrina's life corresponded closely to significant women in the Bible. On the one hand, she lived a virtuous life as did Ruth in the Old Testament and Mary in the New Testament. She remained with and cared for her mother as Ruth did her mother-in-law. In marriage, she was both faithful and a virgin like Mary. On the other hand, while Ruth and Mary gave birth to important sons, Macrina did not. Nonetheless, she provided spiritual direction for her mother's children and became the spiritual mother of her mother and religious community. In addition, Macrina's miracles flowed out of the miracles of Jesus.

Gorgonia	Date: d. ca. 370
	Place: Nazianzus, Cappadocia
	Offices: Wife, Mother
	Biography: *Funeral Oration*
	Biographer: Gregory of Nazianzus (329–89)

Gorgonia was neither a revered ascetic nor a grandiose empress, but a devout Christian wife and mother. In this panegyric, Gregory of Nazianzus, her brother, noted that he utilized an unembellished style to portray an unpretentious life. In fact, her ordinary Christian life made her extraordinary.

Gorgonia was born into a Christian family. Her parents, Gregory (the elder) and Nonna, were a modern day Abraham and Sarah. Gregory left behind his family under God's guidance, while Nonna gave birth to children under the promise. Gregory believed in God, while Nonna called her husband Lord. They were her biological and spiritual parents, giving her temporal life and the hope of eternal life.

Gorgonia lived a virtuous life—she was modest and pious. This was particularly true in her family life. She was a faithful wife, but without pride. Her children and her children's children became the children of God. She was the personification of the woman wisdom in Proverbs who cared for her family above all else (Proverbs 31:10–31). Gorgonia adorned herself with moral simplicity—she wore the "blush of modesty" and the white of temperance. She opened her house to the needy and honored God's priests. She fasted, chanted the Psalms, and prayed on bended knee. In all of this, Gorgonia reflected the image of God.

Gorgonia's life nearly ended prematurely twice. Concerning the first, she was severely injured while riding in a carriage when the mules, pulling it, bolted. The crash was horrific. Her body was bruised terribly and many of her bones were broken. The pain was excruciating, but she refused to let a physician attend to her. She acted so out of modesty, and because she looked not to men, but to the Great Physician for healing. It was concluded that this tragedy happened so that following her suffering she would be glorified. On another occasion, Gorgonia was severely ill with fever and coma and paralysis of mind and body. The knowledge of physicians and the love of her parents were of no effect. While her illness was in slight remission, she left her sick bed and entered the House of God where she prayed and tears flowed. Grasping the altar with one hand while applying these tears to her diseased body with the other, Jesus healed her of her infirmity. In both instances, Jesus watched over and tenderly cared for Gorgonia.

Gorgonia's life ended much as she lived—piously and modestly. She longed to be with Jesus in the heavenly Jerusalem. After she foresaw her death, she was baptized. Because this happened so late in her Christian life, Baptism did not so much grant her forgiveness as seal the forgiveness that she had already received throughout her Christian life. Finally, she lay upon her deathbed. Family and friends surrounded her. In the hushed silence, the psalm she repeated over and over was barely audible. And with her last breath, Gorgonia said, "I shall now recline in peace and rest."[23]

Gorgonia's life was a Christian life. She was portrayed as the daughter of the spiritual Abraham and Sarah. Jesus' healing hand touched her on two occasions. She lived a virtuous life in accordance with the word of God and was baptized into the Word made flesh. This simple Christian woman was an extraordinary Christian as are all who "hear the word of God and keep it!" (Luke 11:28).

Martin	Date: d. 397
	Place: Tours (Turones), Lugdunensis
	Offices: Ascetic, Bishop, Miracle Worker
	Biography: *Life of St. Martin*
	Biographer: Sulpitius Severus (ca. 360–ca. 420)

Sulpitius Severus depicted the sublime life of Martin. He held the prestigious position of bishop, yet lived the humble life of an ascetic. Modesty limited his words primarily to those of Jesus. He served others by performing numerous miracles and also wept for those who persecuted him.

Martin was born and raised in Italy. While his parents were pagans, he became a catechumen in the Christian Church at the age of 10. Although he wished to become an ascetic after two years of study, he was prohibited because of his youth. Not long after this, a Roman law was enacted that required the sons of veterans to become soldiers. As Martin's father had been in the military, Martin, at 15 years of age, followed suit. He served first under Constantine and then Julian. Therefore, a vocational tension unfolded in his youth.

The tensions of Martin's youth escalated in his young adulthood. He was a soldier, but did not wallow in the vices common to this profession. Instead, he lived a virtuous life. One winter in Amiens (Ambiani, Belgica), frigid weather caused great suffering and many deaths. As Martin passed through, he met someone destitute and freezing to death. Others showed no concern, but Martin pitied the man. Not having a spare coat, but a sword, Martin cut his coat in two and gave half to the freezing man. Those looking on ridiculed Martin's actions and his strange new appearance. That very night, Jesus spoke to Martin in a vision. In this dream, Jesus was draped in the half-coat Martin had given to the beggar and said to him: "Truly, I say to you, as you did it to one of the least of these My brothers, you did it to Me" (Matthew 25:40). Shortly after this, Martin was baptized, switching his allegiance from the Roman emperor to the Christian God. Within two years he retired from military service.

Martin quickly came under the spiritual tutelage of Hilary of Poitiers. Martin was first made a deacon, then later installed into the office of exorcist by Hilary. This had far-reaching effects as the devil was never far removed from his life. The evil one attacked Martin throughout his life with threats and lies. On one occasion, a young man in Spain performed many signs and claimed first that he was Elijah and then Jesus. He then traveled to and entered Martin's monastery where he stationed himself next to Martin in prayer. Enveloped in a violet radiance and clothed in the most regal attire, this man said to Martin, "Look at my glory. Confess that I am the Christ." Martin, however, saw through his actions and appearances, and demanded: "Show me the marks of your crucifixion." Immediately this satanic apparition departed.[24]

Martin performed numerous miracles. He gave health to the ill and life to the dead. In one instance, he ordered sacred oil poured into a young girl's mouth, and her voice returned. In another, he kissed a leper, and his malady departed. In yet another, a girl's fever left her after she touched a letter from Martin.

Being first an ascetic, Martin was appointed bishop, but not without difficulty. Unwilling to go beyond the walls of the monastery, a local man falsely begged him to come and heal his wife. Martin left the monastery and was immediately surrounded by a crowd that ushered him into town where he was to be placed into the Episcopal office. Some protested this appointment on the grounds that Martin did not fit the role—his appearance was unpleasant and his clothing was quite shabby. Spiritual judgment prevailed, and Martin was appointed bishop. The people's acclaim manifested God's will for Martin. This bishop did not live in luxury, but returned to his monastery just outside of town and continued his rigorously ascetic life.

Martin lived an extraordinary life that clearly was connected to the life of Christ. Jesus had a profound effect upon him early: first in catechesis, then in a vision, and finally in his Baptism. The remainder of Martin's life was modeled after the life of Christ—both lived simply, fought against the devil, and served the needy with wondrous signs.

Porphyry	Date: 353–421
	Place: Gaza, Palestine
	Offices: Bishop, Miracle Worker
	Biography: *Life of Porphyry*
	Biographer: Mark the Deacon
	(early fifth century)

Porphyry was a notable Christian in the Early Church. He had no desire for ecclesial office, but was nonetheless drawn into it. Although the Roman Empire was very much Christian by the latter half of the fourth century, Porphyry entered a stronghold of paganism in the early fifth-century Gaza where he had to fight tenaciously for the Christian faith and trust in God to deliver him from his enemies.

Born into a noble family in Thessalonica, Porphyry sought solitude and went to Egypt. There he lived for five years with other austere ascetics. Following this, he traveled to Palestine and lived in a cave for five years. He there became quite sick with liver ailment, fevers, and internal pains. He was so weak that he had to use a cane to support himself when he walked, but continued to travel frequently to Jerusalem to worship at the Holy Sepulchre, the place of Jesus' resurrection.

According to Mark, Porphyry was a virtuous man. He studied and understood the Bible well. He had a great love for the poor and was quite compassionate toward the sick. He was a quiet and gentle man, except his anger burned hot against heretics. He clearly spoke the Word of God to them. Even when ill, he trusted in God and His mercy. He distributed his possessions among his brothers in Thessalonica and fed visitors like Abraham.

When word of Porphyry's pious life reached Praylius,[25] Bishop of Jerusalem, Porphyry was ordained an elder. His principle duty was to care for and protect the precious wood of Jesus' cross. This was in fulfillment of a dream that Porphyry previously had. Once ordained, Porphyry continued to live an austere life; he often fasted and drank little. Three years later, when Aeneias of Gaza died, John, the Bishop of Caesarea, declared a fast and three days later the Holy Spirit revealed to him in a dream that Porphyry would be the new Bishop of Gaza. Although Porphyry decried his unworthiness, he was ordained at Caesarea and sent to Gaza.

Porphyry's work in Gaza would prove to be difficult as the area was primarily pagan. The land had suffered a drought that year and the people blamed it on the arrival of the new Christian bishop. Hearing of his imminent arrival, the local pagans tossed thorns upon the road along with all sorts of filth. Their smudges filled the air with smoke. Behind all of this was the devil who was trying to turn away a righteous man.

When Porphyry finally arrived in Gaza and the church called "Peace," he was received by 280 Christians. Porphyry proceeded to proclaim a fast. There was a vigil with much praying and kneeling, hymns and readings. After Porphyry made the sign of the cross in the morning following the vigil, the congregation followed their new bishop out of town to a shrine of the martyr Timothy that contained the relics of another martyr and confessor. Upon their return, the pagans of Gaza had closed the city gates and would not allow the Christians to enter. God, watching over His people and receiving their tears, opened the heavens so that rain watered the land as He had done in the days of Elijah. Witnessing this event, 105 pagans converted to Christianity. Although the pagans of Gaza still sought to harm Porphyry, he continued to pray for them.

Porphyry sought to wipe out paganism in Gaza. On his first try, the emperor answered his request to destroy the pagan temples and their unholy services in town. The local officials, though, took bribes and allowed the temples to remain and their priests to continue their unholy work. When Porphyry traveled to Constantinople and spoke to Empress Eudoxia, action was taken. She ordered the temples destroyed and gave money to Porphyry to construct a new church in Gaza and produce precious vessels for use in it. Porphyry arrived in Gaza to psalm-singing.

In Gaza there was a naked statue of Aphrodite that, at times, provided answers to dreams. When Christians bore the precious wood of Jesus' cross to the statue, the demon that lived in it could not stand the sight of the cross. It came out of the statue and the statue toppled over, harming one man and killing another. Immediately following this, the pagan temples were destroyed. All idols and pagan books were taken out of the town and destroyed. On this occasion, 300 pagans converted to the Christian faith.

The new church was constructed where the pagan temple had stood. Everything from the destroyed temple was an abomination and taken away. The location was sanctified with a procession of clergy that carried the Holy Gospel and sang the Venite. The people so relished in this new project that they sang as they worked. It was completed in five years. Porphyry died after serving as bishop of Gaza for twenty-four years.

Mark the Deacon clearly shows Porphyry to be a member of the Christian family. He fed visitors as did Abraham, and he comforted the poor as commanded by his Lord. Of greater importance, He was a warrior like Jesus. He was attacked by the evil one and was victorious. While he did not cleanse the Jewish temple in Jerusalem, he destroyed the pagan temples and their idols in Gaza. He was responsible for the construction of the House of God where the people of God fasted and prayed, heard the Word of God, and received the Lord's Supper.

Augustine	Date: 354–430
	Place: Hippo, North Africa
	Office: Bishop
	Biography: *Confessions*[26]
	Biographer: Augustine

Augustine's autobiography was a landmark document in Christian biography. It chronicled much of the life of this most eminent theologian in the Early Church who penned biblical commentaries and homilies, apologies and polemics, an ascetic rule and catechetical instruction, letters and treatises. Written by Augustine himself, the autobiography was masterfully constructed. It brought to light many aspects of his life to which he alone was privy. As Augustine looked back and provided spiritual reflections upon various events, he saw the ever-present hand of God upon him.

Augustine was born into a family of which his mother, Monica, was a devout Christian and his father would later convert to Christianity. While he passed over any momentous natal events, he offered a litany of sinful actions in his infancy, childhood, and as a young adult. As an infant, he cried and flailed about his arms to get what he wanted. As a young boy, he preferred stories to studies, prided in winning games and enjoyed bawdy shows, stole from his parents, and succumbed to erotic desires.

At the age of 16, Augustine and some friends saw a pear tree in the neighborhood that was filled with ripe pears. Looking for trouble, they shook the tree and made off with its fruit. They did so neither because they were hungry nor to sell them at the market. Instead, they misbehaved in this manner for the sheer joy of misconduct. Consequently, they tossed the pears into a pigpen.

Augustine aged and his vices matured: vanity, lust, and illicit love. At the age of 18, he fathered a son, Adeodatus, out of wedlock. Following the advice of the orator Cicero, he dabbled in a variety of religious endeavors. For a brief time, he looked to the stars and horoscopes for meaning in life until it was disproved to him. For more than a few years, he delved into the teachings of Mani (ca. 216–76) and Manichaeism. He was very much enthralled with its dualism—physical is evil and spiritual is good—and was adversely influenced by its denigration of the Christian faith. When one of its teachers, Faustus, was unable to answer Augustine's questions, Augustine abandoned it. Finally, he became intrigued with Neo-Platonism. Augustine left no corrupt stone unturned in his early life.

Augustine's spiritual travels were matched by his academic positions. He taught oratory at his hometown in Thagaste, Carthage, Rome, and Milan. In all of these travels, Monica was either praying for his soul or with him, sometimes both.

Not only did Augustine describe his early life in painful detail, but he biblically analyzed it. Job's prayer explained the sin of Augustine's infancy:

"Before Thee none is free from sin, not even an infant which has lived but one day upon the earth" (Job 14:4–5 LXX). Augustine repeatedly compared himself with the prodigal son. Just as this biblical malfeasant had left his father to live a debauched life in a foreign land, only to end up with nothing and desirous of pigs' fodder, so Augustine, time and again, spoke of himself traveling away from his heavenly Father where he wallowed in transgressions and equated his desire for other religions to eating the "husks of the pigs." Without a doubt, Augustine portrayed himself as a descendent of Adam—he had fallen away from God and into the depths of sin. While yet a boy, he fell ill, but before he could be baptized, he recovered and remained unbaptized. Augustine's early life was bleak and he could do nothing to please God.

In his infancy, childhood, and as a young adult, Augustine was searching for something. As an infant and young boy, he sought tangible possessions and physical love. With his own illness and near-death experience, and with the deaths of his father and a close friend, his search continued, but shifted from the physical to the spiritual. Yet of himself, he found nothing good, nothing eternal.

The life of Augustine changed dramatically with his move to Milan, Italy. Through the intercessions of his mother, Monica, the Lord directed Augustine's life and travels. In Milan, he hastened to hear the famed rhetorical style of Ambrose (ca. 339–97) only to be greatly moved by the content of Ambrose's homilies. Flanked by his devoutly Christian mother and friends who were also becoming interested in Christianity, Augustine began to contemplate the Christian faith. He and a group of friends briefly retreated from society. In a garden in Milan, one day, a voice called to him: "Pick up and read; pick up and read."[27] Not unlike Antony, Augustine opened a Bible and read from the thirteenth chapter of Romans. It immediately struck his heart. It condemned his sinful life and called him to be baptized into Jesus. With this, everything changed for Augustine. He informed a friend who was also eager to confess the Christian faith. He then notified his mother, and she rejoiced.

Following Augustine's conversion, biographical data was brief, but not insignificant. He resigned his teaching position and was baptized into the Christian faith at Milan. Augustine, his mother, and friends then departed Milan to return to Africa and live an ascetic life. Passing through Ostia in

Italy, Monica died and was buried there. It was as though the purpose for her life was over—her son was converted.

Augustine's portrayal of his own life was quite intimate and honest. He noted a few positive aspects of his life, like his intelligence and relation to Antony in his conversion. Both of these were the gift of God and not of his own doing. With great personal insight, he very much showed himself to be a descendent of Adam: He was sinful through and through. Because of this, he was in need of grace. God watched over and re-directed his mis-directed life and finally intervened, bringing him to the Christian faith. It was through the waters of Holy Baptism that Augustine's earthly family was supplanted by a heavenly family; that Augustine who had wandered far and away from his heavenly Father was finally united through Christ.

Patrick	Date: ca. 390–ca. 460
	Place: Ireland
	Offices: Missionary, Ascetic, Miracle Worker
	Biography: *Hymn on St. Patrick*[28]
	Biographer: Fiecc (ca. 415–520)

Fiecc, in his hymn, portrayed the missionary work of Patrick in Ireland. Born in Britain, Patrick twice journeyed to Ireland. God's hand was guiding him in this, so he could not do otherwise. Because of his labors there, Patrick has come to be known to all as the Apostle to the Irish.

Fiecc skipped over Patrick's birth and surrounding events, but noted Emptur (Britain) as his place of birth and his parentage, son of Calpurn, son of Otidus. At the age of 16, he was taken captive and held as a slave in Ireland where he had nothing to eat but animal fodder. After six years of servitude to pagans, Victor (the resurrected Christ) commanded him leave. Patrick crossed over to the continent and traveled across the Alps to study under Bishop Germanus. With his studies completed, he was sent back to Ireland as a missionary.

Notable signs in Ireland preceded the missionary work of Patrick. The youth of Caill-Fochladh prayed "that the saint would come, that he would return from Letha to convert the people of Erin from error to life."[29] Heavenly beings visited Patrick and implored him to go. Even the Druids of Loegaire prophesied his homecoming. Upon returning to Ireland, he preached throughout the countryside and baptized many. He healed the sick and raised the dead. Because of the work of Patrick, many were converted to the Christian faith. Although it had been darker than night in Ireland, through Patrick, the Light of the World began to shine upon the people.

Patrick lived an extremely rigorous life. He prayed often. He sang hymns, the Apocalypse, and the Psalms. He wore wet sackcloth. He slept on bare stone with a rock as his pillow. So concerned was he with his work, he neither hungered nor thirsted. Lest his pride overtake him, he would pass the cold nights in a pond.

The death of Patrick was a noteworthy event. The priests in the surrounding area gathered around his bed, as did the heavenly host. Both hymned. Both worked together in harmony—the priests holding a vigil over his decaying flesh of this world and the angels transporting his eternal soul to the heavenly realm.

Fiecc placed Patrick in the family portrait of Christianity. His lineage located him in God's created order. Eating the fodder of animals as a slave in Ireland, he was an involuntary prodigal son. In obedience to Jesus' apostolic command, he preached, baptized, and converted many to faith in the line of Peter, Paul, and other missionaries. His miracles flowed from those of Jesus. Angels directed his life on both sides of death. Jesus spoke to him on more than one occasion. His return to Ireland was prophesied by the Druids, not unlike the birth of Jesus that was made known to the eastern sages.

Daniel	Date: 409–93
	Places: Samosata, Syria; Anaplus.
	Offices: Ascetic (Stylite), Miracle Worker
	Biography: *Life of Daniel the Stylite*

Daniel lived for twenty-five years in a monastery and then atop a column for thirty-three years. While the latter seems odd, he was a holy man who was perched between heaven and earth, between God and man. He not only prayed often to God on behalf of men, but he often spoke and acted on behalf of God toward men.

The events that led up to the birth of Daniel are not unlike those of others in the Christian family. His mother, Martha, was barren and criticized often by her husband, Elias. One night, she prayed to the Lord that He not punish her for her sinfulness, but restore her so she may give birth to a child as Eve was first created to do. After many tears fell from her eyes, she saw in a dream two large lights descend from heaven and remain by her. Within a short time, she conceived and gave birth to a son.

This child was destined to be an ascetic. When he was 5 years old, his parents took him to the local monastery. The abbot asked the parents his name, then responded that another name belongs to him. The abbot sent the boy to a room with books. When he returned with the Old Testament book of Daniel, the name was given to him. His parents wished to leave him there, but the abbot sent Daniel home with his parents. At age 12, he trekked ten miles to a monastery and asked to be admitted, but the abbot sent him home to his parents. Daniel pleaded with the abbot until he and the brothers finally received him into their number. After his parents found him, they praised God for his actions.

After a short time of living an austere life, Daniel traveled with his archmandrite to Antioch. On their journey, they stopped at the monastery in Telanissae where Simeon, the Stylite, had received his ascetic training. The monks there took Daniel to visit Simeon. Daniel ascended the column where Simeon laid his hand upon Daniel's head and blessed him and instructed him to be faithful and persevere.

Not a short time later, Daniel was to become the abbot of his monastery, but left the monastery. He visited Simeon again. After two weeks he departed and headed from the Holy Land even though it was not safe at this time. On his journey, a revered elder directed him away from Jerusalem and toward Constantinople, the Second Jerusalem, to visit the shrine of martyrs.

On his journey to Constantinople, he heard of a church building near Anaplus that was inhabited by a demon. Remembering the words of David, "The Lord is my light and my savior, whom shall I fear?" (Psalm 27:1) and the life of Antony, he entered the building prepared for battle. Holding a cross, he genuflected and prayed at each corner. At night, he would be assaulted by demons who threw stones at him, raised a riotous uproar, and threatened to drown and decapitate him. All of this was done to no avail as Daniel remained steadfast, praying and rebuking the demons. At the name of Jesus he victoriously drove them from that place.

After living nine years in that church, Daniel had a vision. In it, Simeon summoned him atop his column. Once there, Simeon's two companions raised him up to heaven. Everyone understood this to mean that Daniel was to become a stylite. He traveled to Constantinople and then to a monastery of the sleepless ones. Between the capital and the monastery, a government official learned of Daniel and offered to provide a column for him. Where the column was to be placed—near the church in which he lived—he saw a white dove.

From atop the column, Daniel lived a devout life. Myriads visited him because he cast out demons from those possessed and healed the sick. In addition, he blessed the many who came to him and arbitrated between opposing parties. He spoke prophetically and taught the Word of God. When the servants of the serpent attempted to trick him, Daniel always outwitted them and made their deception plain. He became the superior of the ascetics that gathered around him under his column, including one who Daniel freed from a demon. On one occasion, Emperor Leo petitioned Daniel to pray for his wife that she might give birth to a son. After Daniel's prayer and by God's great mercy, Empress Verina conceived and bore a son.

At the behest of Emperor Leo, Patriarch Gennadius of Constantinople ordained him priest upon his column. Leo rejoiced and later visited Daniel upon his column. Later, the emperor built a palace near Daniel's column so that he could live close to Daniel and converse with him often. Upon the death of Simeon the stylite, Leo brought his remains to a newly constructed shrine near Daniel's column where he built a monastery.

After traveling briefly to Constantinople and the Studious Monastery, Daniel returned to his pillar. After a series of illnesses, he died. Before this, he foretold his death and gave spiritual instruction to the ascetics there. Many ascended his column to kiss his body. During the viewing of his body, everyone present saw three crosses in the sky with white doves flying about. He was buried not in a jewel-encrusted coffin, but in the ground, below the remains of Hannaniah, Mishael, and Azariah that Leo had brought back from Babylon.

Daniel was pictured in the family of God. He performed miracles and lived an ascetic life not unlike the life of Christ. He fought against the evil one and was victorious in Jesus. In the end, he was laid to rest with his spiritual fathers of the Christian faith.

Mary	Date: d. ca. 522
	Place: Egypt
	Office: Hermit
	Biography: *Life of Our Holy Mother Mary of Egypt*
	Biographer: Sophronius of Jerusalem
	(seventh century)

Sophronius preserved the extraordinary life of Mary as first learned and handed down by Zosimas, a revered and austere ascetic in Palestine. The occasion was the Season of Lent when the doors of his monastery were opened and many of the monks traveled outside its walls. Zosimas entered the desert east of the Jordan and there encountered Mary. This female ascetic, who lived in the desert with no clothing or protection, narrated the story of her life to him.

Mary's youth was filled with sin and debauchery. At age 12 she disowned her family in Egypt and traveled to Alexandria. There, she had sexual relations with every available man. She was not a prostitute, though, because she refused to be paid for her services. Instead, Mary acted in this fashion simply because she so enjoyed wallowing about in debauchery.

A life-changing event occurred in her life when she met a group of Christians who were traveling to Jerusalem for the celebration of the Exaltation of the Holy Cross. Wanting to go, but having no money, Mary offered sexual favors to the travelers for passage. While aboard the ship, she fornicated with the young men who paid her passage. Even in Jerusalem, Mary continued in her illicit sexual relations with young and old men, locals and foreigners.

When the time came to elevate the cross, Mary joined the throng that was entering the church, but the threshold would not allow her to enter. Time and time again she tried to enter, but an unseen force repelled her repeatedly. Tired and exhausted, she began to understand that her dissolute life kept her out of the church. Mary repented, cried and wept, beat her breast, and gazed upon an icon of Mary, the Mother of God, and petitioned to her that the church would open its doors to her. Finally, Mary entered the church where she saw the life-giving cross of Jesus and His Sacraments.

Upon leaving the church, a stranger gave to Mary three coins with which she bought three loaves of bread. Mary then began to walk east until she reached the Church of John the Baptist at the Jordan River. She washed herself in the holy river and received the body and blood of Jesus. The next day, she crossed the Jordan and entered the desert.

For seventeen years she fought her sinful passions. Her past sins continued to assail and tempt her. She longed for the lavish food and drink that she enjoyed in Egypt. The sinful melodies of her youth sounded in her ears. Sexual passions racked her body. Against these temptations, she wept copiously and beat her breast and lamented her sinfulness. She prayed to the Mother of God to chase them away.

In the desert, Mary ate the little that she could scavenge. The clothes that she wore when she entered the desert gradually wore away. This ascetic suffered not only hunger and thirst, but the cold and frost in winter and the burning sun in the summer. Yet she comforted—fed and clothed—herself with the Word of God.

In the desert, Mary saw Zosimas, the first human being since she walked into the desert forty-seven years previous. While she ordered him to tell no one of her presence, Mary requested that he give to her the Lord's Supper on Holy Thursday the following year at the Jordan River. One year later, he met her at the holy river; he on one side and she on the other. Mary made the sign of the cross over the water and walked across it to receive the precious body and blood of her Savior. Following this, she sang the Nunc dimittis and requested that he meet her in the desert the next year. Returning as she came across the river, she departed into the desert.

The next year, Zosimas crossed the Jordan and entered the desert and found her dead. Unable to dig in the sun-hardened soil, a wild lion approached and began to dig the grave. Zosimas laid her in the grave and covered her naked body with dirt.

The life of Mary of Egypt was extreme as are the lives of many Christians. Mary lived in the desert not unlike John the Baptist. Mary trusted in her Lord to care for her in the desert after the example the Israelites in the Wilderness. She experienced a dramatic conversion similar to that of Paul and Augustine. Most importantly, Mary looked to the cross for her salvation and was nourished, albeit infrequently, upon the body and blood of Jesus in His Holy Supper.

Excursus: *Lives of Illustrious Men*

Jerome penned the Lives of Illustrious Men in 392, and approximately forty years later Gennadius supplemented it with further Christian lives. These two documents briefly chronicle the lives of numerous Christians from the New Testament into the fifth century. According to Jerome, he provided biographical data on authors who had written on Holy Scripture. This was done in part to show that the Christian Church was not devoid of men of letters. Gennadius followed after Jerome and included ecclesial writers from the both the west and the east that Jerome passed over. Concerning the latter, Jerome would in many instances not have been familiar with them and/or their languages.

Jerome's Lives are composed of 135 relatively brief biographical narratives. He included Christians from the New Testament and Early Church Periods, the latter receiving the majority of ink. In so doing, he portrayed both well-known and lesser known figures.

The New Testament figures include the four evangelists—Matthew, Mark, Luke, John—along with other notable characters: Peter, James, Jude, Paul, Barnabas. For these individuals, Jerome faithfully reiterates much biblical data, but also includes extra-biblical data from the early tradition of the Church. For example, he notes that Peter was the Bishop of Rome for twenty-five years and suffered martyrdom in Rome. He requested to be crucified upside down upon a cross because he thought himself unworthy to die identically to his Lord. Very much interested in the perpetual virginity of Mary, he noted two contemporary theories concerning James (who was called the brother of Jesus), a son of Joseph's previous marriage and a son of Mary's sister.

A significant biblical scholar himself, Jerome addresses various canonical issues. The Gospel according to Matthew was initially written in Hebrew as it was penned for the Jews. The canonicity of the Epistle of Jude is questioned by some as it cites the apocrypha, Enoch. Jerome, though, argues that it belongs in the biblical canon because it is an ancient document and used throughout the Christian Church. Though some reject Paul as the author to the Epistle to the Hebrews, Jerome makes a case for Pauline authorship. Paul was well-versed in Judaism and their language, and because he was so well-known among them, it was unnecessary to fix his name to it.

Much more extensively, Jerome depicts the writings and lives of Early Church Christians. He begins with the writings of the Apostolic Fathers, like Hermas's Shepherd, Clement's Letter to the Corinthians, and the multiple epistles of Ignatius of Antioch. He also preserves more explicitly biographical data: Papias and Polycarp not only were ecclesial authors but also hearers of John the apostle; and Polycarp declared the heretic Marcion to be the "firstborn of the devil."[30]

Jerome continued with later Ante-Nicenes. Justin, a philosopher turned Christian author, was martyred in Rome. Irenaeus, a hearer of Polycarp, authored Against Heresies and Apostolic Preaching. Origen, a Christian catechist and well-versed in all of the secular disciplines, constructed the Hexapla and both taught and wrote extensively upon the Scriptures. Of the Post-Nicenes, Jerome primarily limits his comments to the literary achievements of Christians. Nonetheless, he notes Athanasius's exile after the death of Constantine and death during the reign of Emperor Valens. Similarly, Gregory of Nazianzus was exiled for a short time and at the end of his ecclesial career he retired as bishop and became a monk.

Gennadius continued the style of Jerome, primarily noting the ecclesial writings of ninety-nine Christian authors, though, on the rare occasion, he provided more pointed biographical data for these. Interestingly, he noted the ecclesial and secular fame of Augustine's writings, but provided only minimal biographical data. Severus Sulpitius was a man devoted to poverty and humility, and Bachiarius, though a priest, traveled extensively like Abraham. He even noted heretics and their writings: Pelagius' On the Belief of the Trinity and Nestorius' On the Incarnation of the Lord.

These documents were not written simply to preserve biographical data. Nonetheless, they have done so and provided a great service to the Christian Church. First, they serve as a table of contents for ecclesial writings of the Early Church. Though many have been lost to time, their names and titles have been preserved. Second, authorship is not an unimportant aspect of Christianity and Christian lives. Not only did the Word become flesh and dwell among us, but it was preserved by the apostles and evangelists. Later, Christians continued to interpret the meaning of these canoncial writings with their own treatises and letters and sermons. Third,

Jerome and Gennadius show the direct correlation between the life of Christ and the lives of ecclesial authors. Those who twist and distort the word of God are heretics and are not part of the family of God. In contrast, those who faithfully preserve the sacred word and interpret it according to the Spirit of God are part of the divine family.

Summary

The Post-Nicenes portrayed their own in an assortment of offices and with a variety of literary genres, as in the Life of the Blessed Emperor Constantine, Athanasius's panegyric, Funeral Oration for Gorgonia, Augustine's own Confessions, and the Hymn on St. Patrick. Although this array of biographical data was composed by diverse authors at different times and places, there were noticeable likenesses. Some were provided with a lineage and all were situated in specific locations to place them concretely in the creation. Antony and Macrina lived ascetic lives, not dissimilar to the life of Christ. More weighty still, Jesus directly interacted in the lives of each. Jesus visited and directly revealed His will to Constantine and Patrick, causing momentous changes in their lives. Among the multitude of miracles, Jesus worked through Hilarion and Martin. Jesus preserved pure doctrine through Athanasius and Porphyry. Jesus washed away the sins of Gorgonia and Augustine making them children of God in Holy Baptism. Though these Post-Nicene Christians were three and four centuries removed from the Gospel-portrayed life of Christ, their biographers portrayed them as closely connected with Jesus and integral members of the family of God.

Patristic Analysis

Preservation of biographical data in the Early Church was extensive, but not without danger. There was concern from without and within that biographical data had been falsified at worst and exaggerated at best. In addition, Christian lives might be misunderstood or raised to a level beyond divine intent. Guidelines, then, became necessary protective measures. While the Early Church did not produce "official" regulations for biographers, this concern was addressed in numerous fashions.

A danger already among the Ante-Nicenes was the over-glorification of significant Christians. This was particularly true of the martyrs. They followed so closely in the passion of Jesus that some might not be able to distinguish between the two. The Passion of Polycarp provided the needed correction: "He who is the Son of God, we adore, but the martyrs as disciples and imitators of the Lord we cherish."[31] There was a definite hierarchy. Jesus was first and most significant; Jesus alone was worshiped. The martyrs were to be greatly honored, but always in a secondary fashion and in a subordinate relation to Jesus from whom they took their marching orders and after whom they followed.[32]

The foremost component of the Christian life was Baptism. Pontius began Cyprian's life at his Baptism because all that had happened before was of little concern in his Christian life. It also played a life-changing role for Augustine. Though he was almost baptized as a boy, it was not until later, after his conversion, that he was finally baptized and brought into the family of God. Constantine and Gorgonia concluded their lives with Baptism. While Baptism was not explicitly described in every Early Church Christian life, its importance was evident—Baptism created the most intimate connection to the life of Christ.

Faithfulness to the tradition of the Church was of utmost concern. The unknown author of Life of Daniel the Stylite noted that he could not remain silent of the great deeds of the saint. In fact, he argued that the Lord would rightly punish him on the last and dreadful day were he to hide or keep quiet of the saint's life.[33] As a result, he faithfully recorded the life of the saint as had been handed down to him in the church. Not only would he receive divine punishment for his silence, but for distorting the truth of this saint. In addition, God worked the pious actions of the saints. When a visitor observed Daniel upon his column, Daniel reminded him that he was not a spirit, but flesh and blood like him. Not only did he eat and drink, but evacuated his bladder and bowels as do all humans. Or when a leper thought too highly of Daniel's miraculous powers, he was reminded that it was God who healed the sick and performed all of these many wondrous signs.

Imitation, according Gregory of Nyssa, was one of the foremost issues of Christian biography. In his Life of Gregory of Thaumaturgus, he compared the relation of the pious lives of earlier Christians to contemporary Christians as a beacon to a sailor—those who are traveling in darkness need guidance. Moreover, Christian lives were to be analyzed, not according to pagan practices, but those of the Christian Church. Furthermore, the lives of earlier Christians were a living gift of the Holy Spirit to His

Church and revealed God's active participation through the lives of various Christians.

Similarly, Mark the Deacon, in his Life of Porphyry, wrote of the salvific power of Christian biography. The world wasted its words on humor and superstitions and wars that have little or no spiritual value. On the other hand, the Christian Church has copious stories to tell about holy men and women who lived devout and virtuous lives. According to Mark, the lives of these Christians worked both as a medicine which cures one from immorality and a defense against the many temptations that afflict all Christians.

Another early concern was the veracity of miracles performed among Christians. Ambrose (ca. 339–97) did not doubt that miracles were performed in biblical times and in the Early Church. In Letter 22, he noted the circumstances surrounding a specific contemporary miracle to support their authenticity in general. As the relics of two martyrs, Saints Gervasius and Protasius, were being moved, a blind man touched the hem of the cloth covering these relics, and he regained his sight. When the Arians rejected this miracle, Ambrose claimed that they were worse than the Jews and demons in the New Testament, who, though rejecting Jesus, nonetheless recognized the reality of his many miracles.

Augustine also acknowledged the occurrence of miracles in the Early Church, citing a number in his apologetic City of God. In addition, he provided criteria for analysis and validation of post-biblical miracles. First, all Christian miracles attested to the resurrection and ascension of Jesus. Post-biblical miracles were neither arbitrary nor autonomous, but flowed from and pointed back to Jesus. Second, contemporary books in his day had accurately chronicled many miracles and would not be read in church unless they were trustworthy. He noted that he, as well as others, had carefully investigated and assessed contemporary miracles and documented those known to be true. By way of example, Augustine mentioned a miracle that took place just outside of the basilica in Hippo on Easter morning: An ill man was miraculously healed, and the people praised God. Third, the fact that contemporary miracles were less known than biblical miracles was not reason to reject them. Instead, it was all the more reason to tell them to others that they may be believed.

Augustine also addressed the relation between martyrs and miracles in the Early Church, such as the miracle narrated by Ambrose in Letter 22.[34]

Augustine argued that the reason miracles were so often associated with martyrs was that martyrs were "witnesses" of the great miracle of Jesus' resurrected body ascended to heaven. In addition, their martyrdom was a miracle itself. Consequently, miracles often occurred near their relics. Yet it was not the martyrs who were responsible for the miracles, but God who worked through them.

The Christians in the Early Church very much revered and honored the baptized who preceded them in the Christian faith. They carefully collected accurate data and assessed it. Moreover, they believed in miracles that they had witnessed, that others had observed, and that had been preserved in reputable written documents. Furthermore, they rightly emphasized the proper relation between a Christian and Jesus. Whether it was Baptisms or miracles or martyrdoms, the life of Christ was first and foremost, while the Christian life was recognized and understood only in its intimate connection to the life of Christ.

Summary

The Early Church preserved an abundance of biographical data. Over four centuries, Christians filled many diverse offices throughout the Mediterranean world and the differences were manifold. Perpetua died for the sake of the Gospel, but later, Emperor Constantine enacted the Edict of Milan that tolerated the faith. The Ante-Nicenes emphasized martyrdom, whereas the Post-Nicenes exulted asceticism. Lawrence was a deacon in Rome, conversely, Macrina was an ascetic in Pontus. Antony left his family, while Gorgonia remained with hers. Cyprian was raised in a pagan family, but Augustine had a devout Christian mother. Athanasius was a well-known Bishop, while Gorgonia a simple wife and mother.

These many and apparently differing Christians lives very much overlapped one another. Origen's simple lifestyle and self-castration exposed him to be an arch-ascetic before Nicaea, and the asceticism of Antony and Macrina allowed them to be spiritual martyrs after the Edict of Milan. While Cyprian was not brought up in a Christian family, through Baptism, he was made a child of God, and brought into the Christian family. Macrina spiritually supported her mother and family throughout her life, while Augustine's mother prayed for and spiritually encouraged him. Although Roman emperors slaughtered innumerable martyrs in the Ante-Nicene Period, Emperor Constantine in the Post-Nicene Period was baptized in a church dedicated to the martyrs. These examples and others demonstrated that the differences in Early Christian lives were merely apparent. Instead, they exhibited numerous family traits that manifested that they were brothers and sisters in Jesus.

Moreover, these Christian lives shared the family traits of their manifold cousins among the Old Testament people of God and the New Testament Christians. The sinful actions of Origen and Augustine revealed their Adamic ancestry. The Christian heroes, Polycarp and Constantine, were beset by antagonists as were Samson and John the Baptist. Cyprian and Martin were bishops in the line of the apostles. Perpetua was martyred along with Stephen. Cyprian was a quick study like the eunuch. Patrick followed in the missiological train of Paul. And so, Christian lives in the Early Church and those of Bible were portrayed as close relatives.

Furthermore, these Early Church lives intertwined with one another in their relation to Jesus. The genealogies of Origen and Patrick paralleled the genealogies of Jesus by giving them devout parents and placing them in the creation. The Baptisms of Cyprian and Augustine intimately connected them to Jesus. The miracles of Antony and Patrick flowed out of and paralleled the miracles of Jesus. Jesus came to and spoke to Constantine and Patrick. Both the Ante-Nicenes and Post-Nicenes revered the martyrs because of their close connection to Jesus and His passion. Porphyry and Mary of Egypt partook of Jesus' body and blood in the Sacrament of the Altar. In all of these, God was actively involved in their lives, guiding them finally toward their heavenly home.

Thus, the family of God expanded in the Early Church. It grew to include not only patriarchs and Nazarites and forerunners but also bishops and catechists and ascetics, not to mention martyrs and mothers and others. To the same degree, the family portrait enlarged in the centuries immediately following the New Testament. Its collection of Christian lives became more eclectic. At the same time, everyone in the picture had much in common—they were intimately related to the life of Christ through Baptism and faith, through the Lord's Supper and their respective offices.

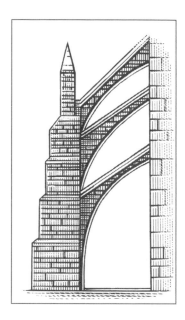

4

WESTERN CHRISTIANITY

AD 500—Present

This chapter of Christian lives progresses from the Early Church into Western Christianity, the western region of the Roman Empire. Movement in this direction had already begun in the Early Church. For example, Irenaeus was a second century bishop in Lyons, and Ireland received Patrick, a missionary in the fifth century. This western branch of Christianity initially revolved about Rome, utilized Latin, and was European; however, this dramatically changed in the sixteenth century. The Protestant reformers, among other things, created new ecclesial capitals: London for the Anglicans, Wittenberg for the Lutherans, and Geneva for the Reformed. Moreover, vernacular languages became standard and missionary endeavors into the new world—North and South America—created new ethnic contexts for Western Christianity. As such, Christian lives in Western Christianity traversed a multitude of geographic regions, linguistic families, and ethnic classifications.

The timeframe of Western Christianity is quite broad and commonly divided into three periods: Medieval (500–1500), Reformation (1500–1650), and Modern (1650–present). While any dating of wide-ranging historical periods can be somewhat arbitrary, these correspond directly to the development of strained family relations within the Western Church. This was partially evident as early as the Medieval Period in which the Church saw power struggles between the popes and Christian emperors, not to mention the growing theological rivalries between competing religious orders. This became unmistakably obvious in the sixteenth century with the Ninety-five Theses (1517) of Martin Luther (1483–1546) that questioned the medieval practice of indulgences. After unsuccessful attempts at reconciliation, Pope Leo X (1475–1521) issued the Exsurge Domine (1520) that excommunicated Luther from the Catholic Church. As a result, the Christian Church in Germany became Lutheran. Similarly, when Pope Clement VII (d. 1534) excommunicated Henry VIII (1491–1547), the Church of England was born. Consequently, the monolithic church of the Medieval Period splintered, and family members became estranged. This fragmentation only escalated in the Modern Period with further denominational fissures.

The biographical literature in Western Christianity is multitudinous and quite diverse. The corpus of related texts grew in direct relation to the ever-increasing numbers of Christians. As they are more recent than those written in the Early Church, more writings have been preserved. The most predominant literary form in the Middle Ages was the "life" of a saint. These generally portray Christians who held significant offices in the Church or through whom wondrous signs occurred. Biographical data also abounded in the Reformation and Modern Periods. Both were a bit more skeptical of the many spectacular events—miracles and visions—that occurred in the lives of Christians, so these later writings focus more upon on true doctrine and the virtuous Christian life. The chronicling of the miraculous in the latter two periods certainly decreased, but by no means ceased. Despite the many denominational estrangements, it is not impossible to see the correlations between Christian lives in Western Christianity. In no uncertain terms, Christian lives continue to be connected intimately with Jesus through Holy Baptism and the Lord's Supper. In addition, numerous family traits remain and common offices shared by many in the family of God.

Medieval Period

The initial chronological period in western Christianity is the Middle Ages. They were not the "Dark Ages" as has been suggested at times, but a time in which Christianity thrived in a culture that was being thoroughly Christianized. In light of this, the most significant Christian offices included pope, emperor, ascetic, scholastic, and mystic. These often overlapped. For example, Gregory I (ca. 540–604) was an ascetic and pope; Peter Abelard (1079–1142) was a scholastic and ascetic. Birgitta (ca. 1303–73) was an ascetic and a mystic. Medieval Christianity employed these and other offices to illustrate the intimate relation between Medieval Christian lives and the life of Christ.

Ascetic. The varied forms of asceticism in the Early Church quickly formalized. As the abbot at Monte Cassino, Benedict of Nursia (ca. 480–550) formulated a Rule for life in an ascetic community. It established order in the community in at least three fashions. The abbot (father) presided over the many brothers. The regulated alternation between prayer and work synchronized the monk's day. Everyday matters such as food, sleep, speech, and possessions were strictly regulated and de-emphasized in amount, and thus, importance. While this rule was not the first, it quickly became the standard in Western Christianity. During this time, a number of distinct ascetic orders formed, such as the Cistercians and Franciscans. Female communities were often attached to these. There, an abbess was the mother-figure among the sisters. Claire of Assisi (1194–1253) founded the order of the Poor Ladies and was an abbess.

Pope. Pope simply means "papa" and was used in the Early Church of the local bishop. Rather quickly, it was relegated in the west to the bishop of Rome alone. Leo I (d. 461), a pope in the waning years of the Early Church, clearly advocated the primacy of the bishop of Rome. Notable popes in the Medieval Period included Gregory I and Innocent III (1160–1216). The latter further delineated the authority of the pope by comparing the relation between the pope and emperor to the sun and the moon—the pope wielded the greater authority, while the emperor the lesser.

Scholastic. While Christianity was a religion of divine mysteries, it also attempted to systematize the doctrines and practices of the Christian faith. Anselm of Canterbury (ca. 1033–1109), a prominent scholastic, explained the necessity of the incarnation in Why God Became Man (1098). Peter

Abelard penned Sic et Non, which compares seemingly contradictory statements from the Bible and earlier fathers, and was used extensively in the theological education of medieval churchmen. The Summa Theologica of Thomas Aquinas (ca. 1225–74) achieved the pinnacle of scholasticism. Exhaustive in scope, it defines the great majority of Christian doctrines and practices from transubstantiation to his "five arguments" for the existence of God.

Mystic. A few Christians intimately encounter God in prayers and visions and the like. These mystics come into the very presence of God, and, in their attempt to communicate their experiences, they often utilize figurative language. Bernard of Clairvaux (1090–1153) wrote of the three kisses: kissing first Jesus' feet, then His hands, and finally Jesus' mouth. Two German mystics included Meister Eckhart (ca. 1260–1327) and John Tauler (ca. 1300–61). Both Bernard and John would positively influence Martin Luther in the Reformation Period. Though women could be not be priests, motherhood and asceticism and mysticism were acceptable in the Medieval Period. Julian of Norwich (ca. 1342–ca. 1413) was an anchorite. As an ascetic, she resided in a cell attached to the local parish building. During her hermit-like life, she received a series of visions and recorded them in Sixteen Revelations of Divine Love. Birgitta of Sweden (ca. 1303–73) was married and had eight children. Following the death of her husband and the raising of her children, she founded the Order of Birgittines in Sweden and recorded her visions in Revelaciones.

The quantity of biographical data from this period is almost without number. While "lives" of the saints are quite common, the number of different literary genres are nearly as numerous as the lives portrayed.

Benedict	Time: ca. 480–550
	Place: Monte Cassino, Italy
	Offices: Abbot, Miracle Worker
	Biography: *Dialogues*[1]
	Biographer: Gregory I

The prominent placement of Benedict in Gregory's Dialogues parallels Benedict's influential role in Medieval Christianity. His asceticism and miracles are not unique, but very much set the tone for Christians who follow after him.

The childhood of Benedict was privileged. He was born into a wealthy family in Italy and was sent to Rome for his education. At school, his life dramatically changed directions when he saw the dissolute life of many of the students. Rather than being learned and impious, he chose to be an uneducated and pious man. Therefore, Benedict fled from this sinful world and sought the devout life of an ascetic.

After performing a miracle that gained him notoriety, he first sought solitude in the Italian wilderness of Subiaco, where he lived in a cave for three years. Initially, no one knew of his whereabouts save a monk named Romanos who brought him bread from time to time. One Easter Day, the Lord appeared in a vision to a priest who was preparing his meal. The Lord chastised him for eating sumptuously while a revered man of God was fasting in the wilderness. The priest packaged up the meal and set out looking for him. Finding him in his cave, the priest informed Benedict that it was the Day of Jesus' Resurrection and a time to feast, not fast. Shortly thereafter, shepherds found Benedict. Because he was clothed in animal skins, they thought him to be a beast. Upon closer examination, they found out that he was a man of God, and many converted from their vices to divine virtues. Once word got out of Benedict's location, many brought him food for his body while Benedict provided food for their souls.

While at Subiaco, Benedict was asked to become the abbot at a local monastery, but it was short-lived as his high standards of asceticism led the monks to bring him poisoned wine. When he blessed it with the sign of the cross, the glass pitcher shattered. Knowing their evil intent, Benedict returned to Subiaco. Because of his austere life and spiritual wisdom, so many ascetics gathered around him that it became necessary for him to establish twelve monasteries with an abbot and twelve monks at each. Leaving these because a priest sought his death, he traveled to Monte Cassino. There, he destroyed the altar to Apollo and upon that spot built a chapel named after John the Baptist. In addition, he rededicated Apollo's temple to Martin of Tours. Immediately, the evil one attacked Benedict, cursing him by name and enveloping him in fire, but to no avail. There at Monte Cassino he established a monastery.

The degree of Benedict's asceticism was astonishing. On one occasion, a bird fluttered about in his face. Making the sign of the cross, the bird flew away, but the evil spirit in the bird attacked Benedict with sinful thoughts of woman. Seeing a patch of stinging thorn bushes, he flung himself into them and thrashed about until his body was torn to pieces and bleeding profusely. In so doing, he extinguished his sinful desires. On another occasion, the monks were attempting to move a large rock in the construction of their monastery. Try as they may, they could not budge it, so they called upon their abbot. Benedict, seeing the devil sitting upon the rock, prayed and made the sign of the cross. This drove the devil from the rock, allowing the monks to easily move the stone.

More than a few miracles fill the life of Benedict, but two examples shall suffice. First, some monks complained to Benedict that they had to traverse a mountainside to get water and requested that they be granted permission to move the monastery. Benedict instructed them to return to their monastery where they would find three stones. Dig there, he commanded them. Upon digging the ground was quite moist and after digging a bit more, water welled up and began to flow out for them. Second, one day a young boy fell into a lake and was carried out from the shore. Knowing of the event, though at a distance, Benedict blessed a monk who ran off to help. When the monk reached the lake, he kept running atop the water until he reached the young boy and pulled him to safety.

The asceticism of Benedict portrays him as a follower of Jesus: both lived an extremely rigorous life. Moreover, the miracles of Benedict show him to follow in the train of biblical miracle workers. Just as Moses caused water to come from a stone and Peter walked on water, so such wonders were attributed to Benedict. Furthermore, Benedict battled against the devil repeatedly and won, not unlike his Savior.

Columba	Time: ca. 521–97
	Place: Iona
	Offices: Abbot, Missionary
	Biography: *Life of St. Columba*
	Biographer: Adomnan of Iona (ca. 628–704)

The life of Columba was organized by Adomnan into three categories: prophesies, miracles, and angelic apparitions. Extensive lists of examples are provided in each category. Common and ordinary events are not mentioned, only those that are extraordinary. Because of the many extraordinary events in his life, Columba is portrayed as a significant individual in the Christian Church.

The birth of Columba was not uneventful. Years before, Mochta, a disciple of Patrick, prophesied that a man of God would be born into the world, and his name would be Columba, which means dove. Immediately following his conception, an angel of the Lord appeared to Columba's mother, Eithne, and handed to her a beautifully arrayed robe. Soon after, the angel took back the robe and let it flutter away. Columba's mother was upset at having the garment for so short a time. This dream, however, foreshadowed the life of her son who would be born shortly, but taken away to do God's work. Columba's father was Fedelmid mac Ferguso, a nobleman who saw to it that his son was trained in divine wisdom.

As a young boy, Columba had been given over to the care of a priest named Cruithnechan. Having left church and returned to his home, Cruithnechan was illumined brightly. He entered his house and saw a bright sphere of light above Columba's sleeping face. Immediately, he interpreted this as a sign of God's Spirit upon this child.

While Columba was a young man and deacon under Uinniau, the bishop of Ireland, he heard the clergy complain that there was no wine for the Sacrament. Because it was his responsibility to bring the wine to the altar, Columba filled a pitcher with water, prayed to Jesus, and blessed it. With the help of his Lord who performed this miracle earlier at Cana, the water turned into wine. Other miracles of Columba were myriad: He turned bitter fruit sweet, healed the sick and diseased, brought water out of a rock, stilled storms, was granted a miraculous catch of fish, caused snakes to leave Iona, and raised the dead to life. While Columba performed other miracles as well, these clearly mirror those of Jesus in the New Testament.

Columba often saw into the future. He saw both blessings for some and death for others. At times, he saw the souls of those translated from earth to heaven. He foresaw the victories and defeats of kings. These and all of his prophesies were granted by the Holy Spirit who worked in him. This was manifested on several occasions when others saw a heavenly beacon enlightening him.

At the celebration of the Resurrection of our Lord in the last year of Columba's life, he had petitioned the Lord to die, but the Lord deemed it unworthy to turn the season of joy into sorrow. A bit later, he foretold a monk that at midnight on the following Sunday—the day of rest—he would die. The monk wept, but promised to tell no one until after his death. Immediately following this, a horse that was familiar with Columba came near him and visibly mourned his upcoming death.

On the night of his death, Columba joyously entered the chapel before everyone else to pray the midnight office. Briefly, the chapel was filled with heavenly light. When the monks entered the chapel, they found Columba lying upon the floor next to the altar. One monk held up Columba's weak hand to bless the others before he died. The monks mourned their loss. Columba's death was revealed immediately to Lugaid mac Tailchain, a man of God in Ireland, who at the same time heard the heavenly chorus joyously hymning. Following the funeral ritual, his body was wrapped in linen and placed in a special grave.

The life of Columba was nothing if not spectacular. In each instance of prophesies and miracles and apparitions, Adomnan portrayed Columba as a man of God through whom the Holy Spirit worked mightily, not unlike the prophets in the Old Testament and the apostles in the New Testament.

Gregory I	Time: ca. 540–604
	Place: Rome
	Offices: Ascetic, Pope
	Biography: *Ecclesiastical History of the English Nation*[2] (731)
	Biographer: Bede (ca. 673–735)

In his church history, Bede highly praised Gregory as one of the foremost popes in the Western Church. Initially an ascetic, Gregory became the bishop of Rome. This ecclesial advancement did not adversely affect Gregory. Instead, he was a faithful servant of God and remained true to his calling—concern for his soul and the souls of others.

Gregory was born into a pious Christian family. Gordian, his father, was a Roman citizen and lived a devout Christian life. Felix, an ancestor, had been highly revered in the Church and was also a bishop of Rome. Gregory faithfully continued in his family line through his ascetic and Episcopal vocations.

As a young man, Gregory left behind all worldly pursuits. He entered a monastery where he could pursue spiritual matters without distraction. He contemplated upon divine matters and spent uncountable hours pondering temporal death and the joys of eternal life. Gregory was snatched from this idyllic life when he was sent to Constantinople as a representative of the bishop of Rome. Although Gregory was there to deal with the Imperial court, he persevered in his spiritual rigors. He remained steadfast in his study and prayer. He began to write a spiritual commentary on Job. When the bishop of Constantinople, Eutyches, rejected the resurrection of a tangible body on the Last Day, Gregory so convincingly opposed this heresy that it was completely silenced.

As the bishop of Rome, Gregory lamented the excessive time and energy he expended on administrative duties. He longed for his earlier days when he had more time to attend to personal spiritual matters, so he continued to live the rigorous life of an ascetic. As a result of becoming a bishop and being faithful to this calling, his interest in the well-being of his own soul turned outward, and he became very much concerned for the souls of others. Though he was often ill, he wrote several volumes for the spiritual care of others. In his Pastoral Office, he advised those who cared for the souls of others. In the Dialogues, he preserved the lives of Italian saints for the edification of Italian Christians. He provided spiritual sermons in Forty Homilies on the Gospel and Homilies on Ezekiel.

Gregory's concern for souls extended beyond the boundaries of Italy and the Church. One day he was at the market and saw some young boys for sale. Gregory inquired as to their origin, and he was told that they were pagans from Britain. When Gregory saw their fair skin and heard that they were called "Angles", he lamented that the Angles knew nothing of the heavenly angels. Gregory then sent missionaries to Britain who converted a people who sat in darkness to the Light of Christ.

Gregory died in the 605th year of our Lord during the reign of Emperor Phocas. He had been bishop for thirteen years, six months, and ten days. His body was interred on the fourth of March in the church of Saint Peter the Apostle.

In sum, Gregory lived a devout Christian life. He prayed, fasted, and meditated upon God's word, living an ascetic life, not unlike that of Jesus. As a bishop, he followed after the apostles, who followed after Jesus. He obeyed Jesus' apostolic commission by sending missionaries to Britain.

Gregory's life was intimately connected to the life of Christ both on earth and in heaven as described in the epitaph on his tomb, which begins: "Earth! take that body which at first you gave, Till God again shall raise it from the grave."[3] It depicted his final hope, eternal life in Jesus.

Hilda	Time: 614–80
	Place: Britain
	Offices: Abbess
	Biography: *Ecclesiastical History*
	of the English Nation
	Biographer: Bede (ca. 673–735)

Bede portrayed a noble Englishwoman who lived an exemplary Christian life as both lay and religious, thirty-three years each. Though little is known about her otherwise, Bede's inclusion of her is notable on at least two accounts: She is one of the few women who are portrayed in his Ecclesiastical History,[4] and she appears to have had some authority and influence over the men in her double monastery, an ascetic community that included both a group of men and a separate group of women.

Hilda was born into a noble family. She was the daughter of Heric who was the nephew of King Edwin of Northumbria. Also, her sister, Hereswith, was the mother of King Aldwulf of the East Angles. Of greater spiritual significance, her mother, Breguswith, had a dream while Hilda was quite young. In it, Heric was taken from her. Though she searched incessantly, she could not find even a trace of her husband, but she found a precious jewel previously hidden under her garments. It shone so brilliantly that its light filled all of Britain. At this time her husband, who had been banished, would soon die of poisoning. Thus, the precious jewel foreshadowed the future virtuous Hilda. In her youth, Hilda was instructed in the Christian faith by Paulinus (d. 644) of York and received the blessed Sacraments from him.

At age 33, Hilda became an ascetic. She first intended to enter the convent at Cale in Gaul, the residence of her sister Hereswith. Before she could embark on her journey, she was called back to her home province where she lived for a year with other female ascetics. Hilda was then appointed as abbess of the relatively new convent at Heruteu. Within a short time she became the abbess at Calcaria. Finally, she established a double monastery at Streanaeshalch. In all of these places, Hilda lived a life of physical and spiritual purity, and she demanded the same from her ascetic companions. Moreover, Hilda became known for her divine wisdom, so bishops and kings and others came to her often for guidance and advice. Furthermore, five monks under Hilda's care and influence later became bishops, such as Wilfrid, who became the bishop of York.

Toward the end of her life, God tested the faith of Hilda with an illness. For six long years, she suffered a severe fever. Like Job, she never complained, but praised her Maker. She also continued her service as an abbess and faithfully taught those under her care. Early one morning, in the seventh year of her illness, she received the precious body and blood of her Lord. Immediately following she instructed those under her care to live with one another in love and peace. Filled with joy, she died. The death of Hilda was immediately revealed to Begu, a nun at Hackness. She looked up toward the heavens and saw the holy angels bearing Hilda's soul upward. Telling her superior of this, all of the sisters at Hackness gathered in the chapel for an all-night vigil of prayer and psalm-singing.

Hilda is very much part of the Christian family. Though the visions surrounding her birth and death suggest her importance, it was through the sacrament of Holy Baptism that she was made a precious child of God. Likewise, she bore many of the traits of the divine and holy family. Through her faithful studies, she grew in divine wisdom. Blessed with divine wisdom, she faithfully instructed all who would listen to her. Through her virtuous life, she exhibited the Christian life. In her illness, she trusted in God alone. Though she was not a mother of flesh and blood, she spiritually cared for those for whom she was responsible.

Charles the Great Time: ca. 742–814
Place: Gaul
Office: Emperor
Biography: *Life of Charlemagne*[5]
Biographer: Einhard (ca. 770–840)

Einhard sang the praises of Charles, king of the Franks and the great emperor of the Holy Roman Empire. Charles the Great, Charlemagne, was a deeply religious man. His Christian faith deeply affected his personal life and his work as a sovereign.

Charles's pedigree was noble and Christian. Both his grandfather and father, Charles Martel and Pepin, held the commanding position of Mayor of the Palace in the Frankish Kingdom, until the pope crowned Pepin king of the Franks. Pepin was interred at the basilica of St. Denis. His only sister, Gisela, was a nun. Pepin's brother, Carloman, established a monastery near Rome to live the quiet and withdrawn life of an ascetic, though it was short-lived. The many Franks making pilgrimages to Rome heard of his holiness and often visited him, disrupting his solitude. Carloman finally sought ascetic refuge at Monte Cassino.

With the death of Pepin, Charles and his brother, Carloman, jointly ruled. Within two years, Carloman died, and Charles became the king of the Franks. Immediately, Charles set upon a series of military campaigns. He defeated Aquitania, the unfinished business of his father. At the behest of Hadrian, the bishop of Rome, Charles crushed the Lombards. He attacked the fierce Saxons and was victorious, not only militarily, but spiritually. The Lombards renounced their pagan beliefs and practices and embraced the Christian faith. Charles also conquered Spain, Bavaria, the Slavs, and Huns, to name a few. During his reign, he extended the borders of the Frankish kingdom from Gaul into much of Europe. His political power and influence reached far beyond his kingdom; he was very much respected by the sovereigns of Scotland, Greece, Constantinople, and Persia.

Though he was a powerful potentate, Charles was a pious Christian. He recognized the significance of the Holy Land and sent emissaries to visit the place of Jesus' nativity and resurrection. Moreover, the churches of the land were repaired and enhanced under his direction. He sent lavish treasures to Rome for the purpose of caring for the Church of St. Peter and other sacred places. In addition, he very much supported the pope and promised to defend him from any enemies. He oversaw the construction of the basilica of the Holy Mother of God at Aix-la-Chapelle, his hometown. The cost of it was monumental—marble pillars and bronze doors were utilized in the construction; gold and silver ornaments abounded. Charles worshiped frequently: He often received the Lord's Supper, and he prayed the morning and evening offices on a regular basis. Furthermore, he distributed alms to Christians under his rule and to Christians in foreign lands.

In Rome, Charlemagne was crowned emperor and Augustus, the successor to the throne of the Roman Empire. Omens pointed to his death—frequent solar and lunar eclipses in his waning years and others—but he chose to disregard them. After more than a decade of faithful governance, he fell ill. In his palace at Aix-la-Chapelle, he crowned his only living son, Louis, emperor. Having received the Lord's Supper, he died on January 28, 814 at 9:00 am. He lived 72 years and reigned 47 years. On the day he died, he was entombed at the basilica in Aix-la-Chapelle.

Charles exhibited numerous traits common to the family of God. His family was quite religious, his uncle and sister being noted ascetics, as was the holy family. He gave alms to the poor as commanded by his dear Lord (Matthew 25:35–40). He cared for the houses of God on earth as had Jesus (John 2:14–16). In his frequent and final reception of the Lord's Supper, Charles's life was connected intimately to the life of Christ.

Peter Abelard

Time: 1079–1142
Place: Brittany, France
Office: Ascetic, Scholastic
Biography: *The Story of My Misfortunes*
Biographer: Peter Abelard

Peter portrayed himself as a tragic figure. He was a wise and good man, but others maltreated him time and again. This was the case with the two loves of his life—academia and Heloise. His purposes were noble, but the consequences were quite tragic.

Peter provided scant data for his birth and youth. He was born in Palets, in Brittany. His father had been a student and a soldier, and wished the same for his sons. Because he was the firstborn son and most loved by his father, Peter was allowed to indulge his academic studies, while the study of weaponry fell to his brothers. Both of his parents later entered the monastic life.

Peter's academic career bounced about France. He began his study of dialectics in Paris under William of Champeaux (ca. 1070–1121). He got on well in his lessons until he successfully refuted the views of his mentor. This caused him much grief because his fellow student's envy of his academic acumen accelerated while William's appreciation for his star pupil dissipated. In addition, his intensive study and the mistreatment he received caused him severe illness, so much so that he had to return home for a few years to recuperate.

Peter turned to the study of theology under Anselm (d. 1117) in Laon, but found that he was like "a fire that fills the house with smoke rather than light",[6] so he stopped attending his lectures. Discussing biblical studies among his colleagues, Peter, as yet untrained in religion, argued that any educated person could read the Bible and ascertain its intent. Chided for his arrogance, Peter lectured on a murky biblical prophecy the next day. Those in attendance praised Peter's spiritual insight and constrained him to continue with further lectures. As students flocked to hear Peter, two prominent professors, seized with envy, orchestrated his removal. He then returned to Paris to continue his biblical lectures.

In Paris, Peter fell madly in love with Heloise (d. ca. 1163), the niece of canon Fulbert. Under false pretense, Peter lodged in the home of Fulbert who then compelled Peter to instruct Heloise. Under the ruse of study, Peter and Heloise embarked upon a love affair. This adversely affected Peter's academic lectures. Though they attempted to hide their tryst, rumors abounded. Their love was surpassed only by their shame. When Heloise became pregnant, she stayed with Peter's sister in the country and gave birth to a son, Astolabe. Incensed at their illicit intrigue, Fulbert finally agreed to a quiet marriage. Heloise entered a convent in Argenteuil and, shortly after, her family castrated Peter during the cover of night. Peter recognized this as a sign of divine justice and entered the monastery at St. Denis.

Peter's hardships continued. When he complained of the lax life at St. Denis, he was denounced privately and publicly. He retreated to a hut and began to teach again. When students flocked to him, other teachers became envious. When he wrote a book on the Trinity for his students, his opponents slandered him and conspired a council to denounce him. Though no heresy could be detected in his writing, he was forced to cast his book into the fire and confess the Athanasian Creed. He was then sent to the monastery at St. Medard where trouble followed. He sought refuge in Troyes in Provins. Students flocked to him once more only to enrage again other professors and their schools.

He considered becoming a missionary, believing pagans would be less troublesome than his fellow Christians, but went instead to the St. Gildas monastery at Ruits. The people there were uncivilized and the monks vile. At this same time, the nuns at Argenteuil were expelled and came to Ruits, Heloise in their band. Peter finally found his refuge. Though the monks relentlessly mistreated him, Peter spent much time with the nuns who appreciated him.

Peter's life was indeed tragic. He was a brilliant theologian (as he often pointed out), but his academic career was time and again sabotaged. Far worse, his intense love for Heloise was illicit. In both of these, Peter recognized his Adamic ancestry. As a son of Adam, he deserved to be punished for his sin; he, like Cain, was destined to be a "fugitive and vagabond" (Genesis 4:14). At the same time, Peter was an heir of Jesus and a member of His divine family. He, like Jesus in Egypt, sought refuge among pagans. He received the trials and tribulations that Jesus promised to His followers (John 15:18–20; 2 Timothy 3:12). In his life of tragedy after tragedy, he was intimately connected to Jesus and could say, no more and no less, than his dear Lord, "Your will be done" (Matthew 26:42).

Ailred	**Time: 1110–66**
	Place: Rievaulx
	Office: Cistercian Abbot
	Biography: *Life of Ailred of Rievaulx*[7]
	Biographer: Walter Daniel (b. ca. 1124)

Walter Daniel, a monk at Rievaulx, portrayed Ailred as a son would his father. The admiration that Daniel and, no doubt, his fellow monks had for Ailred was quite evident. Ailred's gentle care for those over whom he watched was clearly exhibited in Daniel's depiction of this devout Christian abbot.

In his youth, Ailred lived virtuously and lacked vices. This was recognized and appreciated by the king of Scotland under whom he served. The king quickly advanced him to a position of great authority in his kingdom. Ailred administered his duties with kindness and honesty, while remaining a humble servant. He served an earthly kingdom and king, but his mind was always set upon the heavenly kingdom and the divine King. Therefore Ailred was compared to Joseph who worked for the Pharaoh in Egypt, but his mind was ever upon his father in the Promised Land.

Ailred's life abruptly changed when he heard of the Cistercians at Rievaulx, a valley surrounded by hills as by a crown. He was impressed with the relation of their dress and life—both their habit and lifestyle were white and pure. The Cistercians owned nothing, but lived together as one. Uncomfortable with the pomp of the royal court, the Cistercian's simple and ordered life very much attracted Ailred. With his second visit, he forsook his secular vocation and earthly possessions and joined this spiritual community.

The spiritual life of Ailred was quite noteworthy. A "long thread" connected him to Jesus; he saw the Creator everywhere behind the creation. He prayed often and with tears. His strong spirit supported his weak body in his labors. His spiritual exercises consisted of contemplation, piety, and compassion. He constantly fought against his sinful flesh, soaking in ice water and fasting. He often read Augustine's Confessions. In his last years, his face shimmered when he conversed with angels.

Ailred performed many miracles, from mending broken limbs to giving speech to the voiceless. One monk in particular was on the receiving end of these miracles more than once. While still a novitiate, this unbalanced man ignored the counsel of Ailred and departed from the monastery. Ailred prayed to God that his soul would be preserved and that he would be led back to the monastery. This poor man, lost and confused, meandered about until he ended up back at the monastery. Ailred gladly received him back, and he took his monastic vow. Later, an angel made known to Ailred that this monk who was traveling would die shortly. Upon his arrival, Ailred graciously received him and spiritually cared for him as he fell sick. He died six days later.

Spiritual writings flowed from Ailred's pen. In Speculum caritatis, he wrote of love for God and neighbor. He chronicled the lives of King David and King Edward. He published 33 homilies on Isaiah and a volume on spiritual friendship. He put truth before the rules of grammar, but always remained eloquent and true to the Christian faith.

Ailred's career was not without merit. His first assignment at Rievaulx was training the novices. When Rievaulx bore a daughter monastery at Reversby, Ailred became the abbot. Ailred was then brought back to Rievaulx and became the abbot there until his death. During his tenure, Rievaulx became known far and wide for its care of the weak and heavy-laden who were either secular or religious. Rievaulx not only grew in size, but greatly increased spiritually.

The death of Ailred and the events surrounding it were notable. A monk foresaw his death: Ailred's body lay prostrate in a temple while his righteous soul shone brightly above it (cf. Matthew 13:43). Though he was quite ill in his last years, he often preached and worshiped regularly. After he blessed his monks, he was anointed with oil and received the precious viaticum. More than one hundred monks and a heavenly host surrounded him as he lie dying. He repeated: "Hasten, hasten." As was the custom, he was laid upon a rough ash-strewn cloth and died. The monks then prepared his body for burial and noted that his flesh was like that of a child, and his aroma was quite pleasing.

Ailred's life was that of a humble monk and an abbot who faithfully served those under his care. He clearly displayed the traits of others in the family of God: He was a virtuous child similar to John the Baptist; he faithfully served a foreign master as had Joseph; he received an erring brother like the father of the Prodigal Son. Through miracles, angelic messengers, and the Lord's Supper, Ailred's life was intimately connected to the life of Christ.

Francis	Time: 1181–1226
	Place: Assisi
	Offices: Founder of Franciscans, Miracle Worker
	Biography: *Minor Life*[8] (ca.1262)
	Biographer: Bonaventure (1221–74)

Bonaventure, a Franciscan, ordered this relatively short life of Francis into a few neat categories. Each category has a series of short anecdotes that could be easily read liturgically. In this panegyric, Franciscans hear of their famous founder and the many marvelous deeds in his life.

Francis was born in Assisi. Oddly, his mother named him John, but his father renamed him Francis, which he would keep. Francis was kind and gentle in his youth. He was very much concerned with the needs of the impoverished and promised God that he would never turn his back on those in need. After receiving a rudimentary education, he began to work in the world, while never conforming to the world and its ways.

While still a young man, Francis underwent a life-changing event that began with a charitable deed. Happening upon a destitute knight, Francis disrobed to clothe him. It continued in a dream: Jesus showed to him a palace where the armaments were marked with the holy cross and promised Francis that this would be his. Still, these events continued in a vision. Upon the cross, Jesus instructed him, "If anyone would come after Me, let him deny himself and take up his cross and follow Me" (Mark 8:34). Again, Jesus spoke to Francis from a crucifix in the church of San Damiano: "Repair my house. You see, it is all falling down."[9] Finally, Francis sold all of his possessions and gave the proceeds to the priest there to repair the church.

Francis' father was infuriated and forced Francis home where he inflicted severe punishments upon him and would not allow him to depart. No harm inflicted from his father could change Francis' heart or mind. Instead, it only served to strengthen his resolve. When his father demanded that Francis renounce his inheritance, the son immediately presented himself before the local bishop where he stripped himself and stood before the bishop as his Savior had upon the cross.

Unfettered by an earthly family or possessions, Francis began his ascetic life. He lived a life of poverty and frequently fasted. He cared for lepers, cleansing their sores and washing their feet. He became involved with the restoration of the church at San Damiano, soliciting funds and participating in the manual labor. Following this, Francis helped to restore two more churches. These three churches that he repaired symbolized the three fashions in which he repaired the Church of Christ: direction, rule, and teaching. The threefold command of Jesus to repair His Church foreshadowed the three orders Francis founded.

Hearing at Mass the direction of Jesus to His apostles (Matthew 10), Francis received the Holy Spirit and immediately followed suit. Leaving behind his shoes and staff, purse and belt, he set out to preach the precious Gospel of Jesus. Francis was a powerful preacher that greatly affected his hearers. In a short time twelve friars were traveling with him. Francis took his small band to Pope Innocent III. Jesus showed to Innocent in a dream Francis holding up the Lateran Basilica. Innocent greatly supported

Francis, accepted his rule, and sent out he and his followers to preach the Gospel of Jesus.

Francis lived an extremely ascetic life near Assisi. He preached to all in the surrounding area and performed miracles. Francis lived a rigorous life. He ate little and what he ate he mixed in ashes lest he enjoy it. He drank little water and slept upon the ground. He wore the most plain of clothes, and he prophesied.

Francis is well known for his miracles with nature. For example, he turned water into a health-inducing wine and made water come from a rock. At the valley of Spoleto, he preached the word of God to a mixed flock of birds. After he reprimanded them for their incessant noise, they listened carefully to every word he spoke. Though they were wild avians, they were not afraid of Francis and gathered closely around him.

Enrapt in prayer one morning, Francis had a vision of a crucified seraph. Initially uncertain of its meaning, the Lord informed Francis that though he would not follow after Him literally as a martyr, he would, nonetheless, bear the marks of Jesus' crucifixion. Immediately, they began to appear on Francis, on his hands and feet and side. These were not mere marks, but holes that one could place their fingers into and cuts that often bled. They caused not a little pain and suffering. Many miracles flowed out of his stigmatized hands.

The death of Francis was preceded with severe pain. His stigmata did not allow him walk and left his body terribly weak and frail, yet he praised God as had Job. In his last hours of life, he lay upon the ground stripped of his clothing, not to enter the arena of martyrdom, but for one last battle with the evil one. His last words to his friars were to remain faithful to the Crucified One and serve the poor. Holding his arms in the form of the cross, he blessed them. Listening to the Gospel according to St. John, Francis died. One of the friars there saw his soul borne off to heaven.

Francis was an ascetic and a miracle worker like many others in the Christian family. In his nature-related miracles, he shows a very close relation to Jesus restoring post-Genesis 3 life to pre-Genesis 3 life. It is the stigmata, however, which most closely connect Francis to Jesus and serve as visual signs that he is a member of the immediate family of his Savior.

Birgitta	Time: ca. 1303–73
	Place: Sweden, Rome
	Office: Founder of Birgittines
	Biography: *Life of Blessed Birgitta*
	Biographers: Prior Peter and Master Peter

Birgitta was portrayed as the Bride of Christ. She had an earthly husband and family, but heavenly ones as well. She began her life serving her earthly family and concluded serving the heavenly.

Birgitta was born into a noble family, both temporally and spiritually. Her father was Lord Birger of Upper Sweden, but most importantly, he was a spiritual man and regularly practiced penance. In addition, he made pilgrimages to holy sites; he was the fourth generation in his family to visit the Holy Land. Her mother, Lady Ingeborg, was also from noble stock. Lady Ingeborg's father was an aristocrat and patron of the church. One day, Lady Ingeborg's mother was traveling through a convent, when a certain nun began to speak ill of her. That night, an angel appeared to this nun in a dream, admonishing her and foretelling that God would perform amazing signs through this woman's granddaughter.

The birth of Birgitta was preceded and followed by miraculous events. Birgitta's mother, pregnant with her, was traveling aboard a ship when it hit some rocks and began to sink. All perished save her mother. An angel appeared that night in a dream to her mother, explaining that she had been saved because of the divine gift that she carried in her womb. Later when Birgitta was born, a priest saw the virgin Mary sitting in a shining cloud with a book in her hand. She said, "To Birger has been born a daughter whose wonderful voice will be heard throughout the world."[10] Her mother raised Birgitta in a virtuous family and made certain that Birgitta and her siblings had pious teachers. Her mother wept and prayed without ceasing for her entire family.

While yet a child, Birgitta received visions. At age 7, a lady appeared to her, took the crown off of her own head, and placed it upon Birgitta. At 10, she heard a sermon on the suffering and death of Jesus. That night she saw the crucified Jesus and He spoke to her. At 12, she saw a malformed specter of the devil that terrified her. Her aunt, a godly woman, learned of these visions and instructed Birgitta to tell no one.

Birgitta married a nobleman, but they remained virgins in the first year of their married life. Later, however, they conceived a child. During a difficult labor, Birgitta's life was in danger until the virgin Mary, robed in white, appeared and touched her body. The child was then born without any pain to her mother.

Birgitta was a pious Christian woman. She prayed and wept, held nightlong vigils, and genuflected without ceasing. She regularly repented of her sins to her confessor. She often fasted and frequented sermons. She read the lives of the saints and Holy Scripture. She gave alms to the poor, clothed the naked, and cared for the sick. Birgitta lived an exemplary Christian life.

Shortly after her husband's death, Birgitta was enrapt by the Holy Spirit. A voice from a bright cloud, said to her, "Woman, hear me." Frightened, she confessed her sins to her confessor and received the Lord's Supper. This happened a second time. At the third occurrence, the voice identified itself as the one true God, directed her to her confessor, and revealed to her that Birgitta was the bride and messenger of Christ. Brigitta received this vision in 1345.

Her confessor directed her to reside with the Cistercians at St. Mary monastery in Alvastra, Sweden. Once there, Birgitta received special gifts from God. For example, words that offended God tasted bitter in her mouth and smelled acrid in her nose. She received visions[11] and visions proliferated among the religious throughout the land. She disowned her earthly possessions and gave alms to the poor. Birgitta resisted the temptations of the evil one on numerous occasions.

In the final chapter of Birgitta's life, Jesus instructed her to leave Sweden and travel to Rome. Once there, Jesus sent her to visit the remains of the saints in Sicily and then to the Holy Land. She visited the holy places in Rome. There, she continued her devout life, confessing her sins daily and on Fridays mouthing a bitter herb to remind her of Jesus' passion.

Birgitta fell ill in Jerusalem and retired to Rome. There, Jesus appeared to her before the altar in her room. He made known to her that the wedding feast was at hand, the waiting was over. She, the bride, would be joined with Jesus, the bridegroom. After she had received the sacraments at dawn, her spirit departed from her body.

This twofold bride was closely related to Jesus. They shared family traits: pious parents and foretold births and a loving mother. They both lived devout lives. They both experienced demonic temptations and Good Friday. Most importantly for a mystic, Jesus spoke to her.

Excursus: *Golden Legend*

Jacobus de Voragine (1230–98), a Dominican priest, was famed as both a preacher and teacher. He became the Archbishop of Genoa in 1292. However, he is best known for his collection of Christian lives that he entitled Legend Sanctorum, or "Legend of the Saints," which later became more commonly known as the Legenda aurea or Golden Legend (1275).[12] It was loosely styled after the Lives of Illustrious Men by Jerome and Gennadius in that it contained biographical data on Christian lives from biblical times and the Early Church. It differed from the previous in that it included lives from both the Old Testament Apochrypha (Maccabeans) and the Middle Ages, extensively covered the life of Christ, provided far more extensive delineation of the many lives, often defined the saints' names, and included much more questionable biographical data.

Voragine ordered the lives of the saints according the Church Year.[13] These lives fell within four main sections: Advent to Christmas is the time of renewal, Septuagesima to Easter is the period of erring, Easter to Pentecost is the season of reconciliation, and Pentecost to Advent is the time of pilgrimage. A fifth section, from Christmas to Septuagesima, is divided into two sections: the first portion, Christmas to Epiphany, emphasizes reconciliation, while the second portion, Epiphany to Septuagesima is tied to pilgrimage. Consequently, the lives of the saints are read within the liturgical context of the Christian Church.

Commemorated as the herald of Advent and the beginning of the Church Year, Andrew was the first saint portrayed. Voragine first noted the major biblical references to Andrew and then chronicled his post-biblical travels to Scythia, Ethiopia, and Greece. He performed numerous miracles and faithfully taught of Jesus in his travels and converted many to the Christian faith. Prior to his crucifixion in Greece, he was beaten and stripped of his clothing. Rather than fearing the cross, he hailed it as though an old friend. He was tied upon the cross to extend his suffering. Andrew preached to 20,000 people his first two days on the cross. Though the people desired to remove him from the cross, Andrew prayed to God that he would be allowed to die in this manner and receive the crown of glory awaiting for him in heaven. When he breathed his last, the wife of his persecutor revered his body and buried it, while her husband was taken by a demon and died in public.

From the Early Church, Voragine included a miscellany of saints. He mentioned some of those already detailed in the previous chapter, such as Lawrence, Augustine, Patrick, and Martin. He also noted others, like Lucy, Hilary, Hippolytus, and Pelagia. Of Eusebius, he wrote that he was so holy angels could be seen lifting him from the font at his baptism and closing his bedchamber to a lusting noble woman and holding up his arms at Mass. Of Felix, rather than offer sacrifices to pagan deities, he blew upon the statues of Serapis, Mercury, and Diana, and they collapsed immediately. Of Christian, when Emperor Julian tossed her into the fire of martyrdom, she could be seen walking about for five days with angels until she came out unscathed. Of Jerome, a wild lion limped into his monastery one day. While all of the monks panicked and fled, Jerome greeted his guest. Seeing his wounded paw, he instructed his fellow monks to clean and bandage it. The lion then remained at the monastery and shepherded the monastery's flock of sheep.

Voragine portrayed a number of saints from the Middle Ages, many of which are well-known, like Gregory and Benedict, Bernard and Dominic. In particular, he told of the pious life of Thomas of Canterbury. Leaving the court of the King of England, he became an archdeacon and later chancellor and finally the bishop of Canterbury. Despite this most distinguished of offices, Thomas remained humble, fasting and wearing the attire of a penitent underneath his Episcopal vestments. When Thomas would not bend to the sinful desires of the King, he fled to Rome. While the King persecuted his family, Thomas prayed for him and his homeland. Seven years later, Thomas returned to England and became a martyr. At his funeral, an angelic choir interrupted the monks and sang the Mass for the Dead. Later, many were miraculously healed when they merely touched the water that had been used to wash his blood-stained clothing.

Voragine provided biographical data for three historical periods. More than a few of the narratives are somewhat dubious. At the same time, Voragine was not a literary maverick. He frequently utilized earlier documents. For example, he cited the Lives of the Fathers for abbots Pastor, John, Moses, Arsenius, and Agathon. Likewise, many of his narratives concerning Gregory the Great come from John the Deacon and Paul the Longobard. For this reason, his biographical data for Mary of Egypt is merely an abridged paraphrase of Sophronius's Life of Our Holy Mother Mary of Egypt.

The amount of fact and fiction in these biographical narratives is certainly up for argument. Regardless of this debate, Voragine well serves the Christian Church in a number of fashions. He tells interesting and pious stories so as to create devotion among Christians for their spiritual heirs. These earlier Christians must not be forgotten, but honored by contemporary Christians. Likewise, these spirituals ancestors are to inspire their spiritual heirs, and spiritual heirs should imitate their spiritual ancestors. Moreover, Voragine illustrates the unity of the Christian Church in the lives of her saints throughout the ages. Be it martyrdom or God's providential care, the Church is one.

Summary

The Medieval Period contained notable and seemingly diverse Christian lives: Peter was a scholastic and Birgitta a mystic, Gregory was a pope and Charles an emperor, Columba was a miracle worker and Hilda an abbess. The respective authors connected a variety of Christian lives to the life of Christ through differing vocations. At the same time, three themes were prevalent in most, if not all. First, piety played an important role. This, of course, was most evident in the lives of the ascetics who sold all that they had to give to the poor; who fasted and prayed throughout much of their lives. Even Charles I, though he was not a "professional" ascetic like Gregory or Ailred, gave alms and cared for the churches. Birgitta was married and had a family, but later became an ascetic. In addition, the immediate families of these saints were often portrayed as living pious lives, not unlike the pious families of John the Baptist and Jesus.

Second, miracles and visions were quite common. They surrounded the birth of Birgitta and pointed to her spiritual significance. They filled up and flowed out from the lives of Benedict and Columba and Ailred. The miracles of Francis very much reflected those of Jesus. Francis was not shown as simply reproducing them; instead, in miracle after miracle, he restored post-Genesis 3 life to pre-Genesis 3 life. In all of these, the saints are portrayed as being intimately connected to Jesus who reveals Himself to them in visions and reveals Himself to others through their miracles.

Third, the Lord's Supper played a predominant role in the lives of these saints. Medieval doctrine and practice clearly illustrated the Real Presence of Jesus' body and blood in this sacred meal. Eating and drinking of the Lord's Supper was eating and drinking Jesus, and portrayed an intimate relation between a saint's life and the life of Christ. And so, these saints frequently received Jesus' body and blood, and some were fortunate to receive these on their deathbed as their final union with their dear Lord in this world that prefigured their eternal union with Jesus in heaven.

Reformation Period

The chronological midpoint of western Christianity is the Reformation Period. It is commonly suggested to have begun in 1517 with the posting of Martin Luther's Ninety-five Theses. While this inaugurating date is nice and neat, it is also a bit simplistic. Reform had been a matter of interest throughout the Medieval Period. Concerned with corruption in the Western Church, Pope Gregory VII (ca. 1021–85) forbade simony and investiture. Moreover, wealth and prestige often adversely affected the ascetic life of monasteries, resulting in movements to reform monasticism, one at Cluny (909) and another at Citeaux (1098), both in Burgandy. Furthermore, men such as John Wycliffe (ca. 1330–84) in England and John Hus (ca. 1372–1415) in Bohemia began to question the biblical veracity of many of the doctrines and practices of Medieval Catholicism.

These reforms variously blossomed in the sixteenth century. Martin Luther rejected the role of good works in matters of salvation. John Calvin (1509–64) discarded the Mass. Henry VIII shut down monasteries. Even Medieval Catholicism recognized the need to reform herself. In the midst of these and the many other reforms taking place throughout Western Christianity, order was needed. Although the Reformation Period began on a note of change, it quickly shifted to the systematization of the doctrines and practices of the various reformers: each group attempted to define its respective orthodoxy. The Roman Catholic Church did so at the Council of Trent (1545–63), while the Church of England accomplished this with her Book of Common Prayer (1549) and the Lutherans in the Book of Concord (1580).

In the sixteenth century, the Western Church was quite divided by theology and practice, and these divisions were manifested geographically. Germany and Switzerland embraced reform, whereas France and Spain remained within the fold of Medieval Catholicism. England seesawed back and forth. In the midst of these differences, there were a variety of offices.

Reformer. The reformers determined that Medieval Catholicism required change, but all were not agreed upon the degree of change needed. Martin Luther urged major reforms, but not always as extreme as other reformers. For example, he questioned the sacrifice-terminology of the Mass, but he did not totally dispose of the Mass—he edited it. Similarly, while he rejected the doctrine of transubstantiation, he maintained a biblical approach, rather than a philosophical, to the Real Presence of Jesus' body and blood in the Lord's Supper. In contrast, Ulrich Zwingli (1484–1531) and John Calvin abandoned the Mass and transubstantiation, and replaced both with utterly dissimilar alternatives.

Ascetic. Monasticism fell out of favor among the reformers in the Reformation Period, however, it did not die out. Teresa of Avila (1515–82) was a Carmelite nun who initiated the Discalced (sandals instead of boots) Carmelites and advocated a more severe adherence to the Carmelite rule. Ignatius of Loyola (ca. 1491–1556) founded the Jesuits, the Society of Jesus, whose principle concerns were mission work and spiritually counteracting the protestant reformers.

Martyr. With the splintering of the family of God on earth, martyrdom was not far away. Many Christians had lost their lives for the sake of Jesus and the Gospel in Early Church and this was repeated in the Reformation Period. The significant difference was that in the former, the non-Christian Roman Empire was the culprit, whereas it was often other Christians in the latter. The Radical Reformers were put to death by the

Catholics, Lutherans, and Reformed. Martyrdom was a routine occurrence in England. Notables included Thomas More (1478–1535) who was put to death under Henry VIII, and Thomas Cranmer (1489–1556) and John Hooper (d. 1555) who were burned at the stake under Mary.

King/Queen. The Christianization of Europe in the Medieval Period enhanced the role of sovereigns in the church. Charles V (1500–58) was an emperor, yet he was concerned for the spiritual welfare of Europe. For this reason, he was at Augsburg in 1530 to hear the Lutheran confession of faith. Similarly, Elector Frederick the Wise (1463–1525) protected Martin Luther from Charles V when the reformer was declared a heretic and an outlaw. The ecclesial role of a monarch was nowhere more evident then in four successive crowns in sixteenth century England: King Henry VIII allowed only minor reforms to Medieval Catholicism; many more reforms occurred under King Edward VI (1537–53); Queen Mary (1516–58) eradicated the Edwardian reforms; Catholicism was abolished, once and for all, by Queen Elizabeth I (1533–1603).

With the Reformation Period, previous external unity in the Western Church was shattered. Rather than one church with a single leader, both multiplied, and divisions deepened. Despite these schisms, authors continued to portray Christians who exhibited the traits of the family of God and were intimately related to Jesus.

Martin Luther	Time: 1483–1546
	Place: Wittenberg, Saxony
	Offices: Augustinian, Professor, Reformer
	Biography: *History of the Life and Actions of the very reverend Dr. Martin Luther* (1549)[14]
	Biographer: Philip Melanchthon (1497–1560)

Philip Melanchthon, a younger colleague of Martin Luther at the University of Wittenberg, compiled this biographical data from personal and second-hand observations. While Philip was much more genteel theologically than was Martin, he placed Martin in a favorable light. Martin Luther was a great reformer who, following in the train of Jesus and the apostles, led the Christian Church from darkness into the light of the Gospel.

The Luther family name was well known and highly respected throughout the land. The people of the day very much trusted and admired Martin's father, John, who was on the city council in Mansfield. His mother, Margaret, was the model of a devout Christian wife and mother. Margaret knew that her son had been born on November 10 because he was baptized on the following day and received the name of the saint associated with that day, St. Martin of Tours. Though she was uncertain of the year of his birth, his brother, James, was certain that it was 1483.

The parents of Martin were quick to commence his education. Initially, he studied under Father Emilius in Mansfield. Following this, he was sent to Magdeburg for one year of study. His next four years were spent in Eisenach under the tutelage a gifted grammarian. In his studies, Martin excelled far above his fellow students; he learned not because he was required by his parents or instructors, but because of his own love of learning. He yearned to proceed to the university, seeing it as the source of all knowledge. At the University of Erfurt, he studied dialectics; he read Cicero, Virgil, and others. There, he received a Bachelor of Arts and Master in Philosophy. Martin's academic abilities were second to none and applauded by all.

The academic career of Martin leant strongly toward law school, but in his twenty-first year and unforeseen by all, Martin entered the Augustinian monastery at Erfurt. This community lived assiduously: They read at length and studied theology; they frequently prayed and fasted with great austerity. Martin fit in well. He studied more and ate less than his fellow Augustinians. He was the perfect monk, but was deeply troubled.

Martin suffered severe spiritual turmoil. He was an exemplary monk in his studies and piety, however, he feared the indomitable wrath of God. This led Martin to live more devoutly and examine his life even more closely. But the closer he looked at himself, the more he began to fear the divine threats of punishment against his sinfulness. As a result, Martin fell deeper and deeper into spiritual despair.

Martin was not without comfort. An aged monk in his monastery pointed to the Apostles' Creed: "I believe in the remission of sins." What this means, he explained to Martin, is that just as God remitted the sins of

David and Peter so he remits your sins. Fortified by the creed, Martin next read Bernard of Clairvaux (1090–1153): By Jesus your sins are remitted. Martin then realized that Paul wrote of this in the New Testament: We are justified through faith by God's grace in Jesus Christ (Romans 5:1). Even Augustine dealt with this issue. So it was that Martin was slowly but surely being pulled out of his spiritual quagmire.

The University of Wittenberg was established in 1508 and, at the age of 26, Martin was invited to teach there. Faculty and students alike praised his academic acumen. After three years in Wittenberg, he traveled to Rome on Augustinian business. At the age of 30, the university bestowed upon him a doctoral degree in theology.

The doors of reform gradually opened for Martin as he lectured on the Bible—Psalms and Romans. He was now forced to express verbally in the classroom the matters of salvation and the remission of sins with which he had been wrestling in his heart and continued to do so. The true Christian faith was this: The remission of sins is not earned through good works, but is received freely through the merits of Jesus. Luther now saw the relation between the Law and the Gospel—the Law accuses one of sin, while the Gospel absolves one of sin. Luther now saw that all who trusted in the Law were modern-day Pharisees, and must be admonished for their false beliefs. In this fashion, Martin was like John the Baptist in pointing the people to Jesus, the Lamb of God who takes away the sins of the world (John 1:29).

At this very time, John Tetzel (ca. 1465–1519), a Dominican friar, was selling indulgences in the near vicinity. Martin saw a tension between the freely given remission of sins and the vending of indulgences (purchasing the merits of Jesus and the saints so that the temporal punishment deserved for sins committed are remitted). Martin affixed to the door of the Castle Church in Wittenberg ninety-five theses that questioned this practice. While initially he did not outright reject indulgences, Martin pleaded for moderation. Tetzel raised a tumult; he involved the clergy and even the Pope. Polemics flew from either side, and disputations followed. While Martin was painted a heretic for questioning this practice of the Christian Church, he retained the historic faith, never departing from the doctrine of the three Ecumenical Creeds.

Reform swept through the Christian Church; changes were taking place everywhere. Martin sought reform, but only with great care. This was not case with others. While he was in hiding at the Wartburg Castle following the Diet of Worms (1521), Andreas Karlstadt (ca. 1480–1541), a professor at the University of Wittenberg, made extravagant changes, like distributing to the people the body of Jesus and forcing them to drink His blood in the Lord's Supper. It had become the tradition to withhold the cup from the laity, so this caused great consternation among the people. Consequently, Martin felt obligated to return to Wittenberg and oversee the reforms in the Church.

Melanchthon depicted Martin as a reformer in the fourth age. In the first age, the apostles established and maintained the doctrine of the Christian Church (Acts 2:42). In the second, Methodius countered the philosophical dalliances of Origen. In the third, Augustine and his followers—Prosper, Maximus, Hugo, Bernard—offset the heresy of Pelagius. And in the fourth, Martin corrected the superstitions, deceptions, and pollutions of the medieval monastics, bishops, and scholastics. Martin's concern then was for the Christian Church, and he followed in a long line of faithful servants who traced their heritage back to the apostles and He who sent them, Jesus.

Thomas More	Time: 1478–1535
	Place: London
	Offices: Lord Chancellor, Martyr
	Biography: *The Life of Sir Thomas More*
	Biographer: William Roper (1496–1578)

William Roper, the husband of Thomas' eldest daughter, portrayed the life of a valiant Christian. Not clergy, Thomas was a layman who both lived a devout life and was a theologian in his own right. He quickly moved up in the ranks of the English court, but refused to succumb to royal pressure to retain his office and life.

The youth of Thomas was quite notable. After he attended Latin school, he entered the household of Cardinal Morton where his scholarly promise was noted by many. At Oxford, he studied Greek and Law. While there, he delivered a series of lectures on Augustine's City of God at the church of St. Laurence. For three years he was a Reader, then he sequestered himself for four years of prayer and contemplation.

Thomas' family life was exemplary. He was interested in the second daughter of Mr. Colt of Essex. Concerned with how this would negatively affect the eldest and unmarried daughter, he married her instead. Their three daughters excelled in virtue and learning. During the reign of Henry VIII, he was made an undersheriff in London. Following this he was the counsel to the Pope's Ambassador, Treasurer to Exchequer, Speaker of the House of Commons, and Chancellor. In addition, he continued his academic studies. In the midst of his official and spiritual responsibilities, Thomas very much loved his family and would often absent himself from the court to be with them.

Thomas was quite virtuous. He was meek, and Henry VIII greatly respected him for his wisdom and learning. On a daily basis, he prayed and sang psalms, recited the litany and suffrages. He, along with his family, regularly attended chapel. He devoted a special amount of prayer and devotion to Fridays. He exhorted family and household to live a virtuous life. Like an ascetic, he wore a coarse hair shirt under his garments and often flagellated his body into submission.

Henry VIII favorably looked upon Thomas until a series of events changed this. First, Thomas disapproved of Henry's divorce of Catherine and marriage to Anne. After that, he refused to swear the Oath of Supremacy and was imprisoned in the Tower of London. Thomas was courageous. He comforted his eldest daughter by reminding her of God's providential care for him. His wife and others encouraged him to take the oath, as he had so much for which to live, including his family and career. However, Thomas could not be swayed.

Finally, Thomas was removed from the tower and accused of treason: he would not confess that the King of England was the head of the Church of England. Thomas argued that he must obey God rather than man, and because the Oath of Supremacy was the law of man, he could not obey it and remain faithful to God. Before the Lords who condemned him, he compared them to Paul who stoned Stephen. He hoped that just as Paul later converted to the Christian faith and finally joined Stephen in heaven, so would they join him in heaven. Thomas made two final requests: that the king would allow his family to attend his funeral and the people at his execution to pray for him. Finally, he encouraged the executioner in his office and was put to death.

Thomas very much is a member of the Christian family. While Henry VIII was a hero to many, he was a villain in the life of Thomas, while Thomas was the small hero who stood up against a much more powerful villain. Although he lost his life, through faith in Jesus, he had no fear of death. Like the martyrs before him, he trusted in his risen Savior to raise him up on the last day to be with the whole heavenly host unto eternity.

John Calvin

Time: 1509–64
Place: Geneva, Switzerland
Office: Reformer
Biography: *Life of John Calvin* (1564)
Biographer: Theodore Beza (1519–1605)

Theodore Beza, a colleague of John and his successor in Geneva, depicted the harried life of this reformer. John was chased out of his homeland and even out of his future home, yet he persevered. John's writings and actions strongly promoted the reforming movement of his day.

John was born to devout Christian parents, Gerald and Jeanne, in Noyon, Picardy. They sent him to study in Paris. His father obtained a benefice from the Bishop of Noyon for his son at the Cathedral Church and wished him to study theology. John changed directions when he moved to Orleans to study law where he was esteemed by faculty and students alike. He then traveled to the University of Bourges in Italy and continued his studies in law and theology. After the death of his father, John returned to Paris and became interested in the reform movement that was sweeping across Europe.

In 1534, the persecution against the reform movement escalated; some were imprisoned, others were burned alive. John fled from Paris to Strasburg and then to Basle. In Basle, he studied Hebrew and published the first edition of his Institutes of the Christian Religion (1536). After traveling to Italy and France, John was unable to return to Basle because of war and settled in Geneva where he was appointed preacher and professor of theology. Without delay John penned two documents: one defined ecclesial life in Geneva, while the other was a catechism. When the doctrines and practices of John were to become legal statutes in Geneva, Satan stirred up enemies of the Gospel. Finally, John and other like-minded leaders were expelled from Geneva for refusing to administer the Lord's Supper to the ungodly and abolishing the baptismal font and unleavened bread in the Lord's Supper. John returned to Strasburg and was appointed professor of theology and continued with his writing.

In 1541, after John attended conferences at Worms and Ratisbon, he returned triumphantly to Geneva. He established a rigorous system of church discipline and a Presbyterian form of church leadership. Against this, the forces of Satan were impotent. He wrote and preached and lectured, seemingly without ceasing. Battles, though, continued for John. He wrote against the Anabaptists, Libertines, and other heretics of the day. He allied himself with the theology of Philip Melanchthon (1497–1560), Martin Bucer (1491–1551), and Peter Martyr (1500-62). There was, from time to time, unrest in Geneva. Satan himself was often behind these calamities and the like as he valiantly, yet fruitlessly, fought against those who rejected his ways. However, the church in Geneva prospered.

On one occasion, Jerome Bolsec (d. 1584), a former Carmelite monk, preached in Geneva. He maintained free will and denied predestination. His manner of speech was quite arrogant, in part, because he believed John to be absent. During the sermon, John entered the assembly and heard the heresy. Immediately following the sermon, John admonished the preacher with words from Holy Scripture and Saint Augustine. Bolsec was arrested, judged guilty, and expelled from the city. Satan, always working through heretics, sent Michael Severtus (1511–53) to Geneva. John recognized this anti-Trinitarian at once, and he was later burned alive.

John's last years were burdened with poor health. He, nonetheless, never ceased his spiritual labors. He preached his final sermon February 6, 1564. Numerous ailments began to overwhelm him. He would not complain, but look up to heaven and say: "How long, O Lord!" On April 2, he was carried to church on Easter to receive the Lord's Supper. Praying without cease in his last days, he died May 27 at the setting of the sun. The news of his death produced lamenting and tears among the people.

John certainly belonged to the family of God. He was a preacher and teacher following after Jesus and the apostles. Of greater note, John suffered at the hands of his enemies. Satan did not send mere demonic underlings to assault John, but he, himself, caused havoc for and raised up adversaries in this reformer's life as he had in the life of Christ.

Ignatius	Time: ca. 1491–1556
	Place: Loyola, Spain
	Office: Founder of Jesuits
	Biography: *Autobiography*
	Biographer: Ignatius

In his autobiography, Ignatius recorded not only the temporal events during the eighteen years of his life from 1521 in Pamplona to Rome in 1538 but also his spiritual progress. His life changed drastically when he left behind his soldiering to become a pilgrim. Ignatius's travels were filled with numerous Christian experiences.

During a battle against the French in 1521, a cannonball severely injured both of Ignatius's legs. He was taken prisoner and then sent home because of his critical condition. His legs were not mending correctly, so the physicians painfully re-broke them, and he became ill to the point of death. Receiving the Lord's Supper on the eve of Saint Peter and Saint Paul Day, the Lord initiated his recovery that very night. Ignatius now had one shorter leg with a bone hideously protruding from it. Ignatius's agony intensified terribly when the physicians cut off this abhorrent appendage and began to stretch the shorter leg.

While infirmed, Ignatius read the life of Christ and the lives of the saints, and was very much inspired. He began to contemplate upon spiritual matters and weighed in his mind two options: imitation of St. Francis or a barefoot pilgrimage to Jerusalem. One evening, he saw a vision of the Virgin Mary with the infant Jesus, and determined to redirect his life from worldly matters to the spiritual. Shortly thereafter, he donned the garb of a beggar, begged alms, often fasted, and prayed the seven hours upon bended knees.

Ignatius journeyed to Jerusalem in 1523. On the way, he received the blessing of Pope Adrian VI (1459–1523), and Jesus appeared to him from time to time to comfort him. He begged for food and passage the entire way. At Venice, he was one of the fortunate few to receive passage by sea to Cyprus. From Cyprus, he traveled to Jaffa, and finally entered Jerusalem upon a donkey. Seeing Jerusalem, his heart was filled with inexpressible joy, and upon entering, he visited the holy sites. On his return voyage, he was consigned to the smaller ship because he was a beggar, but later, the larger ship wrecked.

Academic studies next enticed Ignatius. After he studied two years in Barcelona, he traveled to Alcala and was there for a year and a half. He studied the works of Albert the Great (ca. 1200–80) and Peter Lombard (ca. 1100–60), and began to teach both his exercises and Christian doctrine. In addition, he helped the impoverished. Ignatius and his companions were wrongly imprisoned in Alcala and then Salamanca. They were interrogated at Salamanca concerning their theology and declared innocent. Ignatius then traveled to Paris to continue his studies, where he was for a short time mistreated. There, he begged and fasted, visited Rouen, and taught his exercises that were much admired.

Ignatius returned home, only to continue his travels and collect alms as he could. He taught his exercises in Venice. After he and his companions unsuccessfully attempted to revisit Jerusalem, they returned to Venice to preach and were well received. Ignatius then journeyed to Rome. For forty days, he taught the exercises to professor Ortiz at Monte Cassino. Back in Rome, false accusations were made against Ignatius, but after he was exonerated, he and his companions continued their pious works.

Ignatius's life was semi-nomadic, yet it was ordered around the life of Christ. The life of Christ was an early inspiration. Like Jesus, Ignatius fasted and was often persecuted. And Ignatius reached the pinnacle of his travels riding into Jerusalem upon a donkey.

John Hooper	Time: d. 1555
	Place: Gloucester and Worcester, England
	Offices: Ascetic, Bishop, Martyr
	Biography: *Acts and Monuments*
	Biographer: John Foxe (1516–87)

John Foxe vividly portrayed this martyr's life. It overlapped the reigns of three English monarchs: Henry VIII (1491–1547), Edward VI (1537–53), and Mary Tudor (1516–58). John's life was faithful to the very end.

As a young man, John was an avid learner. He studied at and graduated from the University of Oxford. In addition, he was spiritually gifted—the Holy Spirit worked in him. He delighted in Holy Scripture and studied it extensively. He prayed often and fervently. In these early years of his Christian life, John increased intellectually and spiritually.

With the Six Articles (1539) of Henry VIII, John's life changed. He opposed their Romish manner and fell into disfavor with certain professors at Oxford, which led to his departure. Following interrogations by his Romish opponents, he fled to the mainland ending up in Zurich. There, Heinrich Bullinger (1504–75) befriended him. John also married.

With the ascension of Edward to the throne, John returned to England where he preached often and splendidly. He reproved the people of their sin and denounced the Romish rituals that had been so recently practiced in England. He proclaimed the Word of God with such clarity and beauty that people flocked to hear him. In addition, John's life was circumspect. Though he was not a monastic, his life was quite devout. He ever maintained a solemn appearance. He did not indulge in sumptuous cuisine, but fed the impoverished. He never spoke improperly of another, taking care to speak simply and with few words.

John's tenure under Edward was not without incident. Appointed bishop of Gloucester and Worcester, John was ill at ease with a bishop's attire: chimere, white rochet, and four-sided cap. Edward allowed him to skirt this practice. When other bishops objected, John robed as a bishop and patiently suffered this ecclesial ignobility. With his twofold bishopric, John was given a coat of arms—a lamb in a fiery bush—that foreshadowed his fiery death.

With the reign of Mary, John's life was upended. He did not flee, therefore became imprisoned and removed from his bishopics. As was the custom, his Romish examiners questioned him on numerous theological issues, but John was unwavering. He pointed to canons from the Council of Nicaea (325) that stated a clergyman should not be separated from his wife. He rejected the corporeal presence of Jesus in the Lord's Supper and the supremacy of the pope. While imprisoned, a blind boy who had been earlier imprisoned for confessing the Christian faith visited him. John comforted him by noting that while God had taken away his physical sight, the same had blessed him infinitely more with spiritual sight.

John was martyred at Gloucester. Prior to this, he praised his guards and did not condemn their actions. They were very much moved by his calm manner. The night preceding his death he slept some, but spent the remainder of the night in prayer. In the morning hours, he maintained his solitary contemplation in preparation for his death. The guards, heavily armed, led him to the stake. The people terribly lamented, while he appeared cheerful and looking unto heaven. After he had bowed down in prayer for half an hour, they stripped him of this clothing and fastened him to the stake with one band about his waist, dispensing with the usual two (neck and legs). The man who approached to start the fire petitioned John's forgiveness and received it. The fire blazed and then subsided, again and again. From this torment, John cried out: "O Jesus, the Son of David, have mercy upon me and receive my soul!"[15] After three quarters of an hour, he died calmly like an uncomplaining lamb, like a child in his bed.

John was an ascetic. Though he did not belong to a Romish religious order, he rigorously exercised his Christian faith by living a devout life. In addition, he was a bishop and martyr. In all of these, John's life was intimately connected to the life of Christ.

Elizabeth I	Time: 1533–1603
	Place: London, England
	Office: Queen
	Biography: *History of the Most Renowned and Victorious Princess Elizabeth* (1630)[16]
	Biographer: William Camden (1551–1623)

William Camden chronicled the career of Elizabeth during her reign in England from 1558–1603. In so doing, he portrayed her actions as a monarch in the realm of the state and the church. The two could not be segregated, but were clearly integrated in Elizabeth's life.

Elizabeth's ascension to the throne of England in 1558 with the death of her half-sister, Mary, was received with unprecedented joy and happiness by the people. In her first year as queen, she addressed essential matters for herself and England. She began with a purging of Roman Catholicism from England and the establishment of Protestantism. To purify the Church of England, it would be based upon Holy Scripture and follow the faithful example of the Early Church. In close connection with this, she remained chaste. King Philip, the former husband of Mary, proposed marriage. God forbade this type of marriage, but Philip promised a papal dispensation. This did not settle well with Elizabeth's antipathy to Roman Catholicism. Earlier, the pope had not annulled the marriage of Henry VIII to Catherine of Aragon so he could marry Anne Boleyn, Elizabeth's mother. Acknowledging the power of the pope in such matters would only confirm her illegitimacy. Freed from such matters, Elizabeth was unbound to serve God.

In the second year (1559), Elizabeth fleshed out the direction began in the previous year. Concerning her interest in Protestantism, she forbade the elevation and adoration of the Host. Moreover, she allowed English for the Bible readings and liturgy. Furthermore, the chalice, along with the host, was given to the people. While Elizabeth removed images from the churches, she forbade any irreverence toward the cross, the saints, and the Lord's Supper. Elizabeth also clearly defined her marital status. When the speaker of the Lower House and others suggested that she take a husband for the sake of England, Elizabeth responded that she was already married to a husband, the Kingdom of England, and the multitudinous fruit of this union was the people of the land. She then provided her own epitaph: "Here lieth Elizabeth, which Reigned a Virgin, and died a Virgin."

In the forty-fifth year (1601), Elizabeth continued to preserve Protestantism in England. She successfully defended her kingdom from the attacks of Roman Catholic Spain. In addition, Jesuits and secular priests stirred up trouble in England. Finally, Elizabeth expelled all of the Roman Catholic malcontents. Religious order was maintained.

Throughout her life, Elizabeth had cared for herself in food and drink, and thus, enjoyed a healthy life, but this changed dramatically in the forty-sixth year of her reign. Elizabeth's health declined; she suffered various ailments. The weather affected her adversely. She knew that her end was near, but refused a physician's care. Her opponents—papists and puritans—anxiously awaited her demise. She fasted and meditated. She chose her successor, James I, King of Scotland. In her last moments, she could no longer lift up prayers with her voice or hand, so she did with her heart. She died on March 24, the eve of the annunciation, and was translated from this earthly prison to the heavenly paradise.

Elizabeth was intimately connected to Jesus as were the sixteenth century reformers. Just as they restored the Christian Church and remained faithful to the doctrines and practices of Jesus, so did Elizabeth. She rejected the authority of the pope and expelled the Jesuits from England. Somewhat more interesting, she was not unlike Mary, the mother of Jesus. Just as Mary was the virgin mother of Jesus, so Elizabeth was the virgin mother of the people of England!

John Gerhard	Time: 1583–1637
	Places: Heidelberg, Coburg, Jena
	Offices: Superintendent, Professor
	Biography: *Life of John Gerhard* (1723)[17]
	Biographer: Erdmann Fischer

Erdmann Fisher portrayed the life of this great Lutheran theologian. Extensive in length and panegyric in scope, John's life is described in great detail, particularly his academic and eccelesial and publishing career. His immense travels are exceeded only by his laborious work for his much loved Church.

John was born in Quedlinburg, a notable city in upper Saxony. John was born to Christian parents. His father, Bartholomew, was a high-ranking government official, and his mother, Margareta, was a paragon of virtue. Margareta was struck in the womb while pregnant with John, and while everyone expected the worst, John was born without injury. Of greater note was the timing of John's birth: He was born at the exact moment when Pope Gregory XIII changed the calendar, portending his future significance. John was baptized four days after his birth.

John was sent to school in Quedlinburg while still quite young. He was a bright student and excelled in his studies. Tragedies, though, followed him. At the age of 15, he lay ill for twelve months. Through he suffered greatly, he prayed much and penned a collection of prayers that were anointed with his own tears. Comforted regularly by his pastor, John recovered from this illness. The following year, he contracted the plague. Physicians administered medicine. Upon returning to health, he knew that it was not the work of men, but the divine word that drove away the disease. Following this, he continued his studies in Halberstadt where he excelled, setting the Passion of Christ to verse.

In 1599, he entered the University of Wittenberg where he studied a broad spectrum of courses, from history to ethics to medicine. Transferring to the University of Jena four years later, John changed his studies from the care of bodies to the care of souls, from medicine to theology. Within the year, he received his master's degree and began to lecture. After a brief, but serious illness, he transferred to the University of Marburg. Because of riotous behavior among the people, he left. Turning down numerous offers of pedagogical employment, he returned to Jena where he once again taught and began to preach the Word of God.

In 1606, John received his doctor's degree at Jena, was ordained in Coburg, and installed as superintendent at Heidelburg. In regard to the last, he regularly taught at the gymnasium in Coburg. While at the last, Princess Christina heard a series of John's sermons. Desirous of more theology, she petitioned his thoughts concerning predestination and the Lord's Supper. While some were offended that John would act thus with a woman, he was finally granted permission and through letters taught to her all of the major doctrines of the Christian faith.

John's constant travel between Heidelburg and Coburg took its toll on his health. Against his wishes, he moved to Coburg where he was both the superintendent and a professor. Finally, John moved to Jena to teach at the university.

The life of John was extraordinary on at least two accounts. First, his publications were monumentous: Sacred Meditations, Loci Theologici, Enchiridion, Daily Exercise of Godliness, and Sacred Homilies, to name a few. Second, his piety was exemplary. He prayed and attended public worship regularly. In addition, he led devotions—scripture, prayer, hymn—in his home two times each day. Obedient to the command of Jesus, he fed the hungry and clothed the naked. Many said of him that he was a meek and kind man.

Numerous events surrounded the death of John. Sick throughout much of his life, he never succumbed to complaints. Nonetheless, he knew that he would not live to be an old man and ordered his affairs even before his last and fatal illness. In his last year, he suffered weakness and fever. He wrote that he not only suffers with Job, but also says along with him: "The LORD gave, and the LORD has taken away; blessed be the name of the LORD" (Job 1:21). Finally taken to bed by a severe fever, he confessed the Christian faith to those at his bedside. His family and friends shed not a few tears. He then confessed his sins and received absolution from Archdeacon Beyer who also nourished him with the precious body and blood of his Savior. Before he died, he gave alms to the poor. A few days later, he breathed his last. The service took place on August 20 at St. Michael Church; Dr. John Mayor preached the sermon.

John became a child of God through Holy Baptism. He followed in the train of Martin Luther and the sixteenth century reformers in faithfully preserving the doctrine and practices of the Christian Church. He acted like Jesus, conversing with Princess Christina as did Jesus with the Samaritan woman at the well, and he obeyed Jesus' command of carrying for the poor. John, though, did not trust in his own good works to be a Christian, but rather God's grace, and he ended his life receiving absolution and the Lord's Supper in which he received God's grace and mercy, life and salvation.

Charles I	Time: 1600–49
	Place: England
	Offices: King, Martyr
	Biography: *Moses and the Royal Martyr*
	(ca. 1683)[18]
	Biographer: Thomas Long

In this sermon, Thomas Long tells of the devout life of Charles I. He noted that the Life of Moses by the patristic author, Gregory of Nyssa, not only preserved biographical data concerning the great prophet, but set high the bar of Christian piety for all who follow after Jesus. Long argued that Charles was Moses par excellence, the life of this king paralleled that of the great prophet.

Long begins by noting a few distinct parallels. Both were born at a time in which the world dealt less than kindly to the people of God. Both were educated in the secular academies of their day. Both were poor speakers and rulers of a nation. Both devoutly worshiped God.

More specifically, Charles was a virtuous man. He was affable and passionless except when the church was under attack. He was innocent and controlled his bodily desires. He opposed wine, women, and tobacco. He ate simply and often fasted. He dressed modestly, yet he outshone Solomon. Like Joseph, he was chaste and had no lust for the women of other men. So holy was Charles that, like Moses, he wore the veil of meekness and humility to shield his glory from the people.

Charles was very much concerned with his responsibilities as a king. He greatly cared for his people. In times of distress, he would have gladly thrown himself overboard, like Jonah, to bring about calm. He loved his enemies dearly—the more they despised him, the greater his love for them grew. He prayed to God for both his people and his enemies, like Moses. He saw to it that justice ruled during his reign. He protected the holy Church from calamity and false doctrine, so much so that the zeal of God's house consumed him (John 2:17).

Both Moses and Charles were martyrs. Moses was a martyr his entire life: from being hidden in the bullrushes to fleeing Egypt to the uprisings of his own people against him. Similarly, and even to a greater degree, Charles suffered. From among his own people rose those who divested him of his possessions and good name, his family and life. His antagonists buried him alive with their mockeries and cruel lies. Finally, he died like Jesus with a crown upon his head and a scepter in his hand.

The life of Charles was not simply an arbitrary pious life. Instead, Moses' spirit was given to Charles and the latter lived a life like the former in more ways than one. In addition, the life of Charles so closely paralleled the lives of so many biblical characters, that he was virtually indistinguishable from them. Consequently, Charles fits into the portrait of the divine family, clearly bearing their many traits.

Summary

The Reformation Period portrayed its own in a number of fashions. On the one hand, a large wedge—Martin Luther's Ninety-five Theses— was driven between the Roman Catholic Church and the reforming churches. In addition, many smaller wedges divided the latter over a number of doctrines and practices. Differences manifested themselves in the church, as well as on the battlefield. On the other hand, numerous similarities rose to the surface in Christian biography. Though Ignatius was a Roman Catholic and Elizabeth I an Anglican, the former was an ascetic and the latter a virgin. John Calvin was persecuted and John Hooper was martyred, though Calvin was Reformed and Hooper an Anglican. All of them were very much concerned with remaining faithful to the teachings and practices of Jesus: Martin Luther emphasized this in the preached word, while Ignatius stressed this in his spiritual exercises; John Calvin and Charles I both had their respective theocracies. As the Western

Church was splintering externally, faithfulness was not only an appropriate characteristic in these Christian lives, but it validated their existence and actions.

Modern Period

The final chronological segment of western Christianity is the Modern Period. Two radically diverse movements had commenced already in the seventeenth century: Pietism and Rationalism. Jacob Spener (1635–1705) inaugurated the first in Germany. His book Heartfelt Desires was the charter of Pietism. It de-emphasized the predominant roles of doctrine, sacraments, and the clergy, instead stressing practical matters and the spiritual development and involvement of the laity. Notable Pietists who followed Spener include August Francke (1663–1727) and John Wesley (1703–88).

Rationalism reared up its head in the midst of intellectual and scientific achievement. The sixteenth century and the first half of the seventeenth had already seen stupendous human achievements, such as circumnavigation of the world and the invention of the telescope. Rene Descartes (1596–1650) declared: I think, therefore I am. With this statement, Descartes began with that which was most knowable—himself—and worked outward in determining truth. Rationalism affected Christianity by de-emphasizing revelation and faith, while stressing instead science and reason to determine truth. This reached its fulfillment first in the Enlightenment and then in Modernism, both of which passed off the miraculous components of Holy Scripture to the erroneous beliefs of ignorant people in primitive times, and thus, more ignorant times and peoples. Notable proponents of modernism include Gotthold Lessing (1729–81) and Rudolf Bultmann (1884–1976).

While Pietism and Rationalism both rejected the authority of the church and her clergy in the Christian life, they were quite different in that the former looked to the heart as a principle source of authority, whereas the latter the mind. In addition, they both affected the preservation and usage of Christian lives in the church. Pietism remained very much concerned with Christian lives in that they served as a model for contemporary Christians. Rationalism was not uninterested in Christian lives, but required critical examination of such. Just as the miracles of Sacred Scripture were rejected, those in the lives of the saints were similarly discarded. The Bollandists, a group of Jesuits, took the lead. Since the seventeenth century, they have not only collected and collated biographical data in Christianity, but critically analyzed these documents and their contents. A notable Bollandist was Hippolyte Delehaye (1859–1941).

Hymnographer. The history of the Christian Church is filled with the writers of hymns. This office received a bit of a revival with the liturgical reformation of the sixteenth century. Each new church body quickly elicited musicians to compose music to coincide with her theology. In the seventeenth century, the Lutheran church had three notable hymnists: Philipp Nicolai (1556–1608), Johann Heerman (1585–1647), and Paul Gerhardt (1607–76).

Pastor. A clerical hierarchy was clearly evident in the Early Church and the Medieval Period. In the former, the local bishop oversaw the ministrations of his priests and deacons. In the latter, the bishop of Rome, the pope, superceded the authority of the local bishop. Consequently, the more prominent clergy were often bishops prior to the Reformation Period. Among the Protestants, clerical hierarchies were de-emphasized, though not in the Church of England. As a result, priests or ministers or pastors, the terminology often differs, became increasingly influential through their preaching and teaching.

Ascetic. Select Christians continued to rigorously exercise their faith. Many did so in their regular lives as a farmer, wife, etc. Others continued to join religious orders. The previously established orders continued their work, and others formed. The Society of Saint-Sulpice was founded in Paris by Jean-Jacques Olier (1608–57) in 1642. Within fifteen years, they were at work in Montreal, Canada. Its principle duty was to prepare men for the priesthood. In America, Elizabeth Seton (1774–1821) initiated the Sisters of Charity whose nuns staffed schools.

Evangelist. Missionary zeal was not lost in the Modern Period. European Christianity sent numerous individuals to preach the Evangel, the

Gospel of Jesus, to the New World. This resulted in the expansion of Western Church beyond Europe and into the Americas. Notable European missionaries to America included Nicholas von Zinzendorf (1700–60) and the Moravians, John Wesley (1703–88) and the Methodists, and Friedrich Wyneken (1810–76) and the Lutherans.

Deaconess. The office of deaconess began with Phoebe in the New Testament and was utilized in the Early Church. While a deaconess did not preach or administer the sacraments, she often assisted the clergy in serving women in various manners, for example, at Baptisms and in hospitals. Whereas nuns became a predominate office for women in the Roman Catholic Church, the office of deaconess resurfaced among the Protestants.

Paul Gerhardt	Time: 1607–76
	Place: Germany
	Offices: Pastor, Hymnographer
	Biography: *Paul Gerhardt—*
	A Life Story (1866)[19]
	Biographer: F. W. Krummacher

F. Krummacher portrayed Paul Gerhardt to be both a faithful pastor and gifted hymnographer. He composed hymns for the church and because he was a member of that church and persecuted because of his faith, he also relied upon his own hymns for spiritual comfort.

Paul was born in Grafenhainichen, near Wittenberg, and received a Christian education. It is thought that the horrors of the Thirty Years' War (1618–48) that devastated the people and the land around him directed him into spiritual matters and the study of theology.

As a young man, he composed and published a number of notable hymns, such as Awake My Heart and Sing and Oh Enter, Lord, Thy Temple. At the age of 45, he was presented as a pastoral candidate to the church at Mittenwalde. He was recommended as well-educated, virtuous, faithful, and dearly beloved by all. Upon his consecration, he pledged his faithfulness to the Book of Concord as a faithful exposition of Holy Scripture. Toward the end of this five-year pastorate, he married Anna Maria.

Paul then became the pastor at Nicolai Church in Berlin. His ministry there was quite successful as the people recognized his love of theology and care of souls. His sermons reached into and turned the people's hearts, and they thronged to hear his preaching.

During this time, the Eucharistic Controversy raged among the Lutherans and Reformed. Each attacked the other as the most vile of heretics, and Elector Frederic William wished to calm the storm. Favoring the Reformed, he saw the Lutherans as the problem. He called a conference of these opposing parties. The Lutherans claimed that their Book of Concord faithfully interpreted Holy Scripture on this issue, while the Reformed argued that this was a non-fundamental doctrine, therefore agreement was not necessary. Paul rejected the position of the latter and remained faithful to the Lutheran teaching. The elector concluded the conference and issued an edict that such theological bickering would not be tolerated. Paul refused to capitulate and was removed from his position at Nicolai Church.

Many petitioned the elector to return Paul to his position. Finally, the elector declared that Paul must have misunderstood the edict and so he could return to his position. Paul, though, refused to acknowledge any misunderstanding and refused his reinstatement. To do otherwise, he would have to reject his confessional oath.

While Paul was enduring a period when he had no means to support himself, his wife died in 1668. His hymn, "Commit Whatever Grieves Thee," that he had written for the church, now comforted him in his time of need. In the following year, he went to Lubben in Saxony and pastored there for seven years, though he was often troubled by the elector. In his will, he left the following instructions for his son Frederic: "Pray diligently, study what is honest, live peacefully, serve faithfully, and remain constant in thy faith and confession; then, when the time comes that thou must die, thou shalt leave this world willingly, happily, and blessedly. Amen."[20] Paul died June 7 and his body was interred in the church at Lubben.

Paul followed in the train of Martin Luther who faithfully proclaimed the Gospel of Jesus at the risk of his own life. This has been true of pastors and bishops and apostles all the way back to Jesus, who Himself faithfully proclaimed the Word of God unto His own suffering and death. In addition, Paul composed hymns for the Lutheran Church of the reformation as had Martin Luther, and he was not unlike David in his composition of Psalms that soothed the soul of Saul. The hymns of Paul have been sung throughout the Christian Church for the spiritual benefit of many and the bringing of salvation for souls.

John Flavel	Time: 1630–91
	Place: Dartmouth, England
	Office: Presbyterian Pastor
	Biography: *Life of John Flavel*

John was a non-conformist in seventeenth century England. As such, he was forcibly removed, for a time, from the Office of the Holy Ministry in the Church of England. Nonetheless, he remained quite close to God. This manifested itself in prayer and his pastoral care for the people in his midst.

John was the son of Christian parents. His father, Richard, was a pastor in three successive parishes. His office was revoked when King Charles II (1630–85) regained the throne of England in 1660. His father continued to preach and care for souls clandestinely until he was arrested. In prison with his wife, they contracted the plague and died shortly after their release.

After studying at Oxford, John was called to serve Devonshire and received a Presbyterian ordination at Salsbury in 1650. In Devonshire, he married his first wife. She died giving birth to her first child, as did the child. One year later, he married his second wife and was called to serve the more prestigious Dartmouth.

John excelled in his pastoral duties. His preaching converted many to the Christian faith. He was more than familiar with the controversies of the day—Lutherans versus Calvinists, Infant Baptism, and Antinomianism. No doubt, his greatest spiritual talent was prayer. On one occasion, he called for a fast during a battle with the French. Wrestling with God in prayer, the Lord answered his prayer and not one of their sailors perished. On another occasion, John journeyed to London by ship. During the passage a dream of his warned of great peril. Following this, the weather worsened, and the ship's captain warned that unless the wind changed they would certainly wreck upon the rocky shore. John called those on board together to pray. He implored God to be merciful to his faithful people; he reminded God that His adversaries would rejoice in the destruction of the people of God. Immediately, the sea calmed, and they arrived safely in London.

The Act of Uniformity (1662) expelled John and other non-conformist pastors from their parishes. Unable to remain in Dartmouth, he withdrew to a small village nearby. Akin to his father, John continued to preach and care for souls privately in and around Dartmouth. On one occasion, he was preaching in Exeter when the local officials disrupted the meeting. Many were arrested, but John escaped to the woods where he continued to preach the word of God. Charles loosed the restrictions against the non-conformists, and John returned to Dartmouth to preach, but this was short-lived.

With the ascension of King James II (1633–1701) to the throne of England, the non-conformists were granted legal status and John flourished. He preached and lectured and wrote, e.g., Reasonableness of Personal Reformation and Sacramental Meditations. He preached his last sermon on June 21, 1691 in Dartmouth. Soon after, he fell ill at dinner and died painlessly on June 26. His funeral and burial took place in Dartmouth; the quantity of those in attendance was exceeded only by the quantity of tears poured out. The pastor of Exeter spoke of John as Elisha had spoken of Elijah: "My father, my father! The chariots of Israel and its horsemen!" (2 Kings 2:12).

John was part of the family of God. He exhibited family traits in that he prayed to God as had Moses (Numbers 14:12–16), and God answered. Similarly, he had pious parents as had John the Baptist and Jesus. In addition, his life paralleled the life of Christ in their analogous care for the souls of the people in their midst and persecution by the ungodly.

George Whitefield	Time: 1714–70
	Place: England
	Office: Preacher, Evangelist
	Biography: *Christian Leaders of the Eighteenth Century* (1869)[21]
	Biographer: John Charles Ryle (1816–1900)

John Charles Ryle wrote about a remarkable evangelist in eighteenth century England who cared for souls inside and outside of church walls.

George Whitefield boldly proclaimed the word of God to all who would hear, and many believed.

George was born at Gloucester where William Tyndale (ca. 1494–1536) was born, Miles Smith (1550–1624) protested, and John Hooper (d. 1555) was put to death. His parents were simple folk. He lived less than a virtuous life while he attended the local school until he was 15. After working in his mother's inn for more than a year, he returned to his studies and was received into Oxford.

At Oxford, George's life changed dramatically. Initially, he read Thomas à Kempis (ca. 1380–1471), among others, and began to embrace asceticism and mysticism. In particular, he regularly fasted and penitently clothed himself. Upon befriending John (1703–91) and Charles Wesley (1707–88) and their band of "Methodists", George began to visit the imprisoned and study the Bible. The doctrine of God's mercy opened a whole new world to him, and he abandoned the legalistic tenets of Medieval Catholicism.

George was ordained by the bishop of Gloucester on Trinity Sunday, 1736, and preached his first sermon at St. Mary-le-Crypt, where he had been baptized and received his first communion. The majority rejoiced at this sermon, while a few disdained it. Immediately following, he continued his studies at Oxford while preaching on occasion. Within a short time, he became renown for his sermonizing.

After preaching briefly in Dummer and Bristol, he journeyed to America at the behest of the Wesleys. Upon returning to England, many of the clergy shunned him for his preaching of repentance and the Atonement and the Holy Spirit. Thereupon, George preached, not from pulpits, but outdoors. His first opportunity took place in 1739 near Bristol. He preached on the Beatitudes to a crowd of un-churched coal miners, a spiritually captive audience. They immediately recognized their own unrighteousness and the great treasure of Jesus' perfect righteousness. Tears smeared the coal dust upon their faces, and many were converted!

George continued to preach outside of church buildings, and multitudes thronged to hear him. The preached word did not return to God without fruit, but rather, thousands of unchurched repented of their sin and confessed Jesus. Not allowed in the majority of pulpits in England, George, nevertheless, preached unceasingly throughout the land. He traveled to Scotland fourteen times and seven to America. Every Lord's day, he administered the Lord's Supper, preached in the morning, afternoon, and evening. He preached regularly during the week. In all, he preached on 18,000 occasions. He lectured and spoke to all manner of men. George's life ended in America. On his way to preach in Newbury Port, New Hampshire, he prayed, "Lord Jesus, I am weary in thy work, but not of thy work. If I have not yet finished my course, let me go and speak for thee once more in the fields, seal thy truth, and come home and die."[22] After preaching a two-hour sermon at Exeter, he finally arrived in Newbury Port. He lay down in bed and never arose. His wife preceded him in death. While he fathered no temporal children, George left a legacy of spiritual offspring.

George was an integral member of the family of God. Born and baptized in Gloucester, he became a spiritual heir of prominent Christian ancestors. Preaching in the open-air, he obeyed the command of Jesus: "go therefore to the main roads" (Matthew 22:9). Through his ministrations, be brought many more into the family of God.

Margaret Jungmann, nee Bechtel

Time: 1721–93
Places: Germany, America
Offices: Wife, Missionary
Biography: *Memoir of Margaret Bechtel, Mrs. Jungmann*[23]
Biographer: Margaret Jungmann

In her memoirs, Margaret related the grace of God in her life. Despite personal trials and doubts and weaknesses, God watched over her and preserved her. In true humility she described her Christian life and, in particular, her missionary work among the Native Americans. In addition, she gratefully praised God for His care and her faith in Him.

Margaret was born in Frankenthal in the Palatinate. Her parents were Reformed. In fact, her mother had been banished from France for her faith. Her parents had Margaret baptized in the Reformed Church. They raised Margaret and her siblings to live righteously before God and provided spiritual literature for them, including the Holy Bible and Johannes Arndt's True Christianity. Daily, the family read scripture and prayed upon bended knee. In her youth, the reading of Jesus' suffering and death elevated her spirit to lofty heights.

At 5 years of age, her family moved to Germantown, Pennsylvania. Her father met Nikolaus von Zinzendorf in 1741 and brought him into their home. Margaret heard him preach that Sunday at the local Reformed Church and knew immediately that he was sent by God and guided by His Spirit. Following the sermon, Margaret gave herself over to Jesus and she received the gift of salvation.

Margaret moved to Germantown, Pennsylvania, at the behest of Zinzendorf. She was quickly received into the Moravian congregation there and married Br. Buttner, a Moravian preacher at Tolpehoken. Immediately after their marriage, they set off to evangelize the Native Americans at Schekomeko. The work was difficult as the Native Americans and the Buttners lived in extreme poverty. This did not dishearten Margaret. Instead, she quickly learned their language and became well acquainted with them. After three years, tragedy stuck—her husband died, she left her mission work, and her newborn son died. Spiritually, Margaret was devastated: God's mercy was unknown to her.

Within the year, Margaret married Johann Jungmann (They would have eight children). Shortly after their marriage, they went to Frederickstown, Pennsylvania, to serve at the Children's School. After giving birth to a daughter, they moved to a congregation for Native Americans in Gnadenhutten, and stayed there for six years. Following this, they served a Native American congregation in Pachgatgoch in New England for three and a half years. After secular employment for ten and a half years, Margaret became a deaconess. They then served successive Native American congregations in Languntotenunk, Muskingum, Lichtenau, and Schoenbrunn. Their work in the third was crippled by the outbreak of the American War of Independence.

As Margaret aged, her work became more difficult. At the age of 64, she began to experience weakness throughout her body, particularly in her arms and legs. This malady brought an end to her missionary endeavors among the Native Americans. In her last years, she remained on bed-rest and suffered terrible pain. The more she suffered, the more she prayed and hymned. Surrounded by her family and friends, she was blessed by the congregation and died on November 22.

Margaret was very much a part of God's family. Not only was she born into and raised in a Christian family, she was born into and raised in the family of God through Holy Baptism and her missionary work among the Native Americans. In the latter, she obeyed the command of Jesus to take the Gospel into all the world and exhibited a family trait common to the family of God.

Charles Porterfield Krauth Jr.

Time: 1823–1883
Place: United States
Offices: Pastor, Professor
Biography: *American Lutheran Biographies* (1890)
Biographer: J. C. Jensson

Charles Porterfield Krauth was raised and educated a Lutheran, but became much more resolute in his Lutheranism later in life. As such, he greatly affected the direction of Lutheranism in nineteenth century America.

Charles was born into a Christian family. His grandfather, Charles J. Krauth (d. 1821), emmigrated from Germany to the United States where he taught school and played the organ in a German Reformed congregation. He married a Lutheran woman; their son was Charles Philip Krauth (1797–1867). Their son studied medicine, but finally entered the Holy Ministry. He married Catharine Heiskell who gave birth to Charles Porterfield Krauth in 1823 at Martinsburg, Virginia; she died the next year.

As an infant, Charles was cared for first by his mother's parents, then by the parents of his father in Philadelphia after his father accepted a pastorate there. He, at age 9, was sent to school at Gettysburg, and he graduated from Pennsylvania College in 1839. He graduated from Gettysburg Seminary in 1841.

Charles initially filled two pulpits successively in Baltimore, Maryland, where his superb preaching came to light. His homiletic preparations included the study of the writings of the Early Church and Reformation Period. Specifically, he diligently examined the homilies of the noted preacher John Chrysostom (d. 347–407). In addition, he was a gifted speaker. People thronged to hear him preach. However, this proved to be his downfall at Second English Lutheran Church. The construction of a church large enough for his hearers proved to be financially debilitating to Charles and he resigned in 1844. He took with him from Baltimore Susan Reynolds as his wife.

Charles served three congregations in Virginia. In a dual parish, he preached at both on alternating Sundays. In a subsequent parish, he administered the Lord's Supper two times each year: each was preceded by three days of evening services. All of his people held him in high esteem.

The theological perspective of Charles shifted with his perusal of the Loci theologici by Martin Chemnitz (1522–86). Charles had already been studying the development of doctrine in the history of the church, and he was more than familiar with the Book of Concord, which includes the Ecumenical Creeds of the ancient church along with sixteenth century confessions of the Lutheran reformers. Since its printing in 1580, it has been the confession of the Christian faith amongst Lutherans. Chemnitz' Loci fit all of these pieces together: extensive citations from Reformation Period Lutheranism, the writings of the Early Church, and Holy Scripture. Charles was won over to the confessional writings of the Lutheran Church—he now saw that they were the most faithful explication of the Word of God.

Charles worked tirelessly in the production of a hymnbook for the people. It utilized the more ancient forms, the historic Epistles and Gospel readings, the Apostles' and Nicene Creeds. In addition, the Augsburg Confession of Philip Melanchthon and the Small Catechism of Martin Luther were to be included. In this fashion, Charles helped to restore true Lutheranism through Lutheran practice in the liturgy.

Two years after the death of his first wife (1853), he remarried and moved to Philadelphia where he served two successive parishes and became the editor of a Lutheran journal. There he opposed the Definite Synodical Platform (1855) and its edited Augsburg Confession (1530). As author and editor, he very much supported the confessional beliefs of the Lutheran Church. In 1864, Charles was elected president of the fledgling Theological Seminary in Philadelphia wherein he was directly responsible for the theological formation of Lutheran pastors.

Charles was instrumental in the General Council. He authored its constitution, and his Fundamental Principles of Faith and Church Polity served as a foundational document. As president for ten years, he was responsible for the design and implementation of the Synod's Theses on Pulpit and Altar Fellowship. In addition, he directly participated in the production of a new hymnal that included the many introits and collects for the Church Year.

Charles "fell asleep in Christ" on January 2, 1883. The faculty of Arts and Sciences at the University of Pennsylvania, where he had been a trustee and professor, lamented his death and consoled his family. Following his funeral service, Beale M. Schmucher (1827–88) spoke at the cemetery.

The apple did not fall far from the tree for Charles. He was theologically connected to the Lutherans of the Reformation Period and the fathers of the Early Church through his extensive studies. More importantly, he was related closely to these and to Jesus as a preacher, teacher, and defender of the Christian faith.

Therese	**Time: 1873–97**
	Place: Lisieux, France
	Offices: Carmelite Nun, Miracle Worker
	Biography: *Bull of Canonization of St. Therese* **(1925)**[24]
	Biographer: Pope Pius XI (1857–1938)

Pius depicted Therese as a flower, plucked too soon. This young woman was a devout model for the Christian life and a cause for celebration. Therefore, he portrayed Therese as deserving of canonization in the Roman Catholic Church.

Therese was born into a devout Christian family on January 2, 1873. Two days later she was baptized into the Christian faith. In less than five years, her mother died, but her family held together. Two older sisters cared for her, while her father lovingly watched over them.

In her youth, Therese was very much interested in spiritual matters. She never tired of conversing about God and resolved to live a holy life before God. At the age of 9, she studied under the Benedictine nuns at Lisieux and fared quite well academically. Her favorite lessons included The Imitation of Christ by Thomas à Kempis (ca. 1380–1471) and Holy Scripture; she committed à Kempis to memory, while she immersed herself in Scripture.

Following a grave illness and miraculous recovery, she continued her studies and joined the Carmelites of Lisieux at the tender age of 15. There, God ordered her holy life. She sought to obey the command of Jesus: "love one another; just as I have loved you" (John 13:34). She taught the novices obedience and humility. She so fully gave of herself to this holy life that it was as though she was wed to Jesus.

Numerous miracles were associated with Therese, both during her life and following. On one occasion, she healed Louise, a Daughter of the Cross, of a severe stomach ulcer, to which three eminent doctors testified to the veracity of this miracle. At a much later time, Gabriella Trimusi, a Poor Daughter of the Sacred Heart, suffered from tuberculosis and Spanish influenza, inflammation of the tibia and spinal pain. Twenty-six years after the death of Therese, Gabriella participated in a novena in honor of Therese. Immediately following this, she was cured and returned to her previous activities.

Therese died September 30, 1897. Immediately preceding this, her dear Lord wounded her heart and enflamed her soul. Completely immersed in divine love, she cried out confessing her great love for her dear Lord. She was buried at Lisieux.

Therese followed in a long line of ascetics who imitated the rigorous life of Jesus through actions such as celibacy and extensive prayer. In devoting her life to Jesus, she connected her life to the life of Christ. Through the many miracles associated with her, Jesus worked in and through her.

Elisabeth Fedde   Time: 1850–1921
Places: Norway and United States
Office: Deaconess
Biography: *The Borrowed Sister* (1953)
Biographer: Erling N. Rolfsrud (1939–93)

Erling Rolfsrud tells the wonderful story of Sister Elisabeth. Though she was an orphan and had little, she desired to serve others. As a deaconess, she cared for the ill and destitute. She was a courageous woman who fearlessly entered into a little-known vocation. Her work would extend beyond her homeland of Norway and into the United States where she heroically persevered and served her Lord.

As an orphan, Elisabeth lived with Dr. and Mrs Siqveland in Fedde Gaard. She always desired to serve others, but did not know how until one day an elderly seamstress suggested that she become a deaconess. Elisabeth knew virtually nothing of deaconesses other than seeing them about town from time to time. Were they not Lutheran nuns? One day she happened to speak to Sister Karen, a deaconess. When Elisabeth acknowledged a bit of interest, Sister Karen warned her that a deaconess must be strong in body and soul, and while the toil is often difficult there are great joys as well. Dr. and Mrs. Siqveland, her employers, supported this idea. Likewise, her pastor, Rev. Oftedal, encouraged her.

Elisabeth enrolled at the deaconess school at Kristiania. She noted their simple clothing: a plain blue dress and a white cap with a black shawl. The life there was quite rigorous. The day began at 5:30 am with devotions and breakfast. The day ended with devotions and bed at 9:30 pm. In between, they worked, feeding and caring for the patients. Every third day, each was required to serve night duty. In addition, their studies included nursing care, deaconess skills, and theology. The living quarters for the deaconesses were quite sparse—one room with a small, but clean, curtained area for each. The deaconesses also attended meetings at Church and in Christian homes where pastors and professors led discussions on spiritual subjects.

At Kristiania, Elisabeth received extensive training in caring for patients: baths and meals and changing linens. On one occasion, she was responsible for caring for the patients in a particular ward when she heard someone knocking at the front door. Knowing that the other deaconesses were busy, she left her patients. On the way, she was severely reprimanded. She was reminded that her responsibility was her patients and not door answering. This was an important lesson that would help her focus on her diaconal calling throughout her career.

Elisabeth worked faithfully in a number of different situations. On two occasions, she served at the State Hospital in Kristiania where she was often mistreated by patients. However, she lovingly served these people, acting like Jesus who was abused before Pilate. When a typhoid epidemic broke out in 1877, she left the safety of her institution to go out and care for a young girl who was ill and survived. Fearful at first, she knew of her heavenly Father's love for her. Sent to the hospital at Tromso north of the Arctic Circle, she and another deaconess worked for Dr. Holmboe. They thoroughly cleaned the hospital and removed all of the vermin. She then demanded that local board of directors for the hospital provide adequate supplies or they would leave. When the board provided the needed supplies, the local women pitched in to help.

Deathly ill, she resigned and returned to Fedde Gaard. Visiting family and friends, her brother-in-law invited her to serve as a deaconess for Norwegians in Brooklyn. After a long trip, she witnessed the great need of the poor and sick Norwegians in Brooklyn, many who were laying in the streets with nothing. She unceasingly begged for food and clothes for the poor. She collected enough money to rent a building with three rooms. She took in patients and continued to travel about visiting and caring for those in need. She organized a Ladies' Aid to provide spiritual and financial assistance to her work. She begged for physicians' care. She started up a Norwegian Sunday School. During her work, she often sang hymns to herself for strength.

In 1885, the Norwegian Relief Society rented a building and the Deaconess Home and Hospital was established in Brooklyn. Elisabeth oversaw all of the work there. There were nine beds, three for the indigent. A physician volunteered his services. A deaconess arrived from Norway to help. In her second year, Elisabeth made 1500 visits to the poor and sick. She was a modern day Phoebe.

On another occasion, Elisabeth overheard two men speaking about her and deaconesses. The first man complained that they were unneeded: there were already too many pastors to support. The second man spoke highly of deaconesses and their works of mercy. The men argued back and forth. A week later she was taken to care for a man who lay paralyzed. Elisabeth recognized him as the man who harshly criticized deaconesses. Rather than leave, she nursed him back to health. When speech returned to the man, he repented of his sin.

In 1888, Elisabeth began to organize a Deaconess Hospital in Minneapolis. The Deaconess Hospital in Brooklyn was completed in 1889. Traveling back and forth from Minneapolis to Brooklyn, Elisabeth kept busy trying to keep both institutions operating. Finally, Elisabeth concluded her service as a deaconess and retired. She returned to Norway and married.

Sister Elisabeth was a devout Christian servant. She served others like Phoebe, the New Testament deaconess, and she gladly suffered shame as had her Lord Jesus. The life of Elisabeth was one of service, not for herself, but others: those who could not care for themselves, but relied upon the grace of God and His work through faithful servants.

Clives Staples Lewis   Time: 1898–1963
Place: Scotland and England
Office: Apologist
Biography: *Surprised by Joy* (1955)[25]
Biographer: Clives Staples Lewis

C. S. Lewis traced the circular course of his early life, which began and ended in the Christian Church. The middle, though, muddled about through friends and a war, books and instructors. In all of this, his dear Lord watched over him and, in the end, guided him back to the family of God.

The family in Belfast into which Clives was born was Christian. Though clergy were common among his mother's family and he learned his religious lessons, he was less than fascinated with the Christian faith. Both of his parents were intellectuals: his mother had been a budding mathematician and enjoyed literature; his father, a barrister, favored oratory and poetry. He was fortunate to have an endearing nanny and a brother with whom he was quite close.

Clives's childhood was idyllic. His brother drew boats and battles, while Clives sketched fauna that spoke and dressed and acted like humans. His brother's pictures took place in India, whereas Clives's land was fanciful. The family house was barren of beauty, however, Clives had his first glimpse of beauty in a miniature garden created by his brother. His parents filled their house with books, and Clives spent many a day reading whatever was at hand. While yet rather young, he received his early schooling at home. Supplementing his studies, this fledgling cartographer integrated the lands of his brother's India and his animals; he penned fanciful stories of the inhabitants in these lands. Clives's childhood was filled with joy, the type of joy that once had and then lost, must be recovered.

With the death of his mother and enrollment at a boarding school in England, C. S. Lewis's life changed dramatically: the joy of his younger days proved quite rare. The headmaster was a tyrant and the others students cruel. Clives fared well, but studied little. Here, he first encountered anglo-catholicism—high church with its incense and kneeling and the like. Such things appalled him, yet he was not unaffected. For the first time, he heard the historic teachings of the Christian Church in sermons, and it began to penetrate his heart.

At the age of 11, Lewis attended Campbell College, near his home. After an illness, he proceeded to Chartres, a school in Wyvern, England, at the age of 13. Here, Clives set aside Christianity. An influential teacher was very much interested in spirituality apart from Christianity, and Clives was already uncomfortable with it. He had been taught the necessity of giving due thought to his prayer, but no sooner had he said, "Amen," then a voice whispered to him, asking him if he was sure he was focusing on what he said. Repetition of the prayer did not comfort him, as thoughtless reiterations only compounded his guilt. Therefore, Clives pushed Christianity out of his life, though he became more interested in higher spiritual realities. Following this, he literally descended the hill from Chartres to Wyvern College, but with little joy.

At Bookham, he came under the tutelage of the "Great Knock", an instructor dearly beloved first by his father. From him, Clives learned to think and speak succinctly. The instructor led his student through ancient Greek and Latin literature, later German and Italian. Clives embraced his studies and devoured books one after another. Knock was an atheist.

Clives went through the rite of confirmation in the church, but under false pretense: he was faithless. He succumbed to this expected ritual and received his first communion. In unbelief, he received the Lord's Supper in an unworthy state and damned himself. He remained resolutely uninterested in the Christian faith. Still, something was askew; the former joy was becoming more frequently absent.

At 18 years of age, C. S. Lewis began his studies at Oxford. Within a year he was a soldier in the first World War. It surprised him, but his military experience was not unpleasant. At this time, he first read G. K. Chesterton (1874–1936), a notable Christian theologian. Clives returned to Oxford at age 21. His circle of friends was not without virtue, but outside the Christian Church. Clives delighted in his atheism until two chums read Rudolph Steiner (1861–1925) and converted to anthroposophy. Unconverted himself, Clives began to read philosophy and became interested in theism. In his continued studies at Oxford, a new friend was a brilliant scholar, but unbelievably a Christian as well.

Lewis stood surrounded. Friends—Owen Barfield and J. R. R. Tolkein—pointed to spiritual realities. The philosophers—Plato and Virgil—attested a greater good. Great literary minds—Edmund Spenser and John Milton—made him look beyond this temporal world. Chesterton was indomitable. His father fell ill and died. In the midst of all of this, his dear Lord moved in for the kill, so to speak. After reading Chesterton's The Everlasting Man, a fellow atheist acknowledged the historical nature of the Gospels, and Clives's life began to fall in on itself. What did all of this mean? And then the great "I am" revealed himself to Clives.

C. S. Lewis's life was not unlike that of Augustine. Both started in a Christian family. Both traveled about on their respective spiritual journeys. Their heavenly Father joyously received both prodigal sons into the divine family wherein both became brothers of Jesus. Clives could then look back over his life and see his heavenly Father's love and guidance, and look forward to his eternal home.

Robert Preus   Time: 1924–95
Place: North America
Offices: Pastor, Professor
Biography: *In Memoriam. Robert David Preus*[26]
and *Commemoration Sermon for
Dr. Robert D. Preus*[27]
Biographer: David P. Scaer

David Scaer, first a student and later a colleague of Robert Preus, portrayed him as one of the more notable Lutheran theologians of the twentieth century. While he confessed that Robert was a sinner, both panegyrics portrayed numerous notable events in his academic and ecclesial careers, not the least being his pivotal role within The Lutheran Church—Missouri Synod during the 1970s Seminex affair at Concordia Seminary in St. Louis, Missouri. Of greater note, Scaer showed that while Robert suffered much persecution in his life, he always remained faithful and, in the end, was delivered by God from the hands of his enemies.

Robert came from a strong Lutheran background. His great-grandfather played an instrumental role in the formation of the Evangelical Lutheran Church. His grandfather was a pastor in the same. Robert followed in their train, being ordained in that church as well.

The academic career of Robert was quite distinguished. His dissertation at the University of Edinburgh was published as The Inspiration of Scripture, and a second doctoral dissertation at the University of Strassbourg was published as The Theology of Post-Reformation Lutheranism. Because of these and his many other publications, he became the foremost contemporary theologian on the sixteenth-century Lutheran Confessions. This complemented the theology of his brother Jacob who was elected president of The Lutheran Church—Missouri Synod in 1969. When Robert became a systematic professor at Concordia Seminary in 1957, he stood contemporary Lutheran systematics on its head, turning it into an exciting enterprise and introducing a confessional revival in the LCMS. He founded the Luther Academy, which was responsible for the journal Logia and a series of volumes on Confessional Lutheran Dogmatics (1989+).

The ecclesial career of Robert was not tragic, but not without pain either. Robert was one of the few faculty who remained on the campus of Concordia Seminary in St. Louis, Missouri, when the liberal professors and students left and formed Seminex, their own "Seminary in Exile." Following seventeen years of teaching at Concordia Seminary, St. Louis (1957–74), in 1974 he became the president of Concordia Theological Seminary in Springfield (1974–75), then moved to Fort Wayne, Indiana (1975–89, 1992–93). There, he founded the Symposium on the Lutheran Confessions. In 1989, he was removed from office by the seminary's board of regents and a charge of heresy was brought against him for the teaching that "all theology is christology." Clearing his name, he returned to the presidency in 1992 for one year, but upon his retirement, he was allowed neither to teach nor preach upon the campus. A new board of regents in 1995 declared him President Emeritus.

At the end of his life, Robert remained interested in Concordia Theological Seminary and was very much wished to return to campus and actively participate in its continued growth. At a conference on Hermann Sasse in St. Catherines, Ontario, he died. Interested in theology unto his dying day, he was very much like Moses who looked into the Promised Land, but was unable to enter.

Robert exhibited many of the traits that are common to the family of God. Like Abraham, his descendants were myriad; he loved theology and taught this love to his students, and his students were his children. Like Martin Luther, he taught and lived the theology of the cross; he was persecuted at both seminaries and deserted by family and friends for his confessional stance. In addition, he bore the marks of suffering. In all of this Robert pointed to Jesus, the center of the Christian faith and that same Jesus strengthened and preserved him through his tribulations.

Summary

Though the Modern Period included Christian lives seemingly beyond number, the few here included in this survey suggest a modest variety. John Flavel was a Presbyterian, George Whitefield a Methodist, Margaret Jungmann a Moravian, Charles Krauth a Lutheran, Therese of Lisieux a Roman Catholic, and Clives Staples Lewis an Anglican. At the same time, one family trait was predominantly apparent: devotion. John preached despite his adversaries. George labored tirelessly. Charles was a loyal proponent of his Lutheran heritage. Youth could not keep Therese from service to her Lord. Clives continually searched for joy. All were portrayed as faithful to their dear Lord.

Western Analysis

The chronological breadth of Western Christianity produced a wide spectrum of biographical analyses. This greatly affected the preservation and utilization of biographical data. For example, miraculous accounts decreased in direct relation to the increase in modern criticism. Hence, the intrinsic value of the saints' lives did not necessarily diminish, but most certainly shifted.

Medieval Period

The Medieval Period was the golden age of the "lives of the saints." Individual lives and collections of lives abounded. Numerous authors vividly portrayed heroes of the Christian Faith. Devotion to their dear Lord super-abounded, with prayers and visions, good works and miracles.

The myriad details of their lives were not arbitrarily thrown together, but purposefully ordered.

Accuracy was a major concern. Already in the Early Church, the saints' lives were quite extraordinary, be it extreme devotion or wondrous signs. These attributes continued to be characteristic of the saints' lives in the Medieval Period. Questions concerning the validity of the data were often addressed by the author. Bede cited ecclesial documents and respected churchmen as his sources. Others claimed firsthand knowledge. Einhard and Walter Daniel were close contemporaries of their subjects, and thus, eyewitnesses of their subjects.[28] This, of course, was also true of an auto-biographical document. In his Minor Life, Bonaventure claimed that many had witnessed the stigmata of Francis and in addition taken an oath that their witness of these were true.

Modeling was one of the chief purposes of these documents. In his Dialogues, Gregory narrated the lives of Italian saints for the express purpose of inspiring the Italian Christians of his day.[29] Past Christian lives were not to be forgotten, but embraced for their spiritual value to later Christians.

Miracles were a rather common trait among these Christians. Gregory showed that Benedict's miracles flowed directly from the miracles of Holy Scripture. In addition, Columba's miracles were accomplished with the divine assistance of Jesus.

The distinction between beatification and canonization of the saints was established during this time. Already in the Early Church, local bishops oversaw the veneration of local martyrs. As the fame of certain martyrs and other Christians grew, their veneration frequently exceeded their local ecclesial boundaries. Pope Alexander III (d. 1181) decreed that no departed Christian was to be venerated throughout the Church without the authorization of the Bishop of Rome. Hence, this distinction arose: beatified Christians were venerated locally at the behest of the local bishop, whereas the Bishop of Rome must canonize a saint if he was to be venerated universally.

Great reverence was conferred upon the saints. In his Summa Theologica, Thomas Aquinas delineated this veneration. First, Christians could pray to saints who were asleep in the Lord. These prayers differed from prayers to God in that the latter were divinely received and answered, whereas the former were no different than petitions to fellow Christians and angels that they would pray to God on another's behalf.[30] Second, Christians could venerate the relics of saints and the Virgin Mary if properly understood. According to Thomas, the highest form of worship (latria) was reserved for God alone, while a lesser veneration (dulia) was to be directed to the relics of the saints. In addition, the Mother of God was worthy of a greater veneration (hyperdulia) than that given to the saints, but remained inferior to the worship offered to the one true God.[31]

Reformation Period

The reformers were very much interested in the roles of Christian lives in the church. On the one hand, they questioned a good part of the Medieval analysis of the saints.[32] In particular, they expressed misgivings of those saints' lives that were obviously exaggerated,[33] if not fabricated. They additionally showed varying degrees of misgiving concerning prayers to the saints and the veneration of their relics. On the other hand, they filled the void they created with a careful analysis of the roles for Christian lives in the church.

Accuracy remained a key issue. Philip Melanchthon used personal experiences and data from Martin Luther's family in his biographical sketches. In portraying John Gerhard, Erdmann Fischer had access to many of John's handwritten manuscripts, as well as numerous funeral sermons and lives.

In Acts and Monuments, John Foxe rejected the medieval practice of praying to Mary as idolatry: He did not make the fine distinction between latria and (hyper-) dulia as had Aquinas. This error manifested itself in the practice of praying more frequently the Ave Maria then the Pater Noster. On a positive note, Foxe commended the martyrs of the church and noted numerous parallels between Polycarp in the Early Church and John Hooper in the Reformation Period.[34]

In the Augsburg Confession (1530) and the Apology of the Augsburg Confession (1531), Philip Melanchthon took the medieval practices to task. On the one hand, he acknowledged that angels pray for us on specific matters, whereas saints in heaven pray for us in general. On the other hand, Holy Scripture nowhere instructed Christians to pray to the saints. Moreover, Melanchthon utterly rejected that the saints in heaven are intercessors or propitiators on behalf of Christians on earth as this is the proper work of the ascended Lord. On a similar note, the notion of patron saints—a particular saint provides a particular service—erroneously directed the Christian's trust away from the Creator to the creation.

Melanchthon filled up the theological vacuum created by his critique of Medieval Catholicism with the proper roles of the saints in the church. Christians now sleeping in the Lord were to be neither forgotten nor slighted. Instead, the Christian Church honored her saints through giving thanks to God for their lives, the strengthening of faith through their lives, and contemporary imitation of their lives.[35]

While the Roman Catholic Church retained her medieval understanding of the saints, the Protestants modified it. As such, the Protestants revered the saints, only according to their understanding, in a manner that remained faithful to Holy Scripture.

Modern Period

The Modern Period variously analyzed the role of the saints for contemporary times. The Roman Catholic Church retained her practice of beatification and canonization of the saints. Likewise, the heirs of the reformers remained more than leery of the remnants of Medieval Catholicism in this area, nevertheless, continued to honor devoutly the saints' lives, particularly those of their respective traditions. Others in the Modern Period much more aggressively examined the biographical data of the Western Church.

The Bollandists were named after John van Bolland (1596–1665), a Jesuit and the first editor of the Acta Sanctorum, a critical edition of the lives of the saints. His work has continued among his vocational heirs, the most recent notable being Hippolyte Delehaye. In The Legend of the Saints, Delehaye examined hagiography. Hagiography, according to Delehaye, does not refer to all documents that contain biographical data concerning the saints. It may be historical, but not necessarily. Instead, hagiography refers to those biographical documents that are "inspired by devotion to the saint and intended to promote it".[36] Hence, hagiographic documents are often legendary in nature: fiction is added to truth to enhance the former life of a saint to inspire more fully the present life of a Christian. According to Delehaye, this is often not done out of a desire to deceive the readers, but rather, to bring attention and honor to one deserving of such.

Summary

The biographical analyses of the Modern Period were quite diverse. Medieval Catholicism revered the saints, so much so, that it flirted with idolatry: they prayed to the saints and venerated their relics and proffered hyperdulia to Mary. The sixteenth-century reformers carefully distinguished between God and His saints, between the Creator and His creation. Yet they recognized the modeling-role of the saints and greatly honored these fathers and mothers of the faith for God's work in and through them. The Bollandists' critical analysis of the saints' lives has proved invaluable for weeding out fanciful stories through textual and academic analyses. Unfortunately, its definition of hagiography has often been applied to the great majority biographical documents in the Church with the tragic result that many of the biographical documents from the history of the Church have been erroneously tossed into the trash heap of historical fiction.

Summary

The Western Church preserved more than a fair amount biographical data. Over a span of fifteen centuries, Christians occupied numerous offices in a church that under went agonizing growing pains: sixteenth century reformation and geographical expansion from Europe to the Americas, Pietism and Rationalism. Serious fissures developed. The pope was greatly revered throughout much of the Medieval Period, but much less honored by the non-Roman Catholics in the Reformation and Modern Periods. Birgitta was a visionary in Sweden, conversely, Charles Krauth was a Lutheran pastor and professor in America. Therese was a devout Christian as a child, whereas C. S. Lewis kicked and fought against Christianity for much of his early life. John Hooper died in England for his anti-Catholicism, while less than a century later, Elizabeth rid England of all that was Romish.

These Christian lives were quite different, yet they can be fitted together as well as any dysfunctional family. Asceticism serves as one fine example. On the one hand, Gregory the Great and Therese of Lisieux were "professional" ascetics. On the other hand, John Calvin and John Hooper were Protestant ascetics who rejected the monastic cowl. All four, nevertheless, lived extremely rigorous lives. Other family traits were common to all Christians in all three periods. Antagonists attacked Peter Abelard, John Hooper, George Whitefield, and Robert Preus. Gregory the Great, Martin Luther, and John Flavel were all pastors. Peter Abelard, John Calvin, C. S. Lewis, and Robert Preus resided primarily within academia. Charles the Great and Elizabeth I were both monarchs. These examples and others illustrate that though their differences were real and significant, they shared common bonds.

Moreover, these western Christians were closely related to their not-so-distant cousins from the Early Church and biblical times. A prime example is the parallel between Augustine and Clives. Both were born into Christian families, but wandered about like prodigals from one spirituality to another. Both were graciously received by their heavenly Father. Both recorded their conversion to the Christian faith in an autobiography. Peter Abelard and Martin Luther and Robert Preus were all academics as had been Origen. Charles the Great and Elizabeth I followed in the train of Constantine in the Early Church and Samson in Bible Times as Christian sovereigns. Similarly, the ascetics of the Western Church and Early Church resembled the lives of Samson and John the Baptist. The comparisons are numerous.

Furthermore, these Western Church lives flowed directly from the life of Christ. The Sacraments of Holy Baptism and the Lord's Supper repeatedly surfaced. In these, Christians living many centuries after Jesus and in faraway lands continued to participate very intimately in the life of Christ. In addition, preachers promulgated the salvific message of Jesus; miracle workers continued those of Jesus; Christian sovereigns were not unlike the King of the Kingdom of God. In these and others, Western Christian lives were intimately connected to and flowed from the life of Christ.

Consequently, the continued growth of the Western church produced a somewhat wieldy family of God. During this time, it appeared that the one family was breaking up into many smaller families. However, when they are forced to stand together in this biographical light, it becomes obvious that they have more in common then at first is apparent: All were intimately related to the life of Christ through Baptism and faith, through the Lord's Supper and their respective offices.

5

EASTERN CHRISTIANITY

AD 500–Present

Early Church Christians in Egypt, Palestine, Greece, and Asia Minor were the progenitors of Christian lives in later Eastern Christianity. This spiritual lineage can be seen in the patriarchs of Constantinople: Paul (d. 350) and Chrysostom (ca. 347–407) in the Early Church were succeeded by Germanus (ca. 634–ca. 733) and Photius (ca. 810–ca. 895). Similarly, the patristic stylites Simeon (ca. 390–459) and Daniel (d. 493) preceded the pillar sitting of Alypius (sixth century) and Luke the Younger (tenth century). Emperor Constantine (d. 337) was the Early Church precursor of Prince Vladimir of Kiev (956–1015). Eastern Christianity directly flowed out of the eastern portion of the Early Church.

Eastern Christianity exhibited a number of distinct characteristics. In contrast to the west, the east began with Constantinople as its ecclesial capital, spoke and wrote Greek, and was Byzantine. All of these changed as Eastern Christianity expanded into Eastern Europe, Russia, and other corners of the world. Mysticism, though, has remained a constant theme and thoroughly pervaded the Eastern Church. Although the east is quite concrete—patriarchs and sacraments and icons—the mystical nature of God and the Church and Christian lives is certainly underscored. This is evident in asceticism in general and in hesychasm and theosis in particular.

The biographical literature of Eastern Christianity is immense. While it is quite diverse, it does not mirror the stark contrasts of the rifts in the west. The east's sustained emphasis upon tradition, to a large degree, safeguards the smooth continuation and close correlation of Christian lives. For example, the nineteenth century Russian wanderer in the Way of a Pilgrim searched for practical advice for his spiritual life from contemporary Orthodox Christians, but was ultimately directed to the sayings of earlier Eastern Christians in the Philokalia. Consequently, the corpus of biographical data in Eastern Christianity depicted Christian lives that were closely related to other Christian lives through the sacraments of Baptism and the Lord's Supper, through common family traits and shared offices.

Byzantium and Russia

The Eastern Church developed according to time and place. It began, in part, with Constantine establishing Constantinople upon the city of Byzantium. For this reason, the east is often referred to as the Byzantine Empire or the Byzantine Church, or even Byzantium referring to both. With Constantinople as the eastern capital of the Empire in the Early Church, this created two distinct ecclesial polls: Rome in the west and Constantinople in the east. Separated by geography, language, culture, and a rivalry over authority in the Church, these two gradually grew apart.

One of the more disruptive issues was the filioque, "and the Son." At the Council of Constantinople I (381), the holy fathers confessed in the third article of the Nicaea-Constantinopolitan Creed that the Holy Spirit proceeded from the Father (John 15:26). At the Council of Toledo III (589), the west amended the creed to confess that the Holy Spirit proceeded from the Father and the Son, filioque. The east rejected this later addition, and the feud began. This theological quarrel, combined with many other issues and differing viewpoints, fully manifested itself in 1054 in what is commonly termed the Great Schism. Each side excommunicated the other—the division between east and west was complete.

Constantinople remained the preeminent center of the east until 1453 when the Muslims finally overwhelmed Constantinople. Eastern Christianity had already sent missionaries into Eastern Europe and Russia. Against many odds, the Christian faith steadily grew, particularly in Russia. With the fall of Constantinople, Moscow became the new ecclesial capital of the Eastern Christianity. The rich theology, asceticism, liturgy, and icons of Byzantium were then translated to Russia where they were given the opportunity to further mature. This is also true of the various offices.

Sovereign. A number of Christian sovereigns in Eastern Christianity integrated their Christian faith with their secular rule. Empress Irene (752–803) reinforced the veneration of icons in the Byzantine Empire following the Council of Nicaea II (787). Prince Vladimir of Kiev more than strongly urged his people to convert to Christianity. Tsar Peter the Great (1672–1725) supplanted the authority of the patriarch with an ecclesial council in Russia.

Patriarch. The highest authority in the Eastern Church was termed a patriarch. The patriarch was not only the bishop of the local church, but oversaw other bishops in the surrounding locales. In the latter half of the Early Church, the five principle patriarchs resided in Alexandria, Antioch, Constantinople, Jerusalem, and Rome, the patriarch of Constantinople being preeminent in the East. Following the fall of Constantinople, ecclesial influence in the East shifted to the patriarch of Moscow. In Moscow, Nikon (1605–81) was responsible for realigning the Russian liturgy with that of the Greeks.

Ascetic. In the Early Church, St. Basil (358–64) produced a Rule (actually two, a long and a short rule) that was commonly utilized in Eastern Christianity. Developments upon this included those of St. Simeon the New Theologian (949–1022) and Joseph Volotsky (1440–1515). Hermits and coenobitic communities abounded throughout the east. Numerous monasteries were located upon Mount Athos.

Fool for Christ. One of the distinct forms of eastern monasticism included the Fool for Christ. Based upon the words of the apostle Paul (1 Corinthians 4:10), these ascetics acted foolishly for the sake of Jesus and the Gospel. For example, they might feast during a fast or vice versa. One would visit a prostitute, not to purchase her services, but to encourage her to repent and change her life. Another would silently suffer for offences not committed. These fools raised important concerns in their day and caused other Christians to give thought to their beliefs and actions.

Hesychast. Hesychasm is defined as silent and inner prayer. It often repeats a short phrase such as a psalm verse. Most commonly, it utilizes the Jesus Prayer: "Lord Jesus Christ, Son of God, have mercy upon me, a sinner" or some variation thereof. This prayer is repeated over and over until it is no longer spoken with the mouth, but ceaselessly recited in the heart. Hesychasts were not required to be hermits, but to recite the Jesus Prayer while they ate, conversed, worked, and slept.

Starets. Staret simply means "elder" in Russian. However, it refers to a wise individual, usually an ascetic, who provides spiritual direction. They are greatly revered for their spiritual acumen in assisting others in their spiritual journeys.

Missionary. Eastern Christianity was not complacent in Byzantium, but extended her spiritual borders. Constantine (Cyril) and Methodius (ninth century) spoke the word of God to the Saracens and Khazars. Later, the patriarch of Constantinople sent them to the Moravians. When their journey to Moravia was briefly delayed, they evangelized the nearby Russians. Ioann Veniaminov, St. Innocent, (nineteenth century) was a Russian priest who catechized, preached, and administered the sacraments among the Aleuts in Alaska.

John the Almsgiver	Time: ca. 550–616
	Places: Cyprus and Alexandria
	Office: Bishop
	Biography: *Life of Our Holy Father, John the Almsgiver*[1]
	Biographers: Sophronius (d. ca. 637) and John Moschus (b. ca. 545)

Sophronius and John Moschus portrayed a most kind and generous Christian man. John took his responsibilities to heart—he cared deeply for and served selflessly those around him. For his faithful and giving service, he has been granted the title of almsgiver.

John's twofold family life was virtuous. He was born into the first. His father, Epiphanius, was esteemed in the civil realm and was an official in Cyprus. In addition, his highly principled life was well known to all in the church. Likewise, his mother was an honorable wife and mother. In this Christian family, John flourished. He received a fine education and was instructed to fear God. He developed not only physically, but spiritually as had John the Baptist and Jesus (Luke 1:90; 2:40). John married into his second virtuous family not because he desired a wife, but under coercion by his father. John highly revered celibacy, so he and his wife abstained from sexual intercourse until his father-in-law demanded that he fulfill his marital vows. John then fathered a host of children.

John's life changed quite drastically. He lost his children to death while they were still young. Shortly after this, his wife died. John was resolute in his response: He forsook temporal matters and embarked upon a more spiritual life. Word of his service to others spread throughout the Empire. At the behest of Emperor Heraclius, Nicetas of Constantinople, and the people of Alexandria, John became the patriarch of Alexandria.

The Episcopal work of John was twofold. On the one hand, he was a faithful proponent of the Orthodox faith. He re-established the use of the orthodox liturgy in the Alexandrian churches. Moreover, he accepted no monies for clerical services performed in accordance with Solomon (Proverbs 15:27) and church law. Furthermore, he required that his clergy reject all heresy and confess the faith of the Ecumenical Councils. On the other hand, his overarching concern was for the poor. He provided homes for the needy and lodging for travelers and hospitals for the sick. He made certain that prisoners were fed and churches were provided for all. When Persia destroyed Jerusalem, John greatly lamented as had the prophet Jeremiah. His sorrow moved him to action and he sent provisions to the Christians there and ransomed thousands of captives from the Persians.

John's death was surrounded by tumult. A certain man named Isaac conspired to kill John, but God intervened and protected him, while Isaac was brutally murdered. As the Persian army closed in on Alexandria, John retreated to his hometown in Cyprus. There, John left this earthly life to be joined to his dear Lord in the heavenly realm.

John was portrayed as part of the holy family. He was born into a devout Christian family. He followed after Jesus in being a patriarch and an almsgiver (Matthew 25) and in being attacked by an antagonist while protected by God. Death for John was not the end, but merely the beginning of eternal life in the Lord.

John of Damascus	Time: 676–ca. 750
	Place: Damascus
	Offices: Ascetic, Apologist, Hymnographer
	Biography: *Great Collection of the Lives of the Saints*[2]
	Biographer: Demetrius of Rostov (1651–1709)

The life of John was blessed both in the secular and sacred realms. With God's help, he was able to withstand persecution and oppression and he persevered. As a servant, John faithfully served God and His Church on earth.

John was born in Damascus of a pious Christian family. They remained faithful to the Christian Church in the midst of the Saracens who ruled the land and persecuted Christians in manifold manners. His father, like Joseph in Egypt and Daniel in Babylonia, held a public office, enabling him to give comfort and aid to fellow Christians. It was in this context that John was baptized and taught the virtuous life by his parents and instructed in the Christian faith by Cosmas, a monk captured by these Muslims and spared for this noble deed.

Under the tutelage of Cosmas, John became academically astute in worldly matters, like astronomy, mathematics, and rhetoric. He also learned to compose ecclesial poetry and studied theology and Christian morality. Though John quickly advanced in his studies and even surpassed Cosmas, he took no pride in his achievements. With the death of his father, John took his position under the Saracen Caliph, though he had his sights set on more spiritual affairs.

At this time Emperor Leo ruled the Byzantine Empire. He was an iconoclast and purged the Christian Church of her sacred images of Jesus and the saints. Unable to bear this demonic attack upon the church of God, John's fervor for the church paralleled that of Elisha. He wielded a pen as a sword in defending the use of icons in the church.

Emperor Leo was an evil man. He had scribes forge a letter from John to Leo in which the former petitioned the latter to send an army to Damascus. Once there, John would deliver the town to Leo. Leo then sent this spurious epistle to the Muslim Caliph in Damascus. Unwilling to listen to John's defense, the Caliph had John's right hand amputated. After hanging it in the public square, the Caliph returned it to John. Kneeling before an icon of Mary, the mother of Jesus, he prayed to her. That night in his sleep, Mary told him in a dream that his hand had been reattached. And so it was in the morning. A red mark on his wrist remained as a sign of this wonder, and the clothe that he used to bandage his severed wrist he wore throughout his life upon his head.[3]

The Caliph repented of his unjust punishment. While he wished to promote John and give to him more authority and power, John begged to be released from his civil service in order to serve his Lord more fully. Granted a peaceful release, John gave his possessions to the poor and set out for the Holy City and there joined the monastery of St. Sabbbas, where he was instructed in asceticism by a elderly sage monk. John listened to him and grew in his spiritual life: fasting and simplicity of dress, humility, and obedience.

One day a grieving monk petitioned John to compose a hymn to comfort him. John refused because he had not been permitted to do so by his elder. Like the judge in relation to the persistent widow, John finally relented and hymned for the man. When his elder heard of this, he imposed a severe penance upon John and forbade him to write or compose. Not long after, Mary, the mother of Jesus, chided the elder in a dream for stopping up a sweet spring. The next morning, the elder instructed John not to speak of legends and lies, but to resume writing books and composing hymns that would benefit the Church. In addition, he penned lives of the saints and sermons and prayers. He also wrote polemics against the iconoclasts. These he composed as he finished his days at the monastery of St. Sabbas.

John is portrayed as a blessed child of God and one among many siblings in the family of God. He was the heir of a spiritual Joseph and Daniel. He acted like Elisha. The Mother of God spoke to him in a dream and healed his injury. In addition, he displayed the virtuous actions of his divine family. Most importantly, John was faithful to his heavenly Father, and his heavenly Father faithfully watched over and preserved His blessed son.

Constantine (Cyril)	Time: 826–69
	Places: Thessalonica, Olympus, and Moravia
	Offices: Professor, Ascetic, Missionary
	Biography: *Life of Constantine*

Methodius	Time: 815–85
	Places: Thessalonica, Olympus, and Moravia
	Offices: Ascetic, Missionary, Bishop
	Biography: *Life of Methodius*

Brothers Constantine and Methodius worked together harmoniously in the Christian Church. Academia called Constantine at first, while Methodius initially lived as an ascetic. In their final mission work, the unique abilities of these Apostles to the Slavs complemented each other: Constantine assigned letters to the spoken Slavic language, while Methodius served them as bishop.

Constantine and Methodius were born into a Christian family at Thessalonica. Their father, Leo, lived piously, like Job. Constantine was the youngest of seven and his parents mutually agreed to refrain from sexual intercourse following his birth. Family and friends spoke well of Methodius. Constantine, at the age of 7, dreamt that when a military officer ordered him to choose a wife from all of the young girls in the city, he chose the most lovely of all, Sophia, which means wisdom. His parents knew that Constantine chose the "wisdom" that is spoken of in the Book of Proverbs, and this dream foretold his life in the service of his dear Lord Jesus.

Early on, their careers took them down divergent paths. The Emperor appointed Methodius a governor. Constantine went to Constantinople and studied with Leo and Photius, future bishops of Thessalonica and

Constantinople, and he mastered all of the arts. Even in his youth, Constantine reveled in learning and his favorite lesson was Gregory of Nazianzus. He lived chastely and withdrew to become a monk, but was persuaded to return and teach in Constantinople.

Constantine's work was difficult if not dangerous. In Constantinople, he disputed the role of images in the church with the iconoclastic patriarch John. He then contended with the Hagarites, Muslims. These Saracens blasphemed the Holy Trinity, but Constantine faithfully defended the Christian faith. When they tried to poison him, his dear Lord protected him as promised in Holy Writ (Mark 16:18).

Their lives crossed paths at Mount Olympus, where both lived as monks. After a short monastic residence, the emperor sent them to the Khazars, who had converted to the Jewish faith, wherein Constantine defended the Christian faith. When they rejected the Holy Trinity, Constantine argued that when you honor a man, you also honor his word and his spirit, i.e., the Father, Son, and Holy Spirit. With many more words and deliberations, 200 Khazars were baptized into the Christian faith, and the Khazan ruler praised Constantine in a letter to the emperor. On their return trip, Constantine turned bitter water sweet as had Moses in the wilderness (Exodus 15:23–25). Though Methodius refused a bishopric, the patriarch of Constantinople assigned him to be the archimandrite of the Polychron monastery at Mount Olympus.

At this time, Rostislav and other princes of Moravia sent an envoy to Emperor Michael in Constantinople. Missionaries from the west were already in Moravia and had converted many to Christianity, but the people desired to be taught in their native Slavic tongue. The emperor sent Constantine and Methodius, and they departed in devoted submission to the apostolic command: "Fear God. Honor the emperor" (1 Peter 2:17). They not only taught the Christian faith to the people in the Slavic language, but Constantine soon created a Slavic alphabet. Holy Scripture was translated into Slavic, as was the holy liturgy.

Distraught that the word of God had been translated into the vernacular and worried that the people might hear and understand it, the devil attacked their labors. In Moravia, the evil one spawned what came to be known as the trilingual heresy: Holy Scripture could be written in no languages other than Hebrew, Greek, or Latin. Thus, according to some, Constantine and Methodius had erred; their labors were a sham. They traveled to Venice and heard more of the same. Constantine responded to this false accusation with the word of God: "Every tongue confess that Jesus Christ is Lord" (Philippians 2:11).

Constantine and Methodius then traveled to Rome. The people of Rome afforded them due reverence, while Constantine and Methodius brought with them the relics of St. Clement. Pope Nicholas placed the Slavic Scriptures upon the altar, and the Slavic liturgy was sung. Nicholas commended their translations. After a brief illness, Constantine died in Rome on February 14.

Nicholas consecrated Methodius a bishop and sent him back to Moravia. Initially, the devil took the upper hand—he turned both civil and ecclesial leaders against Methodius and imprisoned him for over two years. However, the spiritual tide changed. During his captivity, Nicholas banned Masses in Moravia, and four bishops died. Finally, the Moravians drove out the Germans and made Methodius their archbishop. During his tenure, the church in Moravia flourished.

Methodius died April 6, twenty-four years following Constantine. With his last breath, he said: "Father, into your hands I commit my spirit!" (Luke 23:46). The funeral was sung in Latin, Greek, and Slavic, and attended by a throng of the faithful from every station of life.

These two sons of pious Leo were also sons of their heavenly Father. They were born into a Christian family like Jesus. Constantine taught and performed miracles as did Jesus. Methodius lived a rigorous life and was a bishop. Both, as missionaries, carried out the apostolic commission. They suffered under antagonists. In their deaths, Constantine was joined with an early bishop of Rome and Methodius was joined with the many faithful: "He was gathered unto his fathers, unto the patriarchs and prophets, unto the apostles, teachers and martyrs."[4] Therefore, they were closely related to the life of Christ.

Mary the Younger   Time: ca. 875–ca. 903
Place: Constantinople, Vizye in Thrace
Office: Housewife
Biography: *Life of Mary the Younger*

The life of Mary was spectacular in its simplicity. She was a daughter and wife and mother. While these are quite common, she acted in a rather uncommon manner. She loved her children, was faithful to her husband, and cared for those around her who were without financial means. Though she held no official office, she was a devout Christian.

The father of Mary moved from Armenia to Constantinople. There he presented himself to Emperor Basil, who was responsible for the death of the drunkard Michael who preceded him upon the throne. Basil granted Mary's father gifts, placed him into high office, and honored him. Mary was the youngest of five children and married Nikephorus.

Mary's first son was called Orestes. When he died while still a young child, others cried and lamented loudly, but Mary gave thanks to God and patiently bore her suffering as had Job. She acted similarly with the youthful death of Vardanes, her second son. Later, she gave birth to twins, Vaanes and Stephen. Looking upon their birthmarks, Mary foretold that the former would become a soldier, while the latter an ascetic, and so it happened.

The virtues of Mary were quite evident: She had a beautiful soul and fervent spirit. She properly cared for her home and family. She was humble and charitable—she gave alms to widows, orphans, ascetics, and foreigners. She was kind and pious, often praying and fasting. Her greatest love was for God and His Church. She revered the priests and esteemed the monks; she faithfully attended services, and the hymns of the church were ever upon her lips.

Mary's virtues did not go unseen by the tempter. He instigated her sister-in-laws to accuse her falsely of committing adultery with a servant. Her husband believed these falsehoods and turned against her. Also, the steward of the household treated Mary severely. In addition to this, she suffered various illnesses.

On the Sunday that began the season of Lent, Mary warned the women with her that they were beset with evil days. Mary feared that her husband erroneously believed that she had committed adultery. This, according to Mary, was a result of the devil's evil wiles, and so, cursed him. A certain man, overhearing these words, misinformed Nikephorus that Mary called him the devil because of his actions toward her. After he beat her unmercifully, she ran away and fell, hurting her head, after which she became deathly sick. On her deathbed, Mary pleaded for Nikephorus to believe in her chastity. Mary then removed her coat and asked a servant to sell it and give the money to the poor. Surrounded by many of the women from town, Mary saw into heaven—a light and a crown—and died.

Following the death of Mary, a fragrant aroma arose from her corpse. Those present marveled at this. After they cleaned her body, no garment could be found save her last as she kept nothing for herself, but gave all that she had to the poor. Learning of this Nikephorus had one of his garments altered to fit her and look proper upon a lady. Archbishop Euthymios preached at her funeral. The litany of her charitable services brought tears to many eyes.

Numerous miracles occurred in relation to Mary after her death. On one occasion, a mother had a tormented daughter. The girl was out of her mind and acted intolerably. Physicians were unable to cure her. Finally, the mother took her to the tomb of Mary. Removing a bit of oil from the lamp there, she anointed her daughter and immediately she recovered. In the same manner a blind man and a blind woman received their sight. Many pilgrimages were made to Mary's tomb and many miracles occurred.

Mary clearly resided in the family of God. She was a faithful wife and mother. She suffered much in regard to both as does the Bride of Christ, the Church, in her life. Moreover, Mary could not forget the words of Jesus to feed the hungry and clothe the naked (Matthew 25). The signs and wonders surrounding her death attest to the fact that she was a holy one and the heavenly Father's favor rested upon her.

Irene	Time: d. ca. 940
	Place: Chrysobalanton
	Office: Abbess
	Biography: *Life and Conduct of Our Holy Mother Irene*

Irene was portrayed as an extraordinary Christian. Her exceptional character was predicted early in her life and illustrated throughout her career as a nun and abbess. She was too humble to desire the position, but despite and because of her humility, Jesus worked powerfully through her at Chrysobalanton.

Irene was raised in Cappadocia by a Christian family. Not only was she more fair than other women, she was virtuous and faithful to Orthodoxy. Her family sent her to Constantinople in hopes of marrying the son of the empress. On her journey, a holy man prophesied that Irene would become the abbess of the convent at Chrysobalanton. Upon arriving at Constantinople, all thought that she was a perfect match for the heir to the throne. The empress lavished her with gifts, but her dear Lord thought differently. Irene forsook this earthly marriage and sought a spiritual marriage with Jesus.

Irene happened upon the convent of Chrysobalanton in Constantinople and remembered the prophesy of the holy man. Immediately, she shed her jewels, shaved her head, and exchanged her luxurious attire for coarse apparel. Irene took a vow, after which she humbly obeyed her abbess and diligently served her sisters. She studied Holy Scripture and the lives of the saints. Very early in her career, she began her imitation of St. Arsenios—standing through the night with arms outstretched to the east—and treated it not as a burden, but rest.

Irene's humble asceticism—spurning luxury and honor, copiously shedding tears, and often fasting—angered the devil, so he and his evil demons repeatedly accosted her. On one occasion, he appeared to her as a sinister and repulsive specter. To his invectives she merely made the sign of the cross and he took flight. The more he tempted her, the more she immersed herself in the word of God. She invoked the company of heaven and her tears drenched the floor. God sent His Spirit to guard her from Satan.

At another time, a horde of demons assaulted her. They reviled her, however, Irene ignored them as though she was not there but in heaven. One of the demons then kindled a fire that ignited her clothing. Unattentive of this, she was engulfed in flames. A nun, praying during the night, smelled the smoke and extinguished it before the flames consumed Irene. The fire had burned Irene's flesh, but rather than the pungent smell of burned flesh, her wounds were sweet-smelling. Irene's single garment was destroyed, so she received another. Word of Irene's victorious spiritual conflicts spread, and she inspired many to become ascetics.

With the death of the abbess at Chrysobalanton, the nuns visited the renowned patriarch of Constantinople who had suffered under the iconoclasts, received visions, and performed miracles. Guided by God, he selected Irene. After consecrating her, he spoke to these women about their respective responsibilities. He then bade them return to their convent in peace.

Irene faithfully instructed the women of the monastic ideals. They have been called to forsake all: external possessions and internal desires. They must be virtuous and humble, as commanded by Jesus: "Blessed are the poor in spirit" (Matthew 5:3). They must be enemies of the world, rather than enemies of God. The women at Chrysobalanton grew in their asceticism under the tutelage of Irene.

A number of other notable events occurred in Irene's ascetic life. As an abbess, she prayed for "second vision," the ability to know the secrets of her nuns. An angel appeared and revealed to her that God had heard her prayer and would graciously grant her petition. She prophesied of the death of the emperor and his uncle, her brother-in-law. Once she knelt before God outdoors and two cypress trees imitated her. They did not rise until she made the sign of the cross before each of them. She appeared to the emperor in a vision and instructed him to release an innocent prisoner.

On the day dedicated to the archangel Gabriel, the Holy Spirit revealed to Irene that her death was imminent. In preparation, she fasted and received the Lord's Supper; she prayed and shed tears. She told the nuns of her death and gave to them final instructions on spiritual matters. At the moment of death, her face shone brightly. The women greatly lamented as did all the faithful in Constantinople. Many came to touch and view her body, which exuded a fragrant scent. She was entombed in the Chapel of Theodore.

Irene was a faithful member of the family of God. She was a virgin and an ascetic. Though she was not a male, and could not be a priest or patriarch, she faithfully led her community of female coenobitics as an abbess. Like Jesus, the evil foe attacked her, and by the protection of Jesus she survived.

Vladimir   Time: 965–1015
             Place: Kiev
             Office: Prince
             Biography: *Russian Primary Chronicle* (1116)
             Biographer: Sylvester[5]

Vladimir was converted from paganism to Christianity through the sacrament of Holy Baptism. As the prince of Kiev, he facilitated the conversion of his people from godlessness to godliness.

The family of Vladimir was pagan with one exception. His grandmother, Olga (d. 969), was ruthless as were her kin. Upon her visit to the emperor in Constantinople, she was baptized by the patriarch and took the name Helena. There, she prayed and diligently studied the teachings of Christianity. The patriarch prophesied that she would be the precursor of the Christian Church in Russia. This did not happen immediately, as her son and two grandsons, Yaropolk and Oleg, rejected the faith. Her third grandson, Vladimir, was not interested in Christianity at first.

With the death of Vladimir's father and Oleg, Vladimir plotted against Yaropolk and had him put to death. Vladimir then became the sole prince of Kiev. Vladimir erected pagan altars and demonic effigies. He and his people worshiped these false gods.

The villainy and sacrilege of Vladimir was matched, if not exceeded, by his sexual depravity. He impregnated the Greek wife of Yaropolk, to whom he was not married, and she bore a son. He fathered Boris and Gleb by a Bulgarian woman. Rogned, his wife, gave him six children. Moreover, Vladimir spoiled young girls and ravaged married women. Furthermore, his concubines numbered eight hundred. Vladimir followed in the stead of ancient Solomon.

Varying religious proponents approached Vladimir. The Bulgars proposed Islam. Their practices required circumcision and forbade wine and pork. Yet they promised riches and wives beyond compare in the next world. The Germans urged upon him Medieval Catholicism. They believed in the Creator of all that exists and moderate fasting. The Khazars recommended Judaism. They revered the one God, the God of Abraham, Isaac, and Jacob; but also confessed that their God had expelled them from their land and given it to the Christians. Vladimir rejected all three.

A Greek scholar visited Vladimir and spent many days elaborating upon the teachings of the Christian Church. He began with the Creation, commented upon much of the Old Testament, and showed how salvation was fulfilled in the incarnation. Vladimir was quite taken by this Greek scholar, but his advisors implored him to send envoys and inspect the worship of God by each. The worship of the Bulgars was disgusting. That of the Germans was without merit. There was, however, a divine splendor in the Greek liturgy: priestly robes, exquisite choirs, and delightful incense. His envoys reported that while they did not fully understand all that happened, they confessed that God was present! Vladimir was then reminded that this was the faith of his grandmother.

One year later, Vladimir marched upon the Byzantine Empire. Anna, the sister of the Byzantine emperor, was given to him in marriage in exchange for not attacking Constantinople. The single requirement was that he be baptized. Prior to this, Anna promised him that if he was baptized straightway, then his eye ailment would pass. And so it did when Vladimir was spiritually washed at the Church of St. Basil in Kherson. Vladimir's retinue witnessed this miracle and many of them were baptized also. The tenets of the Christian faith according to the early councils and creeds were again expounded to Vladimir.

Upon his return to Kiev, Vladimir had the idols and their altars profaned and destroyed. Many of the pagans lamented, but Vladimir persisted and sought their conversion. He called all to have their sins washed away. Satan's kingdom groaned, while the Kingdom of God rejoiced. Vladimir constructed St. Basil Church upon the former site of the idols. He had churches built throughout his land and sent priests to baptize and teach the people. He dedicated a church to the Virgin Mary, and it was filled with icons. He rejoiced in the conversion of his people and cared for the needy.

At his death, they returned his body to Kiev where it was placed in a costly casket. The funeral service was held in the Church of the Virgin Mary. The people greatly lamented the death of their earthly prince and spiritual benefactor.

Vladimir's life changed dramatically through repentance. Most significant, he was to Russia what Constantine had been to the Roman Empire; he turned an apostate people into the people of God. The Russian Christians gave thanks to God that He worked through this Christian prince to convert so many and extend the kingdom of God upon the earth.

Theodosius	Time: d. 1074
	Place: Kiev
	Office: Abbot
	Biography: *Life of St Theodosius* (ca. 1080)
	Biographer: Nestor (d. ca. 1115)

Nestor described an ascetic who was both pious and humble. Like Jesus, he always made himself last rather than first so that he might serve others to the glory of God. Because of this, Theodosius was constantly tormented by demons, but honored by the people of God who delighted in his Christian faith and life.

Theodosius was born into a Christian family at Vasilev, near Kiev. According to the custom of the day, the infant was brought to the church. The priest there foresaw the spiritual service of this infant and called him Theodosius. Forty days later Theodosius was brought to the church again for Holy Baptism. He spent his youth being spiritually guided by his devout parents and the Holy Spirit.

As a young boy, Theodosius was quite different from his peers. He chose not to play the games of childhood. Rather than wear the attire provided by his parents, he wore rough and worn-out garments. In addition, he loved to study—particularly about the Christian faith.

Theodosius experienced many difficulties while still young. At the age of 13, his father died, so he took to working in the fields, though this upset his mother. The boy remained constant in his theological interests and secretly joined a group of pilgrims traveling to the Holy Land. Three days gone, his mother and brother tracked him down, punished him, and made him return home. She chained him in their house until he promised not to run off again.

On another occasion, Theodosius lamented that the Lord's Supper was not celebrated regularly because of lack of bread. Theodosius then collected grains of wheat and ground them himself. He baked it so that the church could have bread for the altar, and sold the remaining bread to giving the proceeds to the poor. His friends teased him, and when word reached his mother, she admonished him for bringing derision upon their family. Theodosius, though, explained to his mother the holy work that he was doing for the church: providing the bread in which the body of their Lord was present in the divine mysteries.

While still young, Theodosius ran away from home and traveled to Kiev. He went from one monastery to another, but was not permitted to join because of his youth, and he looked to be a pauper. Finally, he happened upon the hermit Anthony. Theodosius begged him to let him remain with him. Anthony allowed him to stay with him in his cave, not because of his begging, but because he foresaw that this young boy would one day lead a great monastery at that site.

Theodosius received his tonsure from the eminent Nikon. At the age of 15, he was ordained and celebrated the Lord's Supper daily. His life in the caves at Kiev was rather rigorous. He consumed only bread and water during the week and on the weekend a bit of porridge or some vegetables. His day was filled with work and worship.

With the departure of Anthony and later Barlaam, Theodosius became abbot. The community there flourished under his guidance. They lived the pious lives of ascetics and many came to receive blessings. Many monks crowded into the small caves. Finally, Theodosius constructed a monastery in a clearing near the caves and it was called the Caves Monastery. They followed the Rule of the Studion Monastery.

The rigors of Theodosius's life were renowned. He wore a coarse horse hair shirt under his garments. During Lent, Theodosius would dwell in the caves where he was assaulted by demons, but they were unable to cause him to waver in his faith. Making the sign of the cross and singing from the Psalter, demons fled from his presence. After the last prayer office of the day, Theodosius instructed each monk to return to his respective cell and pray rather than gather and converse with others. Theodosius, though he was an abbot, always participated daily in manual labor. On one occasion, the cellarer, responsible for the food and drink of the community, informed Theodosius that there was no wood with which to bake. Rather than order a monk, the abbot himself chopped the needed fuel. In addition, the monastery fed the hungry and clothed the naked, and one day a week they sent bread to the local prison.

Learning of his imminent death from above, the abbot called the monks to speak to them. He told of the forgiveness of sins and the Christian life of fasting and prayer, love and obedience. He blessed Stephen, his successor as abbot. Theodosius prophesied of his death that would occur on the following day—his soul would rise with the morning sun. He died on May 3 and, according to his wishes, his corpse was left unwashed and buried in a secret location—the caves where he began his ascetic life.

Theodosius is portrayed in God's family portrait. Like Jesus, he was interested in his father's business as a young boy. A priest and a hermit foresaw his future service for the Lord and to the Church. He was not interested in the world and its ways, but forsook the world and spent his entire life in service for others—the monks under his care and the indigent about him.

Stephen Nemanja   Time: ca. 1114–1200
Places: Serbia and Mount Athos
Offices: Prince, Ascetic
Biography: *Life of Stephen Nemanja*[6] (1208)
Biographer: St. Sava (ca. 1176–1235)

Sava portrayed the life of Stephen, his father and fellow monk. In this panegyric, no one was as austere and devout an ascetic as Stephen. Stephen faithfully served as prince and monk, and he served as a holy example for those over whom he ruled and those who lived under the monastic rule.

Stephen was born into a Christian family. He was baptized first in the Catholic Church. Later, he was baptized a second time in the Orthodox Church. Stephen was a great prince of Serbia. He restored the land to its rightful heirs. Greater still, he instructed the Serbians on the faith of the Eastern Church through his life and actions. He lived devoutly, he fed the hungry, clothed the naked, and provided for orphans and widows. Churches and monasteries were constructed, and they were filled with sacred books and icons and vessels.

After thirty-seven years of glorious rule, Stephen abdicated his throne to become a monk. His son, Stephen, married the daughter of the Byzantine Emperor and took his father's position. The elder Stephen directed the younger to rule the people fairly and care for the church and her spiritual leaders. His other son, Vukan, was placed in a high position. Stephen directed both to love one another according Jesus' command. After blessing the Serbians, they wailed at his departure for he had been like a father and a shepherd to them.

Stephen forsook his possessions and all things. He joined the Most Holy Lady monastery and took the name Simeon on the Feast of the Annunciation. His wife, Anna, took the name Anastasia and entered a convent.

After two years of monastic life with his youngest son, Sava, his son wandered off to Mount Athos. Like the shepherd who leaves the ninety-nine to find the lost one, Stephen journeyed to Mount Athos to find his son. Together, they lived there. Stephen was greatly admired by the many monks at Mount Athos for his religious life.

At Mount Athos, Stephen lay upon his deathbed. He first instructed Sava and then blessed him. Many monks gathered around him in prayer. In his last days, he neither ate nor drank, but received the body and blood of Jesus in the Holy Supper. He requested an icon of the Mother of God for he had vowed to die in her presence. The morning of his death, he woke up and proclaimed: "Praise God in His sanctuary; praise Him in His mighty heavens! Praise Him for His mighty deeds; praise Him according to His excellent greatness!" (Psalm 150:1–2).[7]

In death, his face remained radiant. His body was taken into the church. The initial service took place following Matins where his body was kissed by all. Services were held for nine days until he was buried. Eight years later, Sava exhumed Stephen's undecayed body and carried the remains to Serbia, just as Jacob's body had been returned to the Promised Land. His sons and the Serbians greatly revered the body of their father and former prince.

Stephen was intimate member of the family of God. He was likened to the holy patriarchs: Abraham, Isaac, and Jacob. He cared for others as did the first. He blessed his sons according to the second. His earthly remains were translated and revered by his people as was the third. Most importantly, he benefited from two births and two burials. In birth and death Christians are most closely connected to Jesus, and Stephen had two of each.

Gregory Palamas **Time: 1296–1359**
Places: Constantinople, Mount Athos, Thessa-
lonica
Offices: Ascetic, Hesychast, Bishop
Biography: *Great Collection of the Lives of the*
Saints
Biographer: Demetrius of Rostov (1651–1709)

Gregory was a significant theologian in the Orthodox Church. His writings defended the Christian faith in general and hesychasm and theosis more specifically. While he was a great theologian, Demetrious shows that he lived a devout Christian life both as an ascetic and an archbishop.

Gregory was born in Constantinople. His Christian parents were devout believers. They saw to it that Gregory received an excellent education in the secular and sacred arts. His father died while Gregory was still young, but his mother encouraged him to continue his studies at which he greatly excelled.

At the tender age of 12, Gregory resolved to forsake this world and become a monk. After his mother consented, she and his sisters entered a convent, while he along with his brothers traveled to Mount Athos and there joined a monastery. Under the direction of the devout Nicodemus, Gregory advanced significantly in his spiritual life. Mary, the mother of Jesus, visited him in a dream. After the death of his spiritual guide, he entered the wilderness where he lived a very rigorous life and persevered against the myriad and loathsome temptations of the evil one. At this time, God granted to Gregory the ability to heal bodies and souls of their respective ills.

Gregory was ordained a priest. His celebration of the mysteries of God led many to repent and trust in the mercy of God. During this time, the persecutions of the evil one did not diminish, but increased. These temptations did not dishearten Gregory, but purified him and glorified God.

Gregory's most heinous antagonist was Barlaam of Calabria. The latter professed the ancient heresy of Arius: Jesus was created, and to say otherwise was polytheism. Causing quite a stir among Christians, Gregory was chosen to represent the Church of Constantinople at a council. From his lips flowed words that cleansed the church of Barlaam's heresies. The followers of Barlaam continued to attack Gregory, but to no avail: Gregory routed them one after another. Later being appointed as Archbishop of Thessalonica, Gregory not only cared for the souls in that location, but continued to speak at church councils and write erudite treatises in defense of the orthodox faith against all of the heretics of the day.

Gregory's orthodox doctrine was paralleled only by his pious life. Though he fought valiantly against the devil, he repented often of his sins. He lived a rigorous life in the desert, and he faithfully served the people of God in Thessalonica for thirty years.

The life of Gregory was in sync with many Christians before him. He was born into a devout Christian family as was John the Baptist and Jesus. He defended the Christian faith as had John of Damascus. He lived a rigorous ascetic life like Theodosius. He was a leader of the Church not unlike John the Almsgiver. Above all, Gregory followed in the train of Jesus in all of these offices.

Sergius	**Time:** ca. 1314–ca. 1392
	Places: Rostov and Radonezh
	Offices: Abbot, Miracle Worker
	Biography: *Life and Miracles of Holy Abbot Sergius*[8]
	Biographer: Epiphanius the Wise (d. ca. 1420)

Epiphanius portrayed the ascetic life of the famous Russian ascetic. Though Sergius sought the solitude of a hermit, he became a renowned abbot. However, he remained resolutely humble. Sergius's life was both simple and extraordinary.

Cyril and Mary were virtuous Christians who gave birth to three sons and raised them in the fear and love of God. Sergius, the middle son, was unsuccessful in his studies, and this caused him not a little grief. After praying for divine intervention, he met a revered monk who looked like an angel. This man kissed the boy and asked his desire. Sergius explained his academic difficulties and his desire to comprehend Holy Scripture. After this man fed a sweet bread to him, Sergius brought him back to meet his parents. Then the man straightway took Sergius to the chapel where he instructed him to read the Psalms. Sergius reminded him that he was unable to read, whereupon the man blessed Sergius and Sergius began to read the Psalms. The man then blessed Sergius's parents and foretold them of their son's future service for the Lord in His church. Without notice, he disappeared from their presence.

Sergius began his holy training in earnest. He obeyed his parents and lived a pure life. He participated in the liturgy and examined the holy writings of the church. Because of political strife at this time, his family moved from Rostov to Radonezh.

Sergius wished to become a monk, but promised to care for his parents until their deaths. Forty days after their burials, he gave his inheritance to his younger brother, while he and his older brother sought a desolate place to live an eremitic life. They built a chapel and a local priest dedicated it to the Holy Trinity. (His older brother then went to the Monastery of the Epiphany in Moscow. There he lived a devout ascetic life, and later, he was ordained and became an abbot.) Mitrophan, a priest and abbot, visited Sergius and tonsured him. After this, Sergius received the Lord's Supper and remained in the chapel for seven days singing Psalms and receiving no sustenance save the eucharistic bread.

Never alone in the wilderness, the devil tempted him, and he was surrounded by wild animals. He befriended a bear; they both ate bread and, at times, both went without. Sergius studied the word of God and meditated upon it. After a few years, a small number of monks joined him, and they built more cells. Sergius led them in the prayer offices, while a local priest administered the Lord's Supper to this modest spiritual community. They worked and prayed.

When the abbot who tonsured Sergius died, his fellow-monks begged Sergius to take his place. Sergius adamantly refused at first, but relented because of the monks' need and the command of the bishop who ordained him priest and consecrated him abbot. The monastery grew steadily during his tenure. An archimandrite submitted himself to Sergius's guidance. The Lord's Supper was celebrated daily. Sergius labored exhaustively, from baking the eucharistic bread to upholding zealously the monastic rule, including reprimanding garrulous monks. The laity often gave gifts to the monastery, though Sergius always wore old, worn out clothing.

Sergius performed many miracles. Once, the monks complained because they had to haul water a great distance to the monastery. They inquired of Sergius why he had chosen such an arid location. Sergius responded that he had gone into the wilderness to worship the Holy Trinity in solitude. God, though, had determined that a monastery should be built there. Sergius then went to a low spot near the monastery. He made the sign of the cross over a small puddle, and immediately, it became a spring of fresh water. Many diseased were healed by this water. In addition, Sergius raised the dead, cast out demons, saw visions, and foretold the future.

With Sergius's life drawing to a close, he assembled his monks about him. He encouraged them to remain faithful to their monastic vows and the faith of the Eastern Church, to remain virtuous and humble, to love God and neighbor. After receiving the Lord's Supper, he prayed and died on September 25. The monks mourned and psalmed. A fragrant aroma wafted from Sergius's body as it shimmered in an angelic manner. He was buried at Holy Trinity Church.

The life of Sergius was like Jesus' life. He had devout Christian parents. His miracles stemmed from his care for others. He never sought glory, but disdained it. He was concerned for his "disciples." Finally, he received the Lord's Supper upon his deathbed.

Michael	Time: ca. 1410–ca. 1455
	Place: Klopsko
	Offices: Fool for Christ, Miracle Worker
	Biography: *Life of St Michael*[9]

Michael was a fool for Christ. He often showed himself to be rather foolish, but at the same time was portrayed as quite wise. Through signs and prophesies, in addition to strange actions, he served the people around him on behalf of God.

On the Eve of St. John Day, the monastic community at Klopsko was at prayer in Holy Trinity Church. The priest censed the church and proceeded to the monastic cells. In the cells, an unknown man was found writing. Abbot Theodosius was called, and through a window, he asked the man: Are you human or an evil spirit? To which the man simply repeated the question. Theodosius then entered the cell and queried this time: Who are you and from where do you hail? To which the man repeated the second question. Though his name and origin remained unknown to the community, he was allowed to stay.

On the Eve of Jesus' Transfiguration, Prince Constantine visited the monastic community at Klopsko. When the prince heard this unnamed monk speak, he recognized the voice as his relative Michael. Michael then revealed his name. The prince exhorted the monks to watch over and care for him, which they did.

Michael performed numerous miracles. On one occasion, the land had suffered a drought for four years. As Theodosius and Michael walked along a dry riverbed, someone had written "spring" in the sand. They prayed to God and then began to dig. Water streamed out of the man-made cavity, and did not cease. Michael also miraculously provided food during a famine and changed places miraculously.

Michael prophesied of the future in conjunction with his miracles. Once, the local mayor tyrannized the monastery, forbidding them to pasture their livestock on his land or fish in his river. When the mayor threatened offenders with broken limbs, Michael prophesied that the mayor himself would lose the use of his limbs and almost drown. The next day the mayor found the monks fishing in his river. Attacking a monk, the mayor fell into the water and nearly drowned as his arms and legs had fallen lifeless. The next day, Michael forbade the mayor to enter Holy Trinity Church and the monks to pray for him. Sent away, the mayor was taken from one monastery to another to offer gifts and pray, but he did not receive mercy from God. Finally, the bishop instructed him to return to Holy Trinity Church in Klopsko for a special service. Initially, the mayor could not move his limbs. At the first hymn, his hands regained a bit of life. At the reading of the Holy Gospel, his hand made the sign of the cross and he sat up. Finally, he stood until the benediction.

Michael lived an extremely austere life. He slept upon the ground with no pillow. He consumed only bread and water. At the end of his life, he requested and received the Lord's Supper from Theodosius. He lay in his cell appearing to be asleep, his incense ascending to heaven. On January 11, he was buried at Holy Trinity Church in Klopsko.

In sum, Michael exhibited traits to the family of God. He prophesied and performed miracles. He did not cower before powerful leaders. In the end, his reception of the Lord's Supper and the ascending incense illustrated his eternal abode.

Yuliania Osoryin	Time: d. 1604
	Place: Lazarevo
	Offices: Wife, Mother
	Biography: *Life of Yuliania Lazarevskaia*
	Biographer: Kallistrat Druzhina-Osoryin

Kallistrat Druzhina-Osoryin depicted the extremely devout life of his mother in her biography. Yuliania was neither a nun nor a hermit, yet she lived as an ascetic. As a landowner's wife, mother, and neighbor, she sacrificed much to care for the people around her.

Yuliania was born into a wealthy, Christian family. Her father served in the court of Tsar Ivan the Terrible (1530–84), and her parents lived devoutly. While Yuliania was yet a young child, her mother died. She lived initially with her pious grandmother for six years and then her impious aunt. Yuliania loved God and the blessed virgin. Following the pious models of her parents and grandmother, she obeyed her elders; she abstained from gaiety; she often fasted; she moderated her speech among people, but often prayed to God; she provided for the orphans and widows. For these actions, some scorned her, while others esteemed her. Still, she remained without hatred for her scoffers and humble of spirit.

With her marriage at age 16, Yuliania received her first formal instruction in the teachings of the church. She became a model wife of a landowner as she administered the affairs of the household and treated the servants fairly. Moreover, she continued to provide for the needs of the less fortunate, but always secretly. Furthermore, she was a woman of prayer: When her husband was away on business, she would not sleep, but pray through the entire night.

Yuliania cared for the needy and sick. During a famine, she ate much less and gave away much more to the poor. During a plague, many locked themselves in their homes, but not Yuliania. She washed the sick and was responsible for restoring many to health. She prayed to God for the people and saw to the burial of the dead. When her in-laws died, she ordered their funerals and exchanged the inheritance for alms.

The devil and his evil horde often accosted Yuliania. The devil was directly responsible for the death of two of her sons—one was killed by a servant, the other in a battle. Twice, demons tormented her, and on both occasions, St. Nicholas the Wonderworker appeared to drive them away and calm Yuliania's fears.

Yuliania lived an ascetic life. She was a wife and mother, but was celibate the last years of her marriage. She no longer slept in their marital chamber, but upon a pile of rough firewood. In addition, she fasted and lived in poverty; she often attended church services and prayed the Jesus Prayer.

When she finally fell mortally ill, she wished to take a monastic vow, but considered herself unworthy. After prayer, she received the last rites. She then called her children together and kissed and blessed them. Yuliania made the sign of the cross three times and uttered her last words: "Praise God in all things! Into Thy hands, O Lord, I commend my spirit. Amen!"[10] Those present saw a golden nimbus about her head.

Yuliania's coffin miraculously appeared eleven years later. It was filled with aromatic myrrh. It moved without being moved by anyone. Many were healed of maladies from the myrrh from her coffin and the dirt near it.

The life and death of Yuliania clearly depicted her role in the family of God. Following the commands of Jesus she gave alms and cared for the sick; she prayed and worshiped. Like Jesus, the devil and his evil horde attacked her, but without success. In death, she showed the same trust in her heavenly Father that Jesus showed upon the cross.

Seraphim	Time: 1759–1833
	Place: Sarov
	Offices: Hermit, Staretz
	Biography: *St. Seraphim of Sarov* (1975)
	Biographer: Valentine Zander

A rather modern biographer, Valentine Zander, chronicled the holy life of Seraphim. Utilizing a number of sources, he laid out the life of Seraphim in an orderly fashion portraying Seraphim as a man of God through whom God worked miracles and taught His Holy Word.

Seraphim was born in Kurst to the Moshnin family. The third of three children, he received the name Prokhor, the disciple of the John the apostle. While still a youngster, Prokhor fell from a scaffolding, but was uninjured. A fool for Christ witnessed the event and prophesied that he was one whom God had specially chosen. Though his father died while he was young, his mother provided an exemplary Christian life after which Prokhor modeled his life. Uninterested in secular trades, Prokhor and some friends traveled to the Caves Monastery in Kiev. After this pilgrimage, a staretz foretold to Prokhor that he would travel to Sarov and remain there until his death.

At the age of 23, Prokhor entered the monastery at Sarov. There, he worked as a baker and carpenter, and prayed without ceasing the Jesus Prayer during his labors. He became a reader and studied the holy fathers, such as Basil the Great and John Climacus. In addition, he imbibed frequently from the well of Holy Scripture. After eight years, Prokhor took his monastic vows and took the name Seraphim. That same year, he was ordained a deacon. Seven years later, he became a priest after which he celebrated the liturgy on a daily basis.

On two occasions in his ascetic career, Seraphim lived as a hermit in the forest. Living not too far from the monastery, he often returned on Saturday evening to pray Vespers with the other monks and receive the Lord's Supper the following morning. There, he produced his own food in a garden and often shared it with the woodland creatures. He slept on a sack of rocks and he was attired in the most simple clothing.

As word of Seraphim's holiness spread, many, including Tsar Alexander, journeyed to visit him and petition him for spiritual direction. Though Seraphim dearly loved his time spent in solitude and prayer, this had prepared him to be a staretz. Seraphim had that rare ability of being able to look into the hearts and souls of men and women, and move them to true repentance. In no uncertain terms, he condemned them of their sins and set them on the path of righteousness.

A number of wondrous events were associated with Seraphim. He saw the heavenly host singing and serving at the Divine Liturgy. He was involved in the miraculous multiplication of loaves. On one occasion when food was scarce in the land, Seraphim was sent to the monastic barn to collect the last bit of grain, only to find that it was filled. When he was among the animals with which he lived as a hermit, the small amount of bread that he would bring back from the monastery would feed a myriad of animals. He made the lame walk and the deaf hear. Many with ailments and impairments came to Seraphim, and Seraphim's compassion moved him to heal many.

Seraphim enjoyed a close relation with Mary, the mother of Jesus. On three occasions she visited him when he was ill, and he was healed. Different nuns from Diveyoevo, a convent overseen by Seraphim, told stories of seeing Seraphim conversing with Mary.

Seraphim was a noted teacher of spiritual matters. Of asceticism, he taught that a monk arms himself with patience in prayer. Of faith, it is a most blessed gift granted to the Christian by the Father, Son, and Holy Spirit. Of tears, they are an important component in repentance. Of hope, it brings true peace to the Christian's heart.

In Seraphim's last years, he suffered greatly, but not one complaint was heard from his lips. He withdrew himself more and more from the life of the monastery, but visitors continued to darken his door. On the Nativity of our Lord, he requested of Abbot Niphont that he be buried with an icon of Mary upon his breast. Seraphim picked out his grave sight on New Year's Eve, and a short time later he died. They found him in his cell; he had died reading the Holy Gospels before an icon of Mary. After eight days of reverence to this holy man, he was buried.

The life of Seraphim is portrayed as an important member of the Christian family. Like Jesus and many others, he lived a rigorous life and performed many miracles. Moreover, he faithfully taught the Word of God to all who would listen. Like Jesus, the people flocked to his teaching. Not unique to Seraphim, but distinct nonetheless, he was shown to have special vision, be it seeing the heavenly host at the Divine Liturgy or the presence of Mary in his life.

Anastasia Logacheva Time: 1809–75
Place: Russia
Office: Ascetic
Biography: *Life of Blessed Athanasia*
Biographer: Alexander Priklonsky

The life of Anastasia was quite rigorous. As a child she desired to be a hermit, which St. Seraphim (1759–1833) prophesied. She was a hermit, a coenobitic, and an abbess.

Anastasia was born to Symeon and Mavra, peasants in Kudley. While still a child, she spent many hours in silent meditation to God. When her father left to serve in the military and her mother with him, she remained with her aunt and uncle. Her mother instructed her to pray to Mary, and so she did. She prayed frequently and often sought solitude. At age 12, she abstained from the dress and games of the other girls; she often fasted and frequented the Divine Liturgy. On a trip with her grandfather into the woods to work with his beehives, Anastasia began to dig a cave for the eremitic life she so much desired. The odor of incense lingered in this place.

The blessed ascetic Seraphim entered Anastasia's life on three occasions. In the first, he instructed this young girl to be patient in her desire to be an ascetic. In the second, he sent this girl, now a few years older, on a pilgrimage to Kiev. In the third, he blessed this 23 year old young woman and sent her to live as a hermit in the forest at the place where she smelled incense. With her parents returned and now aged, Anastasia cared for them for seventeen years until their deaths.

Anastasia returned to the cave that she first began to dig as a child. It still smelled of incense, and she extended her previous excavations. She remained there and was frequently visited by two kind women and various forest animals that often howled to frighten her. She fasted and prayed the Jesus Prayer and to Mary. She read one of the Holy Gospels each day of the week. She planted a garden, but a bear repeatedly damaged her efforts. One day she caught up to the bear and sent him away, never to return. Demons wrestled with her. Her asceticism was extreme. On one occasion, she broke apart an anthill and allowed herself to be swarmed by the ants. On another occasion, she stood for forty days upon a rock fasting the entire time.

One day Anastasia and a fellow ascetic sought a spring so that they would not have to haul water. When Anastasia retired to her cell, an unknown nun appeared to Anastasia's companion. The former asked for a pick, made the sign of the cross three times upon the ground, and stuck it thrice with the pick. Immediately water poured out. After Anastasia had been informed of this event, it was revealed to her that the nun was Mary, the Mother of God. Many people were healed from drinking this water.

Anastasia lived an eremitic life. At the same time, other women ascetics occasionally lived with her. In addition, she visited others and received visitors who heard of her rigorous life and desired spiritual guidance from her. She visited neighboring hermits and the local convent, and she called on the local priest to receive the body and blood of Jesus. The priest would, on occasion, visit her and celebrate the Divine Liturgy in the forest.

In 1855 the local authorities dismantled Anastasia's lodging and sent her away. First, she joined the Ardatov Protection Convent. Later, she lived in a cell near the church in Kudley. After a pilgrimage to the Holy Land, she returned to Ardatov Protection Convent and in 1863 was translated to St. Nicholas Convent in Siberia. There, she received the name Athanasia and was an abbess for five years. Repeatedly throughout the day she would make the sign of the cross and say, "Glory to Thee, O Lord!"[11] Though she was the abbess, she dressed poorly and labored as one of the nuns.

Anastasia belongs in the family portrait of the church. Her love of her heavenly Father and the Mother of God paralleled that of Jesus. She forsook the comforts of this world and fought against her demonic antagonist as did her dear Lord. In her last years, her unceasing crossing of herself served as a visible sign of her faith in Christ's life and death.

Ioann Veniaminov	Time: 1797–1879
	Places: Russia and Alaska
	Offices: Missionary, Bishop
	Biography: *Journals of the Priest Ioann Veniamoinov in Alaska, 1823–1836*[12]

Ioann Veniaminov, later in life a monastic taking the name Innocent and then bishop first of Kamchatka and then Moscow, chronicled his missionary work in Alaska. As such, there is mention neither of his birth and youth nor events surrounding his death. Instead, he meticulously recorded his tireless work among the Aleuts, many of whom were Orthodox, though they had no regular Orthodox priest to serve them. His journals illustrate his dedication to this work traveling from island to island and community to community, along with the many accomplishments of the Holy Spirit working through him in Sitka in the Alaskan Panhandle and Unalaska in the Aleutian Islands.

First, Ioann endured difficult travels upon the sea. He often traveled in larger vessels, but at times by much smaller boats called baidarkas. The waters along the Alaskan coast and those among the Aleutian Islands were quite treacherous with strong winds and rocky shores. The weather was often unfavorable for travel. At times, the weather would cause a trip to be canceled, at other times, they began their trip only to have to return to where they had begun. Ioann suffered terribly from seasickness, yet traveled extensively. Often, the Offices were prayed while at sea. On other occasions, he traveled from village to village. By sea and upon the land, Ioann traveled throughout southern Alaska to perform his priestly duties.

Second, he taught and preached extensively. His sermons were based upon the Holy Gospel for the particular day in the Church Year. He generally noted the moral interpretation in his journal. His teachings revolved around a catechism, for example, the Holy Trinity and faith, the Nicene Creed and Sacraments. In 1824, he taught the Lord's Prayer on successive days: January 25—introduction, February 1—2nd and 3rd petitions, February 6—4th and 5th petitions, February 8—6th and 7th petitions. In addition, he taught New Testament history along with grammar and reading in both Russian and Aleut. He also sang and prayed with the students.

Third, he performed a myriad of pastoral duties. He celebrated the liturgy in many places, like the Veselovskoe and Tulik villages, and the Unimak and Akun Islands. In places that had no appropriate building, he raised a tent. He preached at the liturgy. He performed blessings of the waters and breads. He baptized and chrismated and married and buried the people. He held prayer services on Holy Days. He regularly prayed Matins and Vespers. He heard confession.

Fourth, Ioann studied the Aleut language. Some of the Aleuts knew Russian, but most did not. Consequently, he often worked with a translator. Ioann quickly learned Aleut. He translated the catechism and the Gospels into Aleut. Scripture readings were often in Slavonic, Russian, and Aleut at a single service. He also produced an Aleut dictionary.

Fifth, Ioann continued faithfully in his devotional and theological studies. He usually read one book and sometimes two or more each month. For example, he read Thomas à Kempis' Imitation of Christ, Bishop Theofilakt's Dogmatics of the Orthodox Christian Church, Douzetem's Mystery of the Cross and Book of Martyrs, Nikolai Karamzin's History of Russia, and a variety of history books.

Sixth, Ioann dealt with many practical matters. He oversaw the building of a new church at Unalaska. In one village, he was petitioned to address a marriage dilemma. A man had been living with a woman for five years and had promised to marry her. One day, he left her and her children and moved in with another woman who was married to another. After four years, the second woman wished to return to her first. Ioann determined that it was proper for the second woman to return to her first and rightful husband. The man should also return to the woman who he had promised to marry. Should he object, he must nonetheless financially support that woman and her children. More personally, he had a daughter born prematurely. She was baptized and died shortly thereafter.

The missionary zeal of Ioann Veniaminov is a trait of the family of God. His work with foreign people and their language mirrored that of Cyril and Methodius. His travels rivaled that of Paul. His preaching and teaching to the ends of the earth obeyed the command of Jesus.

Alexander Schmemann Time: 1921–83
Places: France, New York
Offices: Priest, Professor
Biography: *A Life Worth Living*[13]
Biographer: John Meyendorff (1926–92)

John Meyendorff's academic panegyric depicted a man of the church: one interested in theological studies, without being a sterile academic; one concerned for the well-being of the church, but not an ecclesial bureaucrat. Alexander deeply appreciated and loved the church and worked at length—teaching and writing and preaching—not for himself, but for the benefit of the Orthodox Church.

Though Alexander was born primarily of Russian stock, he spent most of his first thirty years in France. His family emigrated from Estonia while he was quite young, but was able to retain their ethnic heritage as a large Russian community resided in France at the time. He even attended a "Russian" school. While this hindered his assimilation into the French society, he did not lose his Russian-ness on foreign soil.

In his youth, Alexander was very much taken up into the life of the church. At the magnificent St. Alexander Nevsky Cathedral, he was an altar boy. The eminent clergy there greatly influenced his appreciation for the Orthodox Church. He experienced and began to love the splendor and dignity of the liturgy of the Orthodox Church.

Alexander's advanced academic studies took place in Paris, but again, he retained his Russian-ness. Though he first studied at the French lycée and the University of Paris, he married Juliana Osorguine who was thoroughly Russian. He then continued his studies at the Theological Institute of Paris where eminent Russian Orthodox professors greatly influenced him, such as Father Paul Florensky and Archimandrite Cyprian in the areas of the Early Church and the liturgy. Alexander taught church history there for a few years.

The then-contemporary liturgical renewal in French Catholicism was in full swing. Liturgical scholars, such as Jean Danielou (1905–74) and Louis Bouyer (b. 1913), delved into the ancient Christian liturgies. While Alexander was thoroughly Russian Orthodox, their method of liturgical study significantly affected his own interest and research in the church's rituals.

In 1949 the dean of the Theological Institute of Paris, Georges Florovsky, became the dean of St. Vladimir Seminary in New York. Alexander followed two years later and two other colleagues within a short time. In 1962 Alexander became the dean at St. Vladimir for the duration of his life.

Alexander's accomplishments in the latter portion of his life ranged widely. At St. Vladimir, he integrated the seminary and church through the production of priests with a passion for mission and the liturgy. Moreover, he adamantly appealed for an autocephalous Orthodox Church in America, and he witnessed its first phase in 1970 with the ecclesial recognition by the patriarch of Moscow. Furthermore, his abundant writings and Russian sermons on "Radio Liberty" have inspired and endeared him to many throughout the world.

Alexander belongs to the family of God. Like Jesus, his primary concern was for the church. This was manifested in his preaching and teaching and writing. Not only is he remembered by the church on earth, he is even now with his heavenly Father.

Summary

Christian lives in the Eastern Church revolved around Jesus. Each person was shown to have an intimate relation with Him. Irene and Yuliania were connected to Jesus in humility. Constantine and Methodius obeyed the Apostolic Command in their missionary endeavors. Sergius and Anastasia lived extremely rigorous lives. Gregory and Ioann faithfully taught the Word of God to those who otherwise were ignorant of these divine mysteries. Vladimir and Stephen participated in the death and life of Christ in Holy Baptism. Michael and Alexander joined Jesus in their deaths. Each Christian was portrayed as living and dying in a twofold fashion: Their lives and deaths paralleled those of Christ and, of greater importance, their lives and deaths occurred within the loving arms of their dear Lord.

Excursus: *Way of a Pilgrim*

Hesychasm has been an integral component of the Eastern Church. It was kindled in the New Testament, fanned in the Early Church, and burned brightly throughout the history of Orthodoxy. It became an ascetic model that was practiced by a holy few, but idealized among the vast majority. Hesychasm very much reveals the mystical nature of Eastern Church as her faithful unite with Jesus through continuous prayer.

The Way of the Pilgrim[14] portrayed a hesychast in nineteenth century Russia who was a nameless wanderer. Upon learning to pray continuously, he disclosed this Orthodox teaching and his practice to all he met in his travels. This narrative was written in the first person, though the author's name remains unknown. It was first printed toward the end of the nineteenth century.

This autobiography depicted one who traveled. He was not interested in possessions or prestige, but rather, he sought to obey the apostolic command concerning prayer. He forsook all and searched for this spiritual knowledge. This pilgrim journeyed geographically in his spiritual search to understand hesychasm and assimilate it into his life.

The pilgrim was born into a Christian family. At age 2, his parents died, so a grandfather raised him and his brother. The grandfather, a devout Christian, raised the boys well, regularly taking them to church and reading often to them from Holy Scripture. In a drunken stupor, his grandfather severely injured the future pilgrim's arm. To alleviate his guilt and provide a means of employment, the grandfather educated him using the Bible as a textbook. The future pilgrim grew up and married. When his grandfather died, he left all to the future pilgrim, but nothing to his fallen brother. Enraged with envy, the brother first looted the house of the future pilgrim and his wife and then burned it down. They escaped with their lives and Bible, and they were satisfied. His wife worked and he read the Bible to her as she worked. They fasted and prayed throughout their short marriage until she fell ill, received the Lord's Supper, and died. He sold all of his possessions and distributed it to the poor. He packed his Bible and began his journey.

The word of God greatly affected the pilgrim's life. At a church service, he heard the apostolic command, "pray without ceasing" (1 Thessalonians 5:17). He read his Bible and noted that the apostle Paul said one should be "praying at all times in the Spirit, with all prayer and supplication" (Ephesians 6:18). He knew that this was important, but was as yet unable to comprehend its full extent. He traveled from preacher to preacher, hearing sermons on prayer in general and unceasing prayer in particular, but not enough to satisfy his spiritual curiosity. He happened upon a very spiritual layman who pointed out the value of unceasing prayer, but could not offer concrete advice on attaining it. The same was true of an abbot.

Continuing his journey, the pilgrim was directed to a starets who greatly advocated unceasing prayer. The starets taught the Jesus Prayer—"Lord Jesus Christ, have mercy on me"—to the pilgrim and read to him from the fathers in the Philokalia (1782), such as St. Simeon, the New Theologian (949–1022) and St. Gregory Palamas (1296–1359). The starets agreed to direct the pilgrim on his spiritual quest. In the first week, the pilgrim studied and practiced prayer. His initial results were good, but by the end of the week, he failed miserably by allowing mundane thoughts and lethargy to thwart his prayer. Rather than reprimanding the pilgrim, the starets explained that this was a good thing: Satan did not approve of such prayer, and was attacking him. The pilgrim was then given a prayer rope and instructed to pray the Jesus Prayer 3,000 times a day. At first this was quite difficult, but it became easier with each day. The staretz then directed the pilgrim to pray the prayer 6,000 times each day. It soon became his all-consuming desire. If he stopped for any reason, he was at a loss. The pilgrim was then told to recite the prayer 12,000 times per day. Initially his mouth tired and his hands ached from manipulating the prayer rope. One morning, his mouth prayed the prayer of itself. He was filled with a heavenly joy, and his sole desire was the Jesus Prayer—he prayed when awake and in his sleep.

The pilgrim, learning well his lesson, set off to Siberia to visit the tomb of a bishop. He walked and begged; he studied the Philokalia along with his Bible. The Jesus Prayer became an integral component of his life. He no longer recited the prayer externally, but rather, internally. The prayer was so integrated into his life that it became synchronized with the beat of his heart and his respirations. It warmed him in the cold; it comforted him in pain; it dissipated anger when he was affronted. With the Jesus Prayer, he became conscious of the great beauty of creation and experienced its unceasing praise of the Creator.

During his travels, a church briefly employed him to watch over the offerings for the current building project. This well suited the pilgrim as he sat in church and prayed much of the time. He would at times read the Bible and Philokalia to any interested hearers. One day he overheard a young girl praying unorthodox prayers and instructed her to pray the

Jesus Prayer. People quickly recognized his holiness and flocked to him for spiritual advice. His popularity hastened his departure as he sought solitude, not recognition.

Once, he happened upon a Christian couple that delighted in the care of pilgrims and the needy. They invited him into their home where he was treated like family; they fed and clothed him. One evening, the pilgrim and the husband retired to discuss religion. The husband read widely, like John Chrysostom (ca. 347–407) and Basil the Great (ca. 330–79). He very much valued the Lord's Prayer. His wife read to them from a contemporary book on the Lord's Prayer, and he esteemed it as the greatest of all prayers. The pilgrim then read of its mystical interpretation from his Philokalia. After the pilgrim read a quotation from Peter of Damascus (d. ca. 750) that advocated unceasing prayer, the husband wrote it down and placed it before his icon of the same. Before the pilgrim departed, the couple wrapped his legs and shod his feet as Jesus had washed the feet of His apostles.

The travels of the pilgrim are littered with a number of interesting anecdotes. He had compassion upon those who beat and robbed him, and his prayer rope frightened a wolf. His starets visited him in visions, and he greatly revered the Lord's Supper.

The pilgrim followed in the train of Jesus. While both interacted with people, they often sought prayer in quiet solitude. The pilgrim sought unity with Jesus through prayer. He revered the Lord's Supper and worship.

The Way of the Pilgrim portrayed not only the life of one spiritual wanderer but also a significant example of nineteenth century Russian spirituality. Hesychasm was not for "professional" ascetics only. Granted, the pilgrim was an ascetic, and he prayed the Jesus Prayer. However, he also traveled about Russia teaching the Jesus Prayer to men and women in many different walks of life.

Eastern Analysis

The Eastern Church greatly reveres her saints. This is based first upon the vital role of tradition in Eastern Christianity. An integral link exists between the present and the past: the contemporary generation is to learn from earlier generations. This is not simply a matter of ecclesial doctrines and practices, but affects also Christian lives. In A Supplement to the Life of John the Almsgiver, for example, the reader is informed that he is not merely receiving a history lesson, but more importantly, learning of the life of John the Almsgiver to "gain spiritual profit and a desire to imitate his piety."[15] Hence, the lives of earlier Christians serve as models for and are to be emulated by later Christians. In addition, Nestor, in his Life of Theodosius, notes that when Christians look at the lives of these saints, they glorify not the saint, but the God who has given and preserved this life.

In the Life of Mary the Younger, the author argues that one does not have to be a "professional" ascetic to be a saint and one who is revered in the Christian Church. The Christian life is not based on gender or wealth or freedom or celibacy. These are the standards of the world. For example, in the life of Mary, marriage and children did not exempt her from living a holy and God-pleasing life. Instead, they were the very means by which she lived a faithful life before her God.

This reverence for the saints is based, in part, upon the doctrine of theosis: deification of a Christian. The apostle Paul addressed this rather generally: "[y]ou may become partakers of the divine nature" (2 Peter 1:4). In the Early Church, Athanasius wrote: "God became man, so that man may become God."[16] This doctrine was further developed in Eastern Christianity by Gregory Palamas (ca. 1296–1359) who taught that just as the human nature of Jesus was transfigured to reveal His divinity upon the mount, so can the Christian's human nature be transfigured in this life.[17] This does not imply that Christians are independent gods, but that they participate in the divinity through intensive prayer and the Lord's Supper. One result of this is that Christian lives are quite holy, and should be treated appropriately.

Corollaries of such reverence are inevitable. The biographical data must be accurate. In the Life of Blessed Athanasia, Father Priklonsky repeatedly noted that he utilized eyewitnesses and firsthand accounts. In referring to the miraculous scent of incense at her eremitic cell, he claimed that even a skeptic of such things smelled it.[18]

A second corollary is the relation of God to Christian lives. In the Life of Methodius, it was shown how God has continued to act in His people throughout time. Just as God worked through Abraham and John the Baptist, so He continued to work through the fathers at the Ecumenical Councils in the Early Church and others in Eastern Christianity.[19] For these many manifestations of God's power and mercy in Christian lives, Christians praise the one true God.[20]

Prayer to the saints is a third. Similar to Medieval Catholicism, Eastern Christianity believes that Christians may ask other Christians to pray for them, and Christians are to pray for other Christians. This is true for all Christians be they on earth or in heaven. Consequently, Orthodox Christians pray to the saints, not as they pray to God, but as a petition from one Christian to another to pray on his behalf. At Matins for the Second Sunday in Lent, "O Gregory the Wonderworker, light of Orthodoxy and teacher of the Church, glory of monks and invincible protector of theologians, pride of Thessalonica and preacher of grace, pray without ceasing for the salvation of our souls"[21] is prayed. This is the pattern throughout the many prayers to the saints in the Divine Liturgy and Offices.

Icons are a fourth corollary. They are images of Jesus, Mary, and the many saints. They cover the walls of Orthodox Churches, and the Pantocrator may even be upon the ceiling. These many saintly images are not worshiped as is God. Instead, they serve as a visible reminder of an otherwise invisible reality: The Church on earth and in heaven is one. Just as your Christian sister and friend may be at your sides and are not easily overlooked, the images of John the Baptist and John the Almsgiver are upon the walls lest you forget their place in the church.

Eastern Christianity does not forsake her saints, but embraces them. As the holy people of God through whom He works, they are revered in many different fashions.

Summary

The biographical data of Eastern Christianity is spread across a great expanse of time and place. Each life was rather unique. John the Almsgiver was a bishop in Egypt and Alexander Schmemann a professor in America. Irene was an abbess in Chrysobalanton and Yuliania a wife in Lazarevo. Vladimir was a Prince in Kiev and Ioann Veniaminov a missionary in Alaska. At the same time, they were all clearly portrayed as part of the immediate family of Eastern Christianity and the extended family of the God. The ascetics and miracle workers and missionaries in the Eastern Church reached back through the Early Church and to the life of Christ. Through the sacraments of Holy Baptism and the Lord's Supper, these eastern Christian lives intimately connected them with the life of Christ. Through common traits and offices, they were depicted to be brothers and sisters in the family of God.

6

CONCLUSION

The Holy Bible and church histories overflow with biographical data. This modest study of Christian lives is certainly not meant to be exhaustive in scope, but rather a mere sampling of the broad spectrum of lives in Christianity as portrayed by an assortment of literary types at various times and from different places. Somewhat less modest, this study has attempted to illustrate the intimate relations between Christian lives and the life of Christ. In light of this, connections between sundry Christian lives have been shown as well.

Apology

This study is fraught with difficulties. Its scope of Christian lives—creation to present, Eastern and Western Christianity—is immense, and thus, selecting and ordering these lives is more than challenging. Also, the frequent utilization of ancient documents is problematic in the Modern Period as moderns often question the veracity of ideas, let alone texts, which predate them. The following will address these and related concerns.

The selection of Christians in this study was not completely arbitrary. A major concern was Christian lives that have played significant roles in the history of the Christian Church, such as Augustine, Martin Luther, and Alexander Schmemann. Moreover, a healthy mixture of times and places and offices has been sought. For example, the chapter on Bible Times included lives from the Pentateuch as well as from the days of Judges to postexilic times. Likewise, not only were Russian lives incorporated in Eastern Christianity but also those from Egypt, Serbia, and North America. Similarly, reformers were included in the Reformation Period as well as the founder of the Jesuits, a Roman Catholic religious order. Furthermore, a few otherwise unfamiliar faces with more than lively stories—Gorgonia and Michael of Klopsko—favorably seasoned the mix.

The historical documents utilized in this study have not been critically examined. Times and places have not been altered to align with modern assessments. Similarly, the biographical data, miracles included, have not been questioned, but rather, simply cited. This is not to suggest that the whole of this historical corpus is to be swallowed naively, with the exception of the divinely inspired Word of God. According to the methodology of this study, historical documents have been utilized almost exclusively. The intent behind this methodology was not some sort of historical gymnastics, but to provide then-contemporary perspectives of Christian lives apart from our now-contemporary views. Temporal moderns who are simultaneously spiritual ancients—conservative protestants—are quick to affirm miracles in the Bible, but even more hastily rebuff such actions afterward, particularly those in Medieval Catholicism. They would, however, be well advised to recognize that theologians no less than the Athanasius and Jerome in the Early Church cited the miraculous in the lives of Antony and Hilarion, respectively. Similarly, Ambrose and Augustine attested to such signs.

The emphasis of this study has been to illustrate the unity of these many lives at the expense of their disparateness. There is no intent here to fuel the modern Ecumenical Movement that seeks unity at all costs according to its credo—agree to disagree. The differences of theology and practice within the different branches of Christianity are not insignificant and dare not be overlooked. It would be impious to suggest that the filioque and other issues of the day that led to the Great Schism were of no matter, or to gloss over the significant differences between Lutherans and Jesuits (1 Corinthians 11:19). However, this is not the subject matter of this study. Instead, it is to show the unity of Christian lives in their relation to the life of Christ through the sacraments and their respective offices.

Granted, this study is deficient on numerous fronts. It must be noted, however, that the modern Ecumenical Movement and modern criticism are not without their deficiencies. In regard to this study, both offer an extremely narrow contemporary perspective. In contrast, the historical- and geographical-varied biographical documents of this study emphasize the significance of the common threads that have been sewn through the Christian lives from the first day to this day.

Themes

The harmonious components of these many distinct Christian lives are astounding, particularly when it is remembered that these many biographical documents were not written during one historical period or in a particular location or by a single school of religious thought. The many close relations cannot be disregarded. Instead, a few common themes that illustrate these relations must be elaborated upon more precisely.

First, time and place situate Christian lives in the creation as was the incarnation of the Creator. Jesus was located in first century Palestine where the Jewish sects and the capital punishment of that day greatly affected his life and death. Ruth was a Moabite in Old Testament Times who gleaned fields and married into the messianic line according to Jewish law. Augustine became a Christian only after wallowing about in the religions and philosophies of fourth and fifth century Africa and Europe. The tenth century missionary work of Constantine and Methodius was initiated by Prince Rostislav of Moravia, and Moravia provided the linguistic context for the creation of the written Slavic language. The sale of indulgences in Medieval Catholicism inspired the reforming work of Martin Luther. All were portrayed as historical figures: Their words and actions were understood to be not parabolic or fantasy, but concrete and real. As such, time and place provides the context for Christian lives, and thus, the Christian Church.

Second, all human beings are descendents of Adam, hence, all sin and die. Even the heirs of Jesus through the second birth remain descendents of Adam through their first birth. This Adamic ancestry was most clearly depicted in Holy Scripture. The biblical heroes not only prophesied and performed signs, but their sins were displayed with sharp clarity. Samson, like Adam, had trouble with women, and Paul, following after the serpent, persecuted the people of God. Following the Bible times, the peccadilloes of Christians were treated in one of two fashions. Most literary forms were panegyric in style and chose to ignore such transgressions in favor of an elaboration of their virtues. For example, the courage of the martyrs was clearly displayed, but any doubts or fears were glossed over. Similarly, the virtues of the ascetics were emphasized at the expense of any weaknesses in their Adamic flesh. Autobiographies, in contrast, most faithfully and consistently revealed their flaws, for example, Augustine, Peter Abelard, and Clives Staples Lewis. This was also true of church histories. In his Ecclesiastical History, Eusebius noted Origen's self-castration, and in the Russian Primary Chronicle, Sylvester depicted the early idolatry and sexual perversity of Vladimir.

Third, the sacraments of Baptism and the Lord's Supper most closely connected Christian lives with the life of Christ. While the doctrinal teaching of the Christian Church attempts to define with precision the relation between Christ and the Christian in the administration of these Sacraments, this is illustrated no less clearly, but in different fashions in these biographical documents.

Baptism was not mentioned in each case, but was always implied. Jesus first addressed its magnitude when He said, "unless one is born of water and the Spirit, he cannot enter the kingdom of God" (John 3:5), and the Church has carried this out in the practice of infant Baptism throughout most of her history. When Baptism is mentioned in Christian lives, its significance is clearly shown. It occurred at a pivotal time in the lives of Jesus and the apostle Paul: Jesus' life shifted from hidden to public, and Paul transformed from the arch-persecutor of Christianity to her arch-Missionary. This sacrament clearly marked the beginning of a new life for Perpetua who abandoned her earthly family for one from heaven; for Cyprian who traded in academia for the church; for Martin who exchanged his military garb for that of an ascetic and bishop. It changed the spiritual direction of the Roman Empire and Russia when received by Constantine and Vladimir, respectively. In Holy Baptism, a single, dramatic shift takes place—those of adamic ancestry become the heirs of Jesus; the image of God begins to be restored in fallen humanity.

The Lord's Supper was received frequently and at significant moments in many of these Christian lives. Here again, its worth was first addressed by Jesus: "This is My body . . . This is My blood" (Matthew 26:26, 28), and manifested in the Church with her realistic interpretation—the Christian eats the body of Jesus and drinks His blood. Consequently, Charles I and Sergius frequented the altar for this spiritual nourishment. More commonly noted, Birgitta and Irene and Stephen Nemanja forsook all temporal foods on their deathbeds save the most holy viaticum as they looked beyond this world and to the next.

The second birth, along with the eating and drinking of Jesus' body and blood, were integral components of Christian lives. As such, they were commonly cited and clearly illustrated the intimate relation between Christian lives and the life of Christ.

Fourth, struggle in the lives of Christians is constant and quite fierce. It occurs between those of adamic descent and the heirs of Jesus. This was clearly portrayed in fatal rows between David and Goliath, Eulaia and her pagan persecutors, John Calvin and Michael Servetus. In addition, this struggle occurs in the individual life of each Christian. A Christian is both a descendent of Adam and an heir of Jesus. The fallen nature, inherited from Adam, seeks and delights and wallows in sin. In contrast, the restored image of God, received by the heirs of Jesus, rejoices and delights in the law of God. The two are not a good mix. The apostle Paul experienced this in his own life and warned Christians: "I see in my members another law waging war against the law of my mind and making me captive to the law of sin that dwells in my members" (Romans 7:23). This ongoing struggle finally ends in the life of the Christian when this sinful flesh dies and is buried, and the soul, raised to heaven, is reunited with that same flesh then raised in the glory of Jesus' resurrection.

Fifth, family traits and the many offices in the Church commonly connected Christian lives with the life of Christ. Concerning the former, pious parents, a life-changing event, and a momentous death were quite common. Concerning the latter, these Christians held in common with other Christians and Jesus a variety of offices, like ascetic and bishop and sovereign.

Almsgiving is a significant trait in the family of God. Already in the Old Testament, God revealed His penchant for the impoverished with less costly sacrifices and gleaning (Leviticus 19:10) for the indigent, not to mention the laws prohibiting usury (Leviticus 25:36) and limiting servitude (Leviticus 25:40). In the New Testament, Jesus blessed the poor (Luke 7:20) and commended them to the care of His followers (Matthew 25:34–40). Consequently, Christians followed suit. Lawrence depicted the poor as the treasure of the church. As bishop of Alexandria, John the Almsgiver provided food for the hungry, homes for the homeless, lodging for travelers, and hospitals for the sick. Gorgonia and Charles I and Yuliania distributed alms. Ascetics often sold their possessions and distributed them among the less fortunate. In all times and places, the Christian family has shown little concern for her own physical needs, while generously giving to others.

Martyr is the preeminent office of Christ and Christians. All of the life of Christ culminated in His death. Upon the cross, He offered Himself as a sacrifice for the sin of Adam and the sinfulness of creation, and His heavenly Father accepted it. Upon the cross, God and His creation were reconciled. Jesus promised His followers that the world would treat them as it had treated Him (John 15:18). Those who were persecuted as was Jesus—martyrs—were blessed (Matthew 5:10–11), not because they performed the ultimate God-pleasing act, but in that they participated in the suffering and death of Jesus and became spiritually and concretely connected to the life of Christ and all of the merits associated with and given by Him. Christian lives that fill the office of martyr are thus greatly revered in every corner of Christianity.

Miracle worker is one of the more showy offices in the Christian Church, but that is not its purpose. Jesus performed miracles not on a whim or to flaunt His divine power, but in mortal combat with His enemies and as the Savior of creation. When He healed the sick and calmed storms, Jesus battled against disease and restored the fallen creation. This is no less true for later Christian miracle workers. Martin of Tours healed a leper, and Michael of Klopsko caused water to spring forth in an arid place. While hard evidence of these miracles is lacking, they are portrayed as continuing the work began with Jesus and promised to His apostles (Matthew 10:8).

The offices in the Christian Church are more than plentiful and varied. At times there are Christian sovereigns and at others there are not. On the other hand, bishops and ascetics and missionaries are always present in the church. All, though, have a distinct place and value there. Heaven forbid that they are viewed only as biographical oddities or historical fascinations! Instead, the Christians who fill these offices are granted the opportunity to point back to Jesus and in this fashion, be connected to the life of Christ. Moreover, they provide the opportunity to be connected to those who hold the office in common. Furthermore, they allow Christians to perform Christlike services for others.

Sixth, women have not always filled the most prominent positions in Christianity. They were, however, never absent and filled a variety of supporting and, at times, significant offices. In biblical times, they were neither patriarch nor priest nor apostle, yet judge and prophetess and queen. In post-biblical times, they were not bishop or priest, but martyr and ascetic and mystic and sovereign. Much more fundamental, they were wives and mothers.

Wife was the initial role of woman. According to the creation narrative, Eve was taken from the side of Adam and created to be his helper. Wives did not simply serve their husbands, but complemented them in the family. Gorgonia and Birgitta and Yuliania were wives of husbands. The wife remained faithful to her husband mirroring the relation of the church and her Bridegroom (Ephesians 5:22–33). This was also understood figuratively. Ascetic women like Birgitta and Anastasia devoted their lives to Jesus and became His spiritual brides.

Mother was the subsequent role of woman. Children were a corollary of Eve's relation to Adam. She was, however, more than an incubator. The promise of a Savior began to be fulfilled in her son(s). This promise continued in Sarah's son, Isaac, and that of Ruth, Obed. Mary was the culmination. She was the perfect helper in that she bore the perfect child, the Son of God, the Second Adam. The fulfillment of the promise in Mary did not terminate the significance of the role of Christian motherhood. Instead, Christian mothers continued to give birth to children who were first introduced to virtuous living and the teachings of the church. Spiritual brides were also spiritual mothers. Oftentimes, an abbess, like Macrina or Irene, had no physical children save the nuns under their spiritual care. Even Queen Elizabeth I, a protestant, was a spiritual spouse of Jesus, and the people of England were her spiritual offspring.

Women held other offices. On the one hand, they did not perform priestly functions according to divine decree so as not to reflect improperly the order between God and His people, the divine Bridegroom and His bride. On the other hand, women were martyrs and ascetics and mystics and deaconesses and sovereigns, to mention only a few. Generally, women performed no better and no worse than did their male counterparts in the same office.

Seventh, Christian lives are family. All people are descendents of Adam through their temporal fathers and mothers, and thus, are related to one another: sin and death are the dominant family traits. Christians, though, are born into the family of God through Holy Baptism. As part of this family, Christians do not live their lives for themselves, but for others. This was quite evident in the many Christian heroes who served those around them with words and actions. For example, Christian parents often modeled the Christian virtues and faith for their Christian children: some gave alms, and others preached the Gospel. In addition, the influence of Christian lives upon others extended over many centuries through the faithful preservation of biographical data in the church.

It should be noted that many of these Christians lost one or both of their parents while they were an infant or still quite young. In part, it was the times: lack of modern medicine, wars, and the like. More significant, as tragic as this was, it often accelerated the child's dependence upon God's loving kindness. In the absence of earthly parents, the young Christian's devotion to his heavenly Father deepened and intensified.

Of great importance, earlier Christian "relatives" provided examples of God's mercy and power working and in and through them for the purpose of comforting and strengthening later Christians. If God watched over and graciously protected Polycarp and Perpetua in their passions, then John Hooper, fourteen centuries later, could expect nothing less in his martyrdom. If God so abundantly blessed the motherhood of Mary, then forward-looking Ruth and backward-looking Gorgonia and Birgitta and Yuliania could be comforted in their heavenly Father's care. If God converted the impious Paul and Augustine to the Christian faith, he could do the same for C. S. Lewis. If Elijah was taken up to heaven, then all heirs of Jesus have no reason to fear death, but rather raise their eyes to heaven and praise God for the blessed hope of the "resurrection of the dead and the life everlasting."

All of these Christian lives belong in the family portrait. Accordingly, any attempt to identify a hierarchy among Christian lives—sovereign and bishop, missionary and miracle worker, husband and wife—is misplaced. It is, as Jesus said, "many who are first will be last" (Matthew 19:30). Who is last and thus first, but the crucified and risen Jesus? So there is a hierarchy, but it is extremely simple. Jesus is the single and central figure, and all others surround Him and find their place in relation to Him. Switching metaphors, these Christian lives have been woven together in the one Church like a seamless fabric that is draped upon the Lord Jesus like unto a coat of many colors.

Summary

The study of God must not only be historical but also biographical. God has most fully revealed Himself initially, though only for a short time, in Adam's life and later in the life of Christ. If you would know what God is like, look first and foremost at Jesus. In His birth and baptism, miracles and parables, crucifixion and resurrection, sending of the Holy Spirit, Jesus fully revealed God and the divine will for creation—restore the image of God to a fallen and muddy human image. The pinnacle of this restoration is to wash away the muck and mire under which the image of God in human lives has been buried since the days of Adam.

The study of Christian biography begins then with the life of Christ in the Holy Gospels and proceeds both back into the Old Testament and ahead into the New Testament and beyond. Each and every Christian life is intimately related to the life of Christ. Through Baptism, Jesus washes away the Adamic filth and gives birth to the children of God. Christians are not identical replicas of Christ anymore than a child is of his parents. Nonetheless, they are intimately connected to Jesus through Baptism and the Lord's Supper, and display numerous similarities—family traits and common offices—to one another in their Christian lives.

O almighty God, by whom we are graciously knit together as one communion and fellowship in the mystical body of Jesus Christ, our Lord, grant us so to follow your blessed saints in all virtuous and godly living that we may come to those unspeakable joys which you have prepared for those who unfeignedly love you; through our Lord Jesus Christ, your Son, who lives and reigns with you and the Holy Spirit, one God, now and forever. Amen.[1]

Notes

Chapter 1

1. See Cyril of Jerusalem, Mystagogical Catechesis, 4.3.

2. On a few occasions, God utilizes non-human components of His creation to reveal Himself and His will, for example, Balaam's donkey speaking to its owner (Numbers 22), the angel Gabriel at the annunciation (Luke 1), and the star in the east (Matthew 2).

3. See Athanasius, On the Incarnation, 15.

4. Dr. Andrew Steinmann, a colleague and Old Testament exegete, coined this term during a conversation.

5. Eusebius of Caesarea, Ecclesiastical History, 3.26, 28.

6. See Bede, Ecclesiastical History of the English Nation, 5.24, 4.28, 31–32, Preface.

7. The Hours of the Divine Office in English and Latin, vol. 3 (Collegeville, MN: Liturgical Press, 1964), 1.423.

8. See Edward T. Horn III, The Christian Year (Philadelphia: Muhlenberg, 1957), 179–80.

Chapter 2

1. This list does not include those whose births and/or deaths are included only in genealogies.

2.   The heirs of Jesus in the Old Testament are the circumcised and their families (Genesis 17:10–27; Romans 2:25–29; Colossians 2:11–13).

3.   "My God, my God, why have you forsaken me?" (Matthew 27:46); "Father, forgive them, for they know not what they do." (Luke 23:34); "Woman, behold your son! . . . Behold your mother!" (John 19:26–27); "I thirst" (John 19:28); "Truly, I say to you, today you will be with me in Paradise" (Luke 23:43); "Father, into your hands I commit my spirit!" (Luke 23:46); "It is finished" (John 19:30).

4.   See Isaiah 7:14; Micah 5:2; Zechariah 9:9.

5.   Malachi prophesied of John the Baptist (Malachi 3:1); Isaiah the Magi (Isaiah 60:1–6), and Joel the day of Pentecost (Joel 2:28–32).

6.   See comments in chapter 1, note 4.

7.   With Solomon authoring Song of Solomon and Proverbs, both were written within four generations of the life of Ruth.

8.   This is also supported linguistically. The Song of Solomon intentionally utilizes the Hebrew roots of the names of Ruth and Naomi, which strongly suggests that the author was not only looking ahead to Jesus and the church, but had his eye upon past figures. For example, the root נעם is the basis for the name of Naomi and is used twice in the Song of Solomon by the lovers for the other (Song of Solomon 1:16, 7:6). In addition, the root רעה is the basis for the name of Ruth and is used metaphorically and repeatedly in the Song of Solomon to describe the relation between the lovers (Song of Solomon 1:9, 15, 2:2, 10, 13, 4:1, 7, 5:2, 6:4).

9.   Both Moses and Elijah appear at Jesus' transfiguration in the New Testament, and both ended their lives in the Old Testament under unusual circumstances: Moses was buried by God (Deuteronomy 34:6) and Elijah ascended to heaven (2 Kings 2:11).

10. The short and more valuable list of the Apocrypha includes Tobit, Judith, Wisdom of Ben Sirach, Ecclesiasticus, 1 Maccabees, Susanna, and Bel and the Dragon.

11. See Andrew E. Steinmann, The Oracles of God (St. Louis: Concordia, 1999), 36–39.

12. There is more than an abundance of biographical data for the apostles in the post-New Testament Apocryphal Acts and Epistles, like the Acts of Peter and Acts of John, Paul's Third Letter to the Corinthians, and correspondence between Paul and Seneca.

Chapter 3

1. See William Schoedel, Ignatius of Antioch (Philadelphia: Fortress, 1985), 36.

2. Ignatius of Antioch, Ephesians, 11.2; Romans 1.1–2; Smyrneans, 4.2.

3. Justin, First Apology, 12.

4. See also Irenaeus, Against the Heresies, 3.3.4.

5. In a polytheistic and syncretistic culture such as that of the Roman Empire, a monotheistic and anti-syncretistic religion, as was Christianity, was considered atheistic.

6. Passion of Polycarp, 7.

7. Passion of Polycarp, 9.

8. Passion of Polycarp, 9.

9. Passion of Polycarp, 14.

10. In the Early Church, it was quite common to revere the bones of the martyrs, first in cemeteries and later in altars that served as a visible sign of the invisible reality that the souls of the martyrs reside under the heavenly altar (Revelation 6:9). See J. G. Davies, The Early Church (Grand Rapids: Baker, 1980), 271.

11. See also Augustine of Hippo, Sermons, 280–82.

12. See also Gregory Thaumaturgus, Oration and Panegyric to Origen; Pamphilius, Apology for Origen.

13. Eusebius of Caesarea, Ecclesiastical History, 6.2

14. See also Basil the Great, On the Holy Spirit, 74.

15. See also Augustine of Hippo, Sermons, 302–305A; Leo the Great, Sermons, 85.

16. See also Prudentius, Passion of Cyprian; Augustine of Hippo, Sermons, 308A–313F.

17. See also Augustine of Hippo, Sermons, 313G; Jerome, Letter to Demetrias.

18. Prudentius, "Hymn in Honor of the Passion of the Most Holy Martyr Eulalia," in The Poems of Prudentius, vol. 1 (Washington, DC: Catholic University of America, 1962), 3.1.

19. See also Eusebius of Caesarea, Oration of the Emperor Constantine and Oration of Eusebius Pamphilus in Praise of the Emperor Constantine; Socrates Scholasticus, Ecclesiastical History, 1.1–40; Hermias Sozomen, Ecclesiastical History, 1–2.

20. Jerome, Life of St. Hilarion, 12.

21. Jerome, Life of St. Hilarion, 15.

22. Jerome, Life of St. Hilarion, 45.

23. Gregory of Nazianzus, Oration, 8.22.

24. Sulpitius Severus, Life of St. Martin, 24.

25. The actual Bishop of Jerusalem at this time was John.

26. See also the Life of Augustine by Possidius (ca. 370–ca. 440), an ascetic in Hippo and later Bishop of Calama.

27. Augustine, Confessions, 8.12.

28. See also Patrick, Confessions; St. Secundus, Audite omnes; Muirchu Maccu-Machtheni, Life of Patrick; Tripartite Life; Jocelyn of Furness, Life and Acts of St Patrick.

29. "St. Fiecc's Poem on the Life of St. Patrick," The Irish Ecclesiastical Record (March 1868): 287 [9].

30. Jerome, Lives of Illustrious Men, 17.

31. Passion of Polycarp, 17.3.

32. Sulpitius Severus argued that the life of Martin served not to glorify Martin, but rather, as an example for Christians to imitate, Life of St. Martin, 1.

33. See also Sophronius of Jerusalem, The Life of our Holy Mother Mary of Egypt, 1.

34. Augustine reiterated the miracle note by Ambrose in Letter 22 in both his City of God, 22.8 and Confessions, 9.7.

Chapter 4

1. See also Jacobus de Voragine, Golden Legend, 49.

2. See also the eighth century life of Gregory by an unnamed monk of Whitby; Jacobus de Voragine, Golden Legend, 46.

3. Bede, The Ecclesiastical History of the English Nation, trans. L. C. Jane (London: J. M. Dent, 1903), 63 [2.1].

4. For portrayals of other women by Bede, see Ecclesiastical History of the English Nation, 4.8–10; 4.19–20.

5. See also Monk of St. Gall, Life of Charlemagne.

6. Peter Abelard, The Story of My Misfortunes, 3

7. See also Gilbert of Hoyland, Sermons on the Song of Songs, 41.

8. See also Thomas Celano, First Life (1228), Second Life (1247), Treatise on the Miracles of Blessed Francis (1253); Bonaventure, Major Life

(c.1262); Jacobus de Voragine, Golden Legend, 149; Legend of the Three Companions (c.1300); Legend of Perugia (c.1311); Mirror of Perfection (c.1318).

9. Bonaventure, Minor Life, 1.5.

10. Prior Peter and Master Peter, The Life of Blessed Birgitta, trans. Albert R. Kezel, in Birgitta of Sweden (New York: Paulist, 1990), 72 [6].

11. For a fuller account of her revelations, see Birgitta, Heavenly Book of Revelations.

12. Bernard Guidonis (d. 1331), a fellow Dominican, completed a similar, but more historically accurate, document entitled Speculum Sanctorum, but was not well-received.

13. The later translation and edition of this document (1483) by William Caxton (c.1422–1491) added numerous lives and reorganized them.

14. See also John Bugenhagen, Funeral Oration (1546); Philip Melanchthon's Elegy on the Death of the Rev. Martin Luther and Funeral Oration for the Rev. Dr. Martin Luther; Ludwig Rabus, Accounts of God's Chosen Witnesses, Confessors, and Martyrs (1556).

15. John Foxe, The Acts and Monuments of John Foxe, 8 vol. (London: R. B. Seeley and W. Burnside, 1837–41): 6:658.

16. See also Thomas Heywood, England's Elizabeth her life and troubles during her minoritie, from the cradle to the crowne; Christopher Lever, Queene Elizabeth's Teares: or, her resolute bearing the Christian cross, in the bloodie times of Queene Marie; and M.P., An Abstract of the Historie of the Renouned Maiden Queene Elizabeth.

17. See also funeral and memorial orations for Gerhard by Johannes Himmel, Justus Feurborn, and Michael Schneider; and Johann Zeumer's Lives of the Professors of Theology at Jena (1704). Others are noted in the brief preface of Erdmann Fischer's The Life of John Gerhard.

18. See also A Miracle of Miracles; A Pindaric Ode; Thomas Wilson, A Sermon on the Martyrdom of King Charles I; E. Langford, A Sermon Preach'd before the Honourable House of Commons; Joseph Butler, Sermon III.

19. See also E.G. Roth, Paul Gerhardt, nach seinem Leben und Wirken (Leipzig, 1829); Carl A. Wildenhahn, Paul Gerhardt: A Historical Picture, trans. G.A. Wenzel (Philadelphia, PA: M.J. Riegel, 1881); William Dallmann, Paul Gerhardt, His Life and Hymns (St. Louis: Concordia, 1921).

20. Krummacher, trans. Catherine E. Hurst, "Paul Gerhardt—A Life Story,"

The Ladies' Repository vol.1 (March 1875): 205.

21. See also the journals of George Whitefield; John Wesley, Sermon 53.

22. John Charles Ryles, Christian Leaders of the Eighteenth Century (Edinburgh: n.p., 1885; reprint, Carlisle, PA: Banner of Truth Trust, 1978), 42.

23. The memoirs of Margaret were appended by her second husband, Johann Jungmann.

24. See also the autobiography of Theresa of Lisieux and the homily of Pope Pius XI at her canonization.

25. See also George Sayer, Jack: A Life of C. S. Lewis (Wheaton, IL: Crossway, 1994).

26. David Scaer, "In Memoriam. Robert David Preus," Logia 5 (Holy Trinity 1996): 7–8.

27. David Scaer, "Commemoration Sermon for Dr. Robert D. Preus," Logia 5 (Holy Trinity 1996): 9–10.

28. See Einhard, The Life of Charlemagne, preface; Walter Daniel, The Life of Ailred of Riveaulx, 40.

29. See Gregory the Great, Dialogues, 1.1.

30. See Thomas Aquinas, Summa Theologica, 2.83.4.

31. See Thomas Aquinas, Summa Theologica, 3.25.5-6.

32. See the critical assessment of Guibert of Nogent (d. 1124) concerning the Medieval doctrines and practices surrounding the saints, On the Saints and Their Relics (De sanctis et eorum pigneribus).

33. Ignatius of Loyola noted in his autobiography that an early example of almsgiving in his life was quickly embellished by others during his own lifetime, Autobiography, in Ignatius of Loyola (New York: Mahwah, Paulist, 1991), 18.

34. Stephen R. Cattley, ed., The Acts and Monuments of John Foxe xxvii (London: Seeley and Burnside, 1837–41), 6.661–62, 7.137–38.

35. Apology of the Augsburg Confession, 21.

36. Hippolyte Delehaye, The Legends of the Saints, trans. V. M. Crawford (New York: Longmans, Green, and Co., 1907), 2.

Chapter 5

1. Leontius of Neapolis in Cyprus (590–668) wrote a supplement to this life of John by Sophronius and John Moschus in 641.

2. See also John of Jerusalem, Life of John of Damascus (10th cent).

3.   It is common for John to be wearing a red clothe upon his head in icons depicting him.

4.   The Vita of Constantine and the Vita of Methodius, trans. Marvin Kantor and Richard S. White (Ann Arbor, MI: Michigan Slavic Publications, 1976), 91 [VM, 17]. {sent email}

5.   For a detailed analysis of the possible authors and editors of the Russian Primary Chronicle, see The Russian Primary Chronicle. Laurentian Text, trans. Samuel H. Cross and Olgerd P. Sherbowitz-Wetzor (Cambridge, MA: Mediaeval Academy of America, 1953), 6–23.

6.   See also the Life of Stephen Nemanja by his son Stephen.

7.   Sava, The Life of Stephen Nemanja, in Medieval Slavic Lives of Saints and Princes, trans. Marvin Kantor (Ann Arbor, MI: Michigan Slavic Publications, 1983), 287.

8.   See also Demetrius of Rostov, Great Collection of the Lives of the Saints, 25 September.

9.   See also Demetrius of Rostov, Great Collection of the Lives of the Saints, 11 January.

10. Kallistrat Druzhina-Osoryin, The Life of Yuliania Lazarevskaia, trans. Serge A. Zenkovsky, in Medieval Russian Epics, Chronicles, and Tales (New York: E. P. Dutton, 1963), 319.

11. Alexander Priklonsky, The Life of Blessed Athanasia, 2d ed. (Platina, CA; St. Herman of Alaska Brotherhood, 1993), 85 [11].

12. Journals of the Priest Ioann Veniamoinov in Alaska, 1823–1836 (Fairbanks, AK: University of Alaska, 1993).

13. John Meyendorff, "A Life Worth Living," St. Vladimir's Theological Quarterly 28 (1984): 3-10. See also The Journals of Father Alexander Schmemann 1973–1983.

14. The Way of the Pilgrim, trans. R. M. French, in G.P. Fedetov, ed., A Treasury of Russian Spirituality (New York: Sheed and Ward, 1948).

15. Leontius of Neapolis, A Supplement to the Life of John the Almsgiver, trans. Elizabeth Dawes and Norman H. Baynes, in Three Byzantine Saints (Crestwood, NY: St. Vladimir Seminary, 1977), 207 [preface].

16. Athanasius, On the Incarnation of the Lord, 54.3.

17. See Gregory Palamas, The Triads, 3.1.15–17.

18. See Alexander Priklonsky, The Life of Blessed Athanasia, 3.

19. See Life of Methodius, 1.

20. See Leontius of Neapolis, A Supplement to the Life of John the

Almsgiver, preface.

21. The Lenton Triodion, trans. Mother Mary and Kallistos Ware (Boston, MA: Faber and Faber, 1977), 316. {faxed request}

Chapter 6

1. The collect for All Saints' Day in Lutheran Worship (St. Louis: Concordia, 1982), 116.

Suggested Reading

Anderson, Gerald H., ed. Biographical Dictionary of Christian Missions. New York: Macmillan, 1997.

Attwater, Donald. The Penguin Dictionary of the Saints. Baltimore, MD: Penguin, 1965

Barker, William P. Who's Who in Church History. Grand Rapids: Baker Book, 1977.

Bowden, Henry W. Dictionary of American Religious Biography. Westport, CT: Greenwood Press, 1977.

Butler, Alban. Lives of the Saints. Collegeville, MN: Liturgical Press, 2003

Brown, Peter R. The Cult of the Saints. Chicago: University of Chicago, 1982.

Cartwright, Jane, ed. Celtic Hagiography and Saints' Cults. Cardiff: University of Wales, 2003.

Cunningham, Lawrence. A Brief History of Saints. Malden, MA: Blackwell, 2004.

Delaney, John J., and James E. Tobin. Dictionary of Catholic Biography. Garden City, NY: Doubleday, 1961.

Delehaye, Hippolyte. The Legends of the Saints. An Introduction to Hagiography. Translated by V. M. Crawford. Norwood, PA:

Norwood Editions, 1974.

Duffy, Eamon. Saints and Sinners. A History of the Popes. 2nd ed. New Haven, CT: Yale University 2002.

Dunney, Joseph A. Church History in the Light of the Saints. New York: Macmillan, 1946.

Farmer, David Hugh. The Oxford Dictionary of Saints. 5th ed. New York: Oxford University, 2003.

Hackel, Sergei, ed. The Byzantine Saint. Crestwood, NY: St. Vladimir Seminary, 2001.

Hammack, Mary L. A Dictionary of Women in Church History. Chicago: Moody, 1984.

Head, Thomas. Hagiography and the Cult of the Saints. New York: Cambridge University, 1990.

Kolb, Robert. For All the Saints. Macon, GA: Mercer, 1987.

Lewis, Donald M., ed. The Blackwell Dictionary of Evangelical Biography. 1730–1860. 2 Vol. Cambridge, MA: Blackwell, 1995.

Livingstone, E. A., ed. The Oxford Dictionary of the Christian Church, 3d ed. New York: Oxford University, 1997.

McClendon, James W. Biography as Theology. Nashville: Abingdon, 1974.

Moyer, Elgin S. Who Was Who in Church History. Chicago: Moody, 1968.

Moyer, Elgin, and Earle E. Cairns. Wycliffe Biographical Dictionary of the Church. Chicago: Moody, 1982.

Wace, Henry, and William C. Piercy, eds. A Dictionary of Christian Biography and Literature. Boston: Little, Brown and Company, 1911.

Walsh, Michael, ed. A Dictionary of Christian Biography. Collegeville, MN: Liturgical, 2001.

Suggested Web Sites

Benedictine Saints
www.osb.org/gen/saints/index.html

Biographical Sketches of Christians
www.justus.anglican.org/resources/bio

Christian Hagiography
www.kbr.be/~socboll

Catholic Encyclopedia
www.newadvent.org

Catholic Saints
www.catholic.org/saints

Christian Biography Resources
www.wholesomewords.org/biography/bio.html

Christian Classics Ethereal Library
www.ccel.org

The Dictionary of African Christian Biography
www.dacb.org/

Ecole Initiative
www2.evansville.edu/ecoleweb/

The Great Collection of Lives of the Saints
http://www.chrysostompress.org/collection/index/

Internet Medieval Sourcebook
    www.fordham.edu/halsall/sbook.html

James Kiefer's Christian Biographies
    elvis.rowan.edu/~kilroy/JEK/home.html

Orthodox America
    www.roca.org/oa/saints.htm

Orthodox Christian Lives of Saints
    www.orthodox.net/links/saints-by-date.html

Project Wittenberg
    www.iclnet.org/pub/resources/text/wittenberg/
    wittenberg-home.html

Puritan Biographies
    www.puritansermons.com/hist.htm#bio

Revival Library
    www.revival-library.org

Russian New Martyrs and Confessors
    www.orthodox.net/russiannm/index.html

St. Pachomius Library
    www.voskrese.info/spl/

Synaxarion
    www.rongolini.com/synaxariontoc.htm

Scripture Index